On the Outside

Law and Society Series
W. Wesley Pue, General Editor

The Law and Society Series explores law as a socially embedded phenomenon. It is premised on the understanding that the conventional division of law from society creates false dichotomies in thinking, scholarship, educational practice, and social life. Books in the series treat law and society as mutually constitutive and seek to bridge scholarship emerging from interdisciplinary engagement of law with disciplines such as politics, social theory, history, political economy, and gender studies.

A list of titles in the series appears at the end of the book.

On the Outside

From Lengthy Imprisonment to Lasting Freedom

MELISSA MUNN
AND CHRIS BRUCKERT

UBCPress · Vancouver · Toronto

21 20 19 18 17 16 15 14 13   5 4 3 2 1

Printed in Canada on FSC-certified ancient-forest-free paper (100% post-consumer recycled) that is processed chlorine- and acid-free.

Library and Archives Canada Cataloguing in Publication

Munn, Melissa
    On the outside : from lengthy imprisonment to lasting freedom / Melissa Munn and Chris Bruckert.

(Law and society series)
Includes bibliographical references and index.
Issued also in electronic formats.
ISBN 978-0-7748-2536-8 (bound); ISBN 978-0-7748-2537-5 (pbk.)

    1. Imprisonment – Social aspects – Canada. 2. Prisons – Social aspects – Canada. 3. Ex-convicts – Canada – Social conditions. 4. Sociological jurisprudence – Canada. I. Bruckert, Chris II. Title. III. Series: Law and society series (Vancouver, B.C.)

HV9308.M83 2013   364.80971   C2013-900867-5

Canadä

UBC Press gratefully acknowledges the financial support for our publishing program of the Government of Canada (through the Canada Book Fund), the Canada Council for the Arts, and the British Columbia Arts Council.

This book has been published with the help of a grant from the Canadian Federation for the Humanities and Social Sciences, through the Awards to Scholarly Publications Program, using funds provided by the Social Sciences and Humanities Research Council of Canada.

UBC Press
The University of British Columbia
2029 West Mall
Vancouver, BC V6T 1Z2
www.ubcpress.ca

This book is dedicated to:

Professor Robert Gaucher
whose wisdom inspired us to ask new questions,

to

Robert (Bobby) Brydon
whose struggles inspired us to research life after prison,

and to

Leslie Kennedy
whose words inspired us every time we sat down to write.

Contents

Acknowledgments

Without Barry, Bob, Bobby, Dave, Doc, Ernest, F.G., Fred, Gerry, Gord, Gowan, Jean, Joel, Luc, Marcus, Mr. Flowers, Puzzle, Rick, Tom, and Ziggy, none of this would have been possible. We thank them for bravely sharing their stories and for putting their faith in us to 'get it right.'

Thanks also to the workers at Life Line for helping us to meet some of these men; our friend John Rives who let us 'borrow' his poetry for use in this book, read a very early version of the manuscript, gave amazing feedback, and was an unfailing supporter throughout the project; 'Rick and Rick' who were significant sources of inspiration to us, showed us the power of challenging the system, and followed us in spirit throughout this project; Al 'our pal' Larsen who put up with our countless phone calls, fed us during our marathon writing sessions, and was there to call 'time outs' when needed; Elizabeth Munn for her help with transcription and for her years of encouragement; UBC Press for their enthusiasm and, in particular, our editors Randy Schmidt and Megan Brand who were efficient and encouraging in every way; and our two anonymous reviewers whose detailed and thoughtful review of the manuscript pushed us to expand the analysis and to re-think some of our choices.

We would like to acknowledge the financial support of the Social Sciences And Humanities Research Council.

On the Outside

Telling Tales: State Talk, Con Talk, and Back Talk   **1**

The genesis of this book goes back to the mid-1980s. At that time, we were two eager young undergraduate students studying criminology at the University of Ottawa. The two of us working-class gals came to our studies with some 'baggage' – members of Melissa's family had been incarcerated and Chris's sex work career had certainly exposed her to the criminalized world. Moreover, as active members of the Prisoner's Liaison Group we were politically engaged and, among other things, regularly attended the Lifers' Group at Collins Bay Penitentiary in Kingston, Ontario. Perhaps most importantly, we knew people who had 'done time' and, in some cases, a great deal of it. For the most part, these individuals appeared to lead lives that were no different than those of everyone else we knew – they went to work and/or attended classes, had friends, raised their children, struggled financially, and fell in and out of love. There were, however, moments when the challenges posed by the everyday world were suddenly visible – in, for example, the look of fear and confusion when confronting new technologies, in their antiquated gender role expectations, in their linguistic codes that did not quite 'fit,' and in their evident discomfort with traffic or crowds. Other times, the implications of correctional control were evident – when a weekend break required a parole officer's home visit or when travel restrictions prevented driving across the provincial border to view the changing fall leaves.

We spent long evenings around Melissa's kitchen table drinking countless cups of tea, discussing the conversations we heard everywhere and those we never heard at all. We wondered why no one was talking about the men and women who went to prison, were released, struggled and faced challenges as they resettled back into society, and never returned to prison. Instead, everywhere we looked – in the newspapers, from our classmates, and on television – we heard about the high rates of recidivism and the danger former male prisoners posed.[1] Faced with a disconnect between 'what everyone (appeared to) know' about ex-prisoners and what our own experiences were telling us, we turned to criminology – after all, we had faith that our discipline would provide us with insight and information. Here too we were largely disappointed. With the exception of a couple of (already dated) ethnographies (that is, Erickson et al. 1973; Irwin 1970) and a handful of accounts of former prisoners (that is, Carr 1975; Murphy, Johnsen, and Murphy 2002), most of what we did find was positivist research that sought to 'fix' or rehabilitate prisoners while simultaneously claiming that "nothing works" (Martinson 1974). The critical literature, with its structural focus, spoke of the implications of prisonization (Goffman 1963b) and asserted that prisons fabricate criminals (Cohen 1985; Foucault 1977). Everywhere we turned, however, the experiences of our friends and loved ones were absent. Where was the acknowledgment that individuals successfully endured and transcended the negative psychological and social aspects of imprisonment?[2] Where were their stories – stories that we knew to be filled with accomplishments and setbacks, struggles and triumphs, agency and tenacity, joy and fear.

Twenty years later, by the time Chris was a professor and Melissa a college teacher and doctoral student, these questions continued to resonate. Despite a few notable exceptions (Jamieson and Grounds 2002; Maurna 2001; Maurna and Immarigeon 2004), pathways to crime continued to be a criminological preoccupation. The interest in release and reintegration was largely limited to positivistic searches for the correlates of recidivism (for example, Magura et al. 1993; Schafer 1994; Schwaner 1998). We recognized that the silence regarding those who 'make good' not only contributed to the illusion of the 'dangerous ex-convict' but also meant that the experience of the complex and sometimes treacherous path out of prison and onto the street was invisible. This lacuna pushed us to think about the politics of knowledge, and so we turned to the insights of Michel Foucault (1984/89, 462-63):

> The work of an intellectual is not to mould the political will of others; it is, through the analyses that he does in his own field, to re-examine evidence and assumptions, to shake up habitual ways of working and thinking, to dissipate conventional familiarities, to re-evaluate rules and institutions and to participate in the formation of a political will.

Foucault's words speak to the importance of engaging with questions of truth and power, of reflecting on knowledge and politics, and of destabilizing the false theory/practice binary. They push us to think about the intersections and interplay between these dynamics, and they challenge us to be subtly subversive. We have taken Foucault's words to heart, and in this book we seek to make the invisible visible by recounting a story that is rarely told: the journey of men who have successfully resettled (Correctional Service of Canada 1998) into the community after spending long periods of time incarcerated in some of the most punitive and secure institutions in Canada.

In putting these men's stories 'on the record,' we are seeking to present counter-narratives that challenge the dominant discourse.[3] This undertaking can be destabilizing because it obliges us to navigate the tension between 'truths' – what we 'know' and what the men 'know.' Indeed, so ingrained is the moral condemnation of 'the criminal,' that merely validating the stories of ex-prisoners and attending to their experiences can be disconcerting. Here again we are inspired by Foucault's work. His studies on mental illness (1964), the prison (1977), and sexuality (1978) excavated the conditions of possibility that allowed particular understandings to emerge and others to disappear. In the process, he challenged the historical record with its embedded supposition that we are progressing by demonstrating that current ways of knowing/doing/being are neither inevitable nor, in some absolute sense, 'better.'

Destabilizing 'what we know' brings to the fore the question: why are some truths 'true'? Put in terms of this book, why are some stories (of recidivism and violence) always told and others (of struggle and success) so rarely recounted? Does it speak to a conspiracy of mind control? Is it indicative of an Orwellian ministry of 'thought police'? We firmly reject such a notion and instead recognize the need to attend to the economic, social, political, and technological contexts in which ideas become thinkable or, more to the point, unthinkable. This possibility alerts us to the intersection of truth, knowledge, and power – in short, "each society has its regime of truth, its 'general politics' of truth: that is, the types of discourse which it accepts and makes function as true" (Foucault 1980b, 131). This assertion is supported when we trace Western penal discourse.

The Contemporary Tale

A particular narrative about 'the criminal' is recounted in movies, newspapers, websites, and political discourse. There are some minor variations in the details but, for the most part, it states: "Criminals are not like us. They are dangerous. The criminal justice system fails and these predators keep committing new offences because we are soft on crime. The solution is to *get tough* – to have more *law-and-order*." This narrative is repeated often enough that it becomes common knowledge – presumed to be the truth – it must be so because we hear it everywhere. It is further legitimated when our elected leaders authoritatively, and unquestioningly, reproduce this 'knowledge.' As a case in point, in Prime Minister Stephen Harper's (2011) *Speech from the Throne*, he offered up the following words:

> The Government of Canada has no more fundamental duty than to protect the personal safety of our citizens and defend against threats to our national security. Our Government will move quickly to reintroduce comprehensive law-and-order legislation to combat crime and terrorism. These measures will protect children from sex offenders. They will eliminate house arrest and pardons for serious crimes. They will give law enforcement officials, courts and victims the legal

tools they need to fight criminals and terrorists. Our Government will continue to protect the most vulnerable in society and work to prevent crime. It will propose tougher sentences for those who abuse seniors and will help at risk youth avoid gangs and criminal activity. It will address the problem of violence against women and girls. Our Government has always believed the interests of law-abiding citizens should be placed ahead of those of criminals.

The Conservative Party of Canada put rhetoric into law when they pushed the Omnibus Crime Bill (C-10) through Parliament. The (euphemistically named) *Safe Streets and Communities Act* came into effect on 12 March 2012.[4] Ironically, these laws are being implemented at a time when even conservative Texas lawmakers, long advocates of 'law-and-order' policies, are declaring the approach a social and fiscal failure and are moving to repeal minimum sentences and adopt community solutions (Milewski 2011).

Given that crime rates have been falling steadily for the last two decades (Statistics Canada 2010a), Prime Minister Harper has shrewdly drawn on common 'knowledge' to invent a social problem for political currency (Mallea 2010). To this end, he is evoking the most primal of emotions (fear) and employing an ancient conceptual frame (good versus evil) when he vows that his government will protect the innocent, the victim, and the law-abiding citizen from the threat embodied by 'the criminal.' Perhaps because this binary thinking is so primordial, it is also appealing – a straightforward problem and self-evident solution to ensure safety and security for all 'deserving' Canadians.

As is so often the case, common (non)sense collapses on reflection. First, who is the criminal? By definition, it is someone who has broken the law – something that applies to most, or more likely all, Canadians (Gabor 1994). Indeed, the large amount of unknown criminal activity – the 'dark figure of crime' – illustrates that very few *Criminal Code* violations actually make it through the funnelling and filtering process (recognized, reported, found by police, charged, and convicted) to be recorded in official crime statistics (Winterdyk 2006).[5] If we take a more legalistic approach, we can say the criminal is someone who has broken the law, been apprehended by law enforcement, and been found guilty in court. Yet, even this designation applies to 3.8 million Canadians (Public Safety Canada 2011, 107), so that, in other words, approximately one in every seven adult Canadians is, legally speaking, a criminal![6]

Second, there is the question of the get-tough-on-crime 'solution,' which is essentially to protect 'good' citizens by putting more 'bad' people in prison and keeping them incarcerated for longer periods of time.[7] This powerful rhetoric is substantively bankrupt, something Justice Minister Rob Nicholson implicitly acknowledged when he noted "unlike the Opposition, we do not use statistics as an excuse not to get tough on criminals" (quoted in Galloway 2011). Those individuals who are amenable to evidence-based research have pointed out that Canadians will not be safer from crime under the new regime because longer sentences and mandatory minimums do not reduce offending (Durlauf and Nagin 2011). Criminologists have also drawn attention to the implications of an overburdened correctional system wherein overcrowding leads to violence, and effective prison programs (for example, literacy, anger management, and vocational training) are cut (Mallea 2010).

Finally, the cost of the *Safe Streets and Communities Act* is estimated at a staggering $19 billion (IRIS 2011) – money that as Irvin Cotler (2011), former minister of justice and attorney general of Canada, pointed out "cannot be used to invest in a social justice agenda, child care, health care, crime prevention, seniors or social housing. At the end of the day, we will have ... more crime and less justice." Indeed, the abandonment of the rehabilitative ideal rapidly became evident. For example, on 16 April 16 2012, the Correctional Service of Canada announced that the award-winning Life Line program, which has helped life-sentenced individuals (including many of the men in this research) reintegrate back into society after prison, will no longer be funded due to federal budget cuts (Munn 2012).

The tale of the criminal, and the appropriate response to him, has not always been told using the imagery of Prime Minister Harper. Indeed, a review of the discourses that have emerged since Canada's first penitentiary was erected in 1835 demonstrates that particular eras have had their own narratives and accompanying practices.

The Stories Told

For most of Western history, wrongdoing has been sanctioned by expulsion, indentured servitude, corporal punishment, or death – jails were largely holding places for those awaiting trial or the execution of their sentence. The prison as a form of punishment in its own right emerged in the context of eighteenth-century dissatisfaction with public spectacles of corporal and capital punishment and the need for an 'enlightened' approach to 'justice' (Foucault 1977). This idea was espoused by classical theorists such as Cesare Beccaria (1764 [1986]) who thought that by ensuring swift, certain, and proportional punishment, rational persons, engaging in a cost-benefit analysis, would be deterred from committing crimes. The goal of the prison was to neutralize the 'dangerous classes' – those that posed a threat to the emerging bourgeois order (Goff 1999). Early places of confinement, which were characterized by disorder, filth, dismal overcrowding, and the total absence of classification, were condemned by reformers such as John Howard (1777 [2000]) as breeding grounds of disease, criminality, and immorality. His calls for reform were heeded by governments of the day who introduced a new type of institution "based on the principles of solitary confinement, religious instruction, and hard labour" (Garcia, 2005, 416).

By the nineteenth century, the penitentiary was an accepted response, and the story was that the system could be improved if punishment had "humanity as its 'measure'" (Foucault 1977, 75). In practice, reformers were committed to 'fixing' the criminal through coercive policies that would "act upon the body, a calculated manipulation of its elements, its gestures, its behaviour" (138). To this end, they employed regulation and surveillance in institutions that "mimicked the discipline necessary for the factory system" (Scull 1977, 26) in order to produce corrected and reformed disciplined workers capable of enduring, and willing to endure, the labour conditions of nineteenth-century factories. In short, the prison was not only about 'enlightened' punishment through the deprivation of liberty but also about the "recoding of existence" (Foucault 1977, 236) by "organizing and training people into normalcy" (Goff 1999, 68).

In this context, there was a period of rapid prison expansion throughout Europe and North America that lasted into the twentieth century.

In the process, the 'truth' of prisons as a solution to the problem of crime became ever more entrenched, although the justifications for it were reconfigured. By the 1930s, positivism, which sought to identify the causes of crime through the scientific method, asserted new 'truths.' The resulting story of physiological, psychological, and/or social determinism was one that co-existed, and sometimes displaced, classicalism as the prevailing penal tale. Crime came to be envisioned as the symptom of an underlying individual defect, with prisoners needing treatment and cure under the watchful eyes of 'experts' in prison. While the approach appears more 'humane,' it was, in practice, characterized by repressive and brutal punishment in the name of treatment – for example, restricted diets became euphemistically reframed as "behaviour modification meatloaf" (Ross and McKay 1980, 45). More to the point, the reification of the criminal as 'a different kind of person' is complete when the reform of rational actors (the classical model) is replaced by the rehabilitation of 'sick,' defective, or deficient beings who must be confined until they are 'fixed' (the positivist model).

By the 1960s and 1970s, a different 'truth' had taken hold and a new story was being told. The zeitgeist of this period was one of cynicism grounded in a discursive trope that the state was ineffective, the government's efforts to reform prisoners were illusory, the correctional discourse mere rhetoric, and penal institutions more harmful than beneficial. Not surprisingly, this period was characterized by efforts to minimize the role of the 'repressive' state by encouraging more inclusive and community-driven responses to crime and deviance. In practice, elements of previous discourses remained and a bifurcated system emerged with corresponding divisions in the classification of criminals (Pratt 1999). On one end of the correctional continuum, less serious types of crimes received interventions aimed at diverting the most 'deserving' out of the penal apparatus. On the other end of the continuum, the 'undeserving' (those convicted of serious crimes) were locked away in prisons for increasingly long sentences (Cohen 1985).

By the 1980s, the idealism of the welfare era, with its commitment to the 'social,' was quickly disappearing and the social safety net became increasingly tattered as states shifted to the conservative right. Governments of the day employed the language of economic rationalism to argue that the high cost of welfare programs was crippling the economy, leaving them with few options but to cut expenditures and rely on families and the private sector to fill the inevitable chasm in services and support. As Maureen Baker (1997, 2) explained, "the ideology of economic rationalism has been used by employer's groups and financial organizations to promote their own interests of global trade and higher profits for the business sector. Yet, these groups have successfully persuaded governments that what is good for the business sector is beneficial to the nation." As Nils Christie (2004) pointed out, the increased privatization of prisons and the off-loading of rehabilitative services are the result of this process. In other words, it is precisely this rationality that gave rise to the prison industrial complex.

By the turn of the millennium, market-driven neo-liberalism – characterized by individualization and the off-loading of responsibility and concurrent responsibilization of individuals, communities, and professionals – was firmly entrenched (Rose 1996).[8] At the same time, the story of risk came to dominate both criminal justice and political rhetoric; governments were expected to engage with risk management techniques and act accordingly. The search for a way to predict and control crime (and consequently criminals) became a significant preoccupation, and, as a result, an unquestioning reliance on statistical analysis for decision making emerged. In this actuarial context, the criminalized individual was no longer a subject to be reformed or aided but, instead, was a threat to be minimized. To meet this goal, the correctional system endeavoured to reduce the likelihood of recidivism by discovering and preventing risk factors or by creating and installing protective factors. These techniques afforded the Correctional Service of Canada, the Parole Board of Canada, and other parts of the penal justice apparatus significant power and control justified on the premise of recidivism reduction (Thurber 1998).

Reflecting on these discursive shifts, we see that the criminal is being constituted in very specific ways in each time period – from one who can be corrected, to one who can be rehabilitated, and, finally, to one who must be managed. These linguistic and conceptual shifts mask consistent underlying themes. Over and over again, the stories have been predicated on the criminal as 'other' and pivot on the (modernist) confidence in progress. Perhaps this should not surprise us since, as Stanley Cohen (1985, 157-58) cautioned:

> The language which the powerful use to deal with chronic social problems like crime is very special in its banality. Invariably, it tries to convey choice, change, progress, and rational decision making. Even if things stay much the same, social-control talk has to convey a dramatic picture of breakthroughs, departures, innovations, milestones, turning points – continually changing strategies in the war against crime. All social policy-talk has to give the impression of change even if nothing new is happening at all.

The Story Not Told

In this book, we aim to tell a different story by recounting the success and resettlement of those who have previously been criminalized. This story is not rooted in folklore but, rather, in evidence and experience. In direct contrast to the dominant discourse, data indicate that the former long-term prisoner is able to resettle into the community without jeopardizing the safety of other citizens. At this juncture, we need to emphasize that we are not referring to all of the individuals who have been incarcerated and released in Canada. Indeed, given that in 2008-9 alone, almost 90,000 adult criminal court cases resulted in custodial sentences for the accused, the full contingent of imprisoned people is well beyond the scope of this inquiry. We exclude the majority of prisoners, those who have received provincial sentences (less than two years) and instead focus on those individuals who have received severe federal sanctions (Thomas 2010). This choice was deliberate as it has usually been this smaller group, or rather their crimes, which have dominated the get-tough rhetoric and have strongly informed the tales we have been told.

By and large, the individuals who because of their crimes have received much media and political attention do not re-offend and return to prison. Over the past ten years, over 80 percent of day paroles,[9] over 70 percent of full paroles, and between 58 percent and 62 percent of statutory releases were successfully completed.[10] Therefore, it is reasonable to conclude that the great majority of the approximately 7,100 men on conditional release from the federal system will never return to life behind the penitentiary wall (Public Safety Canada 2011). It would seem that success is the norm – recidivism the exception. This finding is even more evident when the data on revocation of conditional release (failure) are scrutinized – most of these returns to prison are for technical violations (for example, breach of conditions), and less than 2.5 percent are for new *Criminal Code* offences (Statistics Canada 2010b).

Despite this evidence, success is largely absent from the conversation. For example, the *Report of the Correctional Service of Canada Review Panel* acknowledges that "failures are far less than the successes" (Correctional Service of Canada Review Panel 2007, 129). Yet, the failures are the sole focus of the document. To counter this obsession with recidivism, we offer an alternative focus, a grounded methodological approach and an integrated theoretical framework that provide a point of entry to another story.

Our point of departure mirrors that of the United Nations' *Standard Minimum Rules for the Treatment of Prisoners,* which was ratified by Canada in 1975 and which state: "The suffering that results from the loss of liberty and freedom by the fact of incarceration is punishment enough."[11] In other words, we believe that individuals are sentenced to prison as punishment, not for punishment, and, having served their deprivation of liberty sanction, are entitled to 'move on.' Embedded in this approach is a categorical refusal to perceive criminalized behaviour as indicative of a 'kind of person.' This positioning is not a valorization of criminalized individuals but, simply, an acknowledgment of their humanity. Accordingly, this book does not concern itself with the psychology of the respondents, does not focus on their pre-prison lives or crimes, and does not engage with philosophical reflections about the role of punishment. Instead, we suspend judgment and give meaningful consideration to the challenges that these formerly incarcerated men have faced and to the strategies that they have employed to overcome these obstacles. Simply put, it is an examination of the common experience of success. It is the story of men who, like Alice from Lewis Carroll's (1865) famous children's tale *Alice's Adventures in Wonderland,* plummet into a bewildering environment in which they must make sense of their surroundings and the interactions therein and, after a considerable period of time, 'fall out of the rabbit hole' and back into the real world, where they must re-adapt to the mundane.

Hearing and Writing This Story

In order to tell this story, we sought out a research method that would shed light on the lived experiences of former prisoners. While quantitative data demonstrate that success is the norm, they do not illuminate the texture and nuance of the journey from sparse prison cell to one's own home. To do so, we employed the Canadian government's definitions of both long-term incarceration and successful reintegration and conducted twenty in-depth semi-structured interviews with men who had been incarcerated for periods of ten years or more and had been in the community charge-free for at least five. These men very generously took the time to share their stories and respond with remarkable candour to our often tedious probes. We asked them about their experiences preparing for release from prison, about their re-entry, and about the years since. We wondered what factors had helped or hindered them in finding a new place in the community after years of being removed from the social body.

The majority of the respondents (sixteen) were serving life sentences, and the amount of time in prison ranged from ten years to more than thirty – the median was seventeen years. Some of the men had been out of prison for considerably longer than five years; two had spent more than twenty years in the community post-prison. Although predominantly middle-aged, two were senior citizens and one was under the age of forty; most were white, although one man self-identified as Aboriginal; some had university degrees, while others had not completed grade school; some were married, while others were common-law, and still others were single. For the interested reader, an appendix at the end of this book details the methodology employed in this research and some of the ethical issues we confronted.

We had come to know the men as individuals, and we want to afford the reader this opportunity as well. In order to bring the men 'to life,' the next chapter introduces them through a series of vignettes designed to capture their individuality and, in some cases, their quirkiness. Moreover, throughout the book we present, to the best of our ability, their complexity, their insights, and their struggles. Accordingly, we anchor our analysis in the men's narratives.

Precisely because we had come to know the men as people who were not defined by their crime or by their imprisonment, we struggled with terminology in the writing of this text. We had learned too much from the men about the negative impact of labels on their self-concept and on their public identity to replicate the language that informed a discourse that we were motivated to shift. Terms such as 'offender,' 'murderer,' and 'inmate' were obvious problems and easily avoided. Others such as 'parolee,' 'convict,' and 'former' or 'ex-' prisoner, which were used frequently by the men during their interviews, proved more difficult to resolve. If the men felt comfortable using these terms, could we? Using this language implied something that had happened to the men (to be convicted and imprisoned) rather than an inherent quality or master status. However, over time we came to appreciate that our writing was not in keeping with our political and research goals if we consistently used these words.[12] We then considered following the lead of the Correctional Service of Canada's Taskforce on Federally Sentenced Women, which eschewed the negative terms (for example, female offender or female inmate) and instead adopted federally sentenced women as their descriptor (Canada 1990). As such, we played with using the term 'formerly federally incarcerated men,' but this term also felt like a form of 'othering,' albeit one that was gentler and perhaps softer. Ultimately, while some stigma-loaded terms appear in the narratives, we refer to these individuals simply as "the men" and accept that this terminology is sometimes textually tedious.

"Making Sense" of the Stories

At the same time as we recognize that social actors are the experts of their own lives, we are committed to situating these individuals within broader social and discursive contexts. As we endeavoured to make sense of what the men were telling us, we found ourselves turning to the theories and concepts of our academic disciplines. While we have strived to make this text accessible to a wide audience by not weighing each assertion down in heavy theoretical prose, we nonetheless believe that some preamble about the main philosophical and theoretical traditions that inform this work is needed. The purpose of this section is two-fold: first, we want to demonstrate the importance of using an integrated theoretical framework that, in our case, draws on sociology, criminology, and geography; and, second, we want to ground the reader in our understanding of the principal theoretical traditions employed in order to provide a basis on which they can consider our analysis.

The first strand that we weave into our theoretical tapestry emerges from the work of critical human geographers. We begin with an understanding that place (in both cartographic and symbolic senses) is enmeshed in our daily lives. That is, locations and locales influence our actions and thoughts rather than being mere backdrops and, in turn, the geographic places themselves are transformed. For example, the discussion in Chapter 8 highlights the difference between having a 'place to live' and having a 'home' and how regulatory frameworks and normative social expectations condition this subjectivity. Ultimately, we concur with Tim Cresswell (1996, 16), who recognized that place mirrors and shapes the hegemonic landscape:

> Place is produced by practice that adheres to (ideological) beliefs about what is the appropriate thing to do. But place reproduces the beliefs that produce it in a way that makes them appear natural, self-evident, and commonsense ... Thus places are active forces in the reproduction of norms – in the definition of appropriate practice. Place constitutes our beliefs about what is appropriate as much as it is constituted by them.

Appreciating that place creates, reflects, and disrupts power relations, and of course influences all social interactions, opens up a conceptual space for the work of symbolic interactionists. This theoretical tradition focuses on the way symbols (some of which are spatialized, gendered, racialized, or classed) create meaning and allow individuals and groups to situate themselves within a social milieu. This literature demonstrates that, through interactions with others, the individual comes to assume a role (or roles) that mediates how he sees himself (personal identity) and how he is seen by others (public identity):[13]

> The self, then, as a performed character, is not an organic thing that has a specific location, whose fundamental fate is to be born, to mature, and to die; it is a dramatic effect arising diffusely from a scene that is presented, and the characteristic issue, the crucial concern, is whether it will be credited or not credited. (Goffman 1959, 252-53)

As Erving Goffman's quote suggests, symbolic interactionists have also alerted us to the consequences of being labelled, which includes confronting a constellation of stigmatic assumptions. For those who are criminalized, the rituals and ceremonies surrounding their conviction are designed to strip them of their "social citizenship" and burden them with a tainted identity (Bosworth 1999, 116). In Chapters 7 and 8, we will see how ex-prisoners negotiate multiple identities and manage the implications of stigmatic designations.

Of course, interactions (symbolic or otherwise) do not occur in a vacuum and must be contextualized within socio-economic discourses, practices, and structures, including social, interpersonal, and intrapersonal regulation "beyond the state" (Dean 1991). As Elizabeth Comack (2008, 26) has pointed out, criminalized men "encounter structural inequalities that operate to contour and constrain their lives." Therefore, social actors navigate and position themselves within "a set of pre-existing cultural categories some of which are hierarchically arranged" (Schrock and Schwalbe 2009, 280). Put another way, social stratifications speak to systems of privilege and constraint that condition the 'possible' through highly gendered, classed, racialized, and sexualized structural limitations and normative pressures. Moreover, intersectionality theorists have drawn our attention to how these axes of inequality are bound together into "interlocking systems of oppression" that condition the experience of social actors (Collins 1990, 221).

In addition, the men are situated within a particular insidious regulatory framework. Earlier in this chapter, we presented the 'stories that have been told' in order to trace the ways prisons and prisoners have been constituted in discourse and practice. It is important, in order to make sense of the experiences of the men, to explore the complex assemblage of techniques that constitute the regulatory context. To this end, Foucault's work on governmentality affords us a complementary, albeit more theoretical, lens through which to think about the configuration of regulation. He identified three regimes of governance that are still in evidence today (Foucault 1980a [1991]). The first, which he termed sovereignty, pertains to the state's power over individuals. In contemporary society, we see sovereignty in the justice system's ability to take the life (metaphorical and social) of subjects (or to pardon those deemed worthy).

At the same time, the state also has the ability to monitor and assess the individual until such a time as he is transformed into a self-disciplining subject – one who is 'normalized' into conformity.[14] This regime is referred to by Foucault as disciplinary power. The third regime, articulated in Foucault's (1980a [1991], 1982, 2004) writings on governmentality, draws our attention to the complexity of governance in neo-liberal society and alerts us to significant shifts in the regulation of disaffiliated populations (Rose 1996). While the state retains the sovereign authority to criminalize and sanction, regulation is diffused throughout the social body by the state "governing at a distance" through initiatives that, though supported through state funding, appear to operate independently (Rose and Miller 1992). The burden of managing risk shifts from the state onto non-governmental agencies, outside experts, and perhaps, most significantly, individuals. We see this dynamic exemplified in the recent *Speech from the Throne* in which Prime Minister Stephen Harper (2011) pledged to:

> Give law enforcement officials, courts and *victims* the legal tools they need to fight criminals and terrorists ... Canadians who are victimized or *threatened* by crime deserve their government's support and protection, and they should have the right to take reasonable steps to *defend themselves and their property* when the police cannot be there to assist them. Our Government will reintroduce legislation to clarify and strengthen laws on *self-defence, defence of property and citizen's arrest.* [Emphasis added]

We contend that cultural geography, symbolic interactionism, and governmentality provide a useful analytic point of entry. However, in order to do justice to the complexity of the men's experiences, we also draw on other theoretical lenses. For example, in Chapter 9 we utilize labour theory to make sense of the men's relationships to work and in Chapter 10 we use feminist theory to consider how gender is implicated in carceral and post-carceral relationships.

Organization of This Book

After introducing the men as individuals and as a collective in the next chapter, this book is divided into two sections that reflect the temporality of the ex-prisoner's journey: the first part, entitled "Inside Out," concerns itself with imprisonment, with the process of release (when an individual is discharged from prison), and with the early period in the community (re-entry). The first chapter of this section, "Being In: Negotiating Prison," examines the men's experience of prolonged incarceration. We provide an overview of the correctional system in Canada in order to situate the men's experiences within penal eras – from rehabilitation to the more contemporary risk management characteristic of neo-liberalism.

Using Foucault's (1988) concepts of technologies-of-the-self and technologies-of-domination as an organizing frame, Chapter 4, Getting Out: Finding a Way to the Street," examines the process of release from prison. We reflect on the negotiation of the penal bureaucracy by prisoners and attend to their resistance of the actuarial techniques that removed their individuality. Once released from prison, the men began adapting to 'free' society. In Chapter 5, "Starting Out: Halfway There," we consider the tumultuous transitional period in the community residential facility when the men are on parole – halfway in and halfway out of prison. We will see that the planning done while in prison becomes muddled once the stark reality of re-establishing life on the outside is confronted.

Part 2 of the book, entitled "Outside In," is about resettlement, which is the period when an individual is able to decide where he will live without daily monitoring by representatives of the state. In much of the American and Canadian literature, the term 'reintegration' is used to connote a similar meaning, but we have rejected this language as it is often bound to ideas of rehabilitation and behaviouristic discourses.

We also use the term resettlement differently than do some British scholars (see, for example, Maruna, Immarigeon, and LeBel 2004), who regularly employ it to refer to all activities and programs from sentencing onward. In order to reflect broader contextual issues surrounding an ex-prisoner's location in the community, our use of resettlement closely mirrors that employed in the literature on political prisoners. More specifically, we contend that the ex-prisoner's ability to return to, and find, a sense of community is bound up with regulatory frameworks and political trends. The paroled men do not simply reintegrate back into their previous communities but, instead, must negotiate, resist, and respond to the penal apparatus and other government agencies. In this way, the notion of resettlement, which is the relocation of individuals after an upheaval of sorts, is particularly apt.

Part 2 is comprised of six chapters, each of which addresses a particular issue encountered as the men seek to settle into society. In order to provide a nuanced analytic lens that renders visible the layers of experience, each of these chapters foregrounds a specific conceptual framework. Chapter 6, "Negotiating 'Freedom': Echoes and Reverberations," focuses on how the men grapple with the nebulous nature of 'freedom.' Drawing heavily on the work of governmentality theorists, we contend that power relations are rendered visible in the lives of these men who consciously engage in self-regulation and responsibilization as they endeavour to remain out of prison.

In some ways, this self-governance requires the individual to reconceive himself as a social citizen rather than as an ex-convict, and in Chapter 7, "Identity: Fractured and Fragmented Selves," the complex nature of both the personal and public persona of the 'ex-prisoner' is examined. This chapter also considers the multitude of identities that are enacted by the men as they endeavour to 'fit in.' In Chapter 8, "Stigma: Negative Expectations and Amazing Reversals," we extend the analysis from the previous chapter in order to address questions about 'marked' identities. We see that the men engage with their expectations of stigmatization and that they develop strategies to manage their discreditable status (Goffman 1963b).

Critical human geographic theory is employed in conjunction with symbolic interactionism in Chapter 9, "Home and Homelessness: Being

In and Out of Place," in order to explore the ways that place is entangled in the resettlement of formerly incarcerated individuals. We consider how the men's experiences in various locations sometimes leave them feeling profoundly out of place and, at other times, comfortably in place. Chapter 10, "Work and Finance: Navigating the New Economy," incorporates labour theory to examine how the men's struggle to 'catch up' plays out in their efforts to be fiscally stable and to forge 'meaningful' places for themselves in the wage economy. We end the chapter with reflections on those who 'opt out' of this normative expectation.

Chapter 11, "Interactions: Etiquette, Intimacy and Fitting In," examines the challenges those who have been incarcerated confront as they endeavour to negotiate interpersonal relationships. Using Goffman's dramaturgical theory as a conceptual point of entry, we consider the way prisoner-generated scripts, and the constraints imposed by state surveillance, undermine their ability to realize social and interpersonal intimacy.

In the conclusion to the book, "Final Thoughts: Understanding Life outside 'the Rabbit Hole,'" we tie together the theoretical strands to consider on the significance of successful resettlement. Here we reflect on the narrative themes that emerged over and over again and that weave through the book – masculinity and 'being a man,' the aspiration for 'normalcy,' and the profound need to feel 'in place.' This synthesizing chapter is organized along a major theme – struggle – as we contemplate the ways in which struggle has manifested itself for the men in their attempts to find meaningful lives after prison.

We wrap up the text with a brief epilogue in which we reflect on our journey since the research was completed. Like the men we interviewed, we also grappled with the relativity of success. For us, however, the tension pivoted on our ability to put committed scholarship into practice and make the research meaningful to men who were dreaming of, planning for, or on the road to resettling in the community after many years in prison.

Introducing the Men

2

"Who are YOU?" said the Caterpillar.

This was not an encouraging opening for a conversation. Alice replied, rather shyly, "I – I hardly know, sir, just at present – at least I know who I WAS when I got up this morning, but I think I must have been changed several times since then." (Carroll 1865, Chapter 5)

In *Alice's Adventures in Wonderland*, the title character, once in the rabbit hole, must figure out who she really is, how others see her, and, more importantly, what she believes in. The men discussed in this book confronted the same anxieties and existential dilemmas when they fell into the hole (prison) and again, years later, once they fell back out into society. As a result, their often tumultuous journeys are complicated by transforming senses of self, shifting public personas, and a geographic and social 'dis-ease.' While the reader will get to know the men (who have been anonymized) throughout this text, introducing them in this chapter offers an opportunity to relate to each of the men individually and as part of the collective as well as providing some demographic information (see Table 2.1).

Table 2.1 Respondent demographics

Interviewee	Age range	Highest level of education	Children [C]/ Step-children [S]	Current marital status	Employment status	Years served in prison	Years since release
Barry	50-54	university	C/S	common-law	full time	13-15	20+
Bob (lifer)	55-59	university	No	single	unemployed	19-21	5-7
Bobby (lifer)	55-59	college	S	common-law	disability pension	13-15	20+
Dave (lifer)	60-64	college	S	married	retired	19-21	14-16
Doc (lifer)	45-49	high school	No	common-law	full time	16-18	5-7
Ernest (lifer)	65-69	vocational	C	single	retired	13-15	14-16
F.G. (lifer)	65-69	elementary	No	single	disability pension	22-25	5-7
Mr. Flowers	50-54	university	S	married	self-employed	19-21	5-7
Fred (lifer)	40-44	college	C	married	unemployed	13-15	8-10
Gerry	65-69	unknown	No	single	full time	29+	11-13
Gord (lifer)	50-54	elementary	No	single	disability pension	22-25	5-7
Gowan (lifer)	45-49	vocational	C/S	married	full time	10-12	14-16
Jean (lifer)	50-54	university	C/S	common-law	full time	22-25	8-10
Joel (lifer)	45-49	university	No	divorced	full time	10-12	11-13
Luc (lifer)	60-64	unknown	No	common-law	full time	29+	11-13
Marcus	30-34	unknown	C	common-law	full time	10-12	5-7
Puzzle (lifer)	40-44	unknown	C	common-law	unemployed	10-12	8-10
Rick (lifer)	50-54	university	C	married	full time	19-21	8-10
Tom (lifer)	50-54	university	C/S	common-law	disability pension	19-21	8-10
Ziggy (lifer)	50-54	university	C/S	married	full time	13-15	11-13

Getting to Know the Men

Our first meeting with one of the men took place some twenty-five years ago when we walked into a long-term prisoners' group at an Ontario penitentiary and saw a room filled with men serving life in prison – some were starting their time and others were decades into their sentences. Joel was in this room, and he looked both in and out of place. Indeed, his atypical middle-class background was apparent despite the prison greens he wore. Before beginning his life sentence, Joel was, until his arrest for murder, a law-abiding individual with little or no contact with the criminal justice system – the quintessential 'straight-john.' Many years later, we contacted Joel to participate in this research, and during his interview he remembered being pleased about having been invited to join the prisoners' group because it confirmed his acceptance into the convict cohort. His insecurity about belonging was a theme that ran throughout his interview.

Well educated prior to his incarceration, Joel has been employed full time since his release thirteen years ago. In spite of his ability to 'pass,' his impressive intellect, and his generosity of spirit, he struggles with the guilt he carries for the crime that gave him a life sentence, with the daily implications of being an ex-convict, and with the difficulty in finding new friends after prison. He worries about his 'lifer' label and the resultant stigmatization (see Chapter 8). Not surprisingly, while he has retained some of his pre-prison friends and married (and divorced) after prison, his closest relationships are with his family and those with whom he served his time in prison.

One of those friends is Rick, who was also in the prison group all those years ago. Rick served nineteen years inside and has been working steadily since he was released over ten years ago. Divorced and remarried while in prison, he, unlike many of the others, enjoyed the significant support of family, friends, his wife and his ex-wife throughout his incarceration. As a result, he was able to foster a relationship with his child and now with his grandchildren. It is this continuity that helped him retain his pre-prison identities of father, brother, and son. Throughout the interview, Rick positioned his own experiences within the broader socio-political context and drew our attention to the contradictions between the stated objectives of punishment and how these objectives 'played out' in reality. Given that Rick maintains that he was wrongfully convicted, it is not surprising that a major theme of his narrative is one of struggle with injustice. He is not only instrumental in ensuring that his own needs are met but is also willing to challenge the system and 'pay the price' for actively resisting human rights violations.

Another man who saw himself as a resistor was Bobby. He was savvy, academically and street smart – he could read a room and adjust his presentation-of-self accordingly. He considered himself to be a good judge of character, who valued trustworthiness and honour above all else. He was, in the most positive sense, a 'con's con,' and he did his time with integrity, did not have a 'bad beef,' and did not 'rat' on other prisoners.[1] Bobby could have done more time in prison if it had been necessary, and this was the crux of his character. This middle-aged white man was willing to suffer in order to draw attention to needlessly intrusive or arbitrary rules. He would, quite literally, put his body on the line – for example, at one point, he went on a lengthy hunger strike until correctional officials reviewed his dossier. He recognized that his obstinacy made his journey more arduous than it might otherwise have been. Keeping his focus and doing what was most expedient or useful was not always easy for Bobby. His struggles with mental health issues and his own tenacity sometimes got in the way of his succeeding in the community. Unfortunately, Bobby died before this book went to press. He had served fifteen years in prison and had been on parole for over twenty years.

Ziggy has also struggled with mental health issues throughout his life, and his conversation about this challenge was frank, powerful, and self-reflective. Sensitive to people's unease with the mentally ill, he asked his wife to sit in on the interview in order to prevent the interviewer from feeling any uneasiness. He spoke of the profound impact that his illness had had on him as a child, as an adolescent, and as a young man and how it had factored into the crime that led to his life sentence. Indeed, his mental health diagnosis might have made it possible for him to mitigate his crime and avoid responsibility, though he never took this route. Instead, he used his time in a psychiatric facility and in prison to come to grips with his disease and credits workers in the system with providing coping strategies to him: "I was really screwed up but no one did anything. Prison offered me something that nothing else has ever. They offered me so that I wasn't locked in my mind. You know, they offered me that. There was a lot of caring inside." Ziggy is a particularly appreciative individual who readily acknowledges not only the efforts of mental health professionals but also the opportunities afforded him to acquire an education and other valuable skills during incarceration. He is, however, frustrated with the resilience of the stigma. Since his release over a decade ago, he has met all of the expectations placed on him (he has continued therapy, formed pro-social relationships, and worked full time) and is therefore discouraged with the unrelenting surveillance by the state.

Mr. Flowers also speaks to the government's over-involvement in his life. Since no topic is taboo for this smart and articulate individual, conversations can be disconcerting. Not only is he capable of very sophisticated analysis but, just when think you have figured out where he is going, he will also take you in another direction. In the process, he assaults your senses with vivid imagery that makes his arguments almost visceral. He is bold, direct, controversial, and, most definitely, unapologetic. He very clearly sees himself as someone who did more time than could be reasonably justified for non-violent offences and projects the confidence, even arrogance, of someone who has stared the system down and, despite the pains of imprisonment, remained true to his beliefs. This is a man for whom being able to maintain control, regardless of the situation, is critical. It is difficult to capture the essence of Mr. Flowers, who is profoundly insightful and sensitive to the people and environments he encounters and yet clearly wants to be seen elsewise. We are sure he would find it appropriate to have him speak for himself: "I'm a salty motherfucker. And I think my greatest asset is to tell people 'don't get me mixed up with someone who gives a fuck.'"

In sharp contrast to Mr. Flowers, Bob is very soft-spoken. In many ways, he epitomizes the problem of stereotypes by challenging our assumptions about the 'kind of person who goes to prison for long periods of time.' In person, Bob is rather non-descript – neither outgoing nor diminutive – he is simply a disconcertingly 'average' middle-aged white man. Bob is aware that there is nothing about his presentation- of-self that makes him stand out in the crowd and understands when people are surprised to learn that his past includes a violent childhood and twenty years in prison. Bob, who earned a university degree during his incarceration, is self-reflective and thoughtful. Throughout the interview, he never strayed from the topic we were discussing and seemed to really want to make amends in some way for the harm he had caused. He struggles with having committed the crime that sent him to jail and initially expressed concern that his "high profile" would reflect badly on the research. Ultimately, Bob told us a story of struggle and disappointment: "I felt very inferior in some senses when I would talk to people and guys my age ... I thought I'm never going to have what these guys have now. What am I going to have? ... Real men raised their families and worked, you know, for 25 years."

Gowan is another unassuming mild-mannered and soft-spoken middle-aged man. A screenwriter would salivate over Gowan's story, which seems ready-made for a movie adaptation. Like Bob, his presentation-of-self belies the fact that he comes from a large family for which serving prison time is the norm: "It's just a really, really horrific family that was netted into criminal activity from the beginning and we all got busted up when we were young ... We all went to foster homes all over the place." Not surprisingly, he is profoundly ambivalent about having a relationship with his family of origin. Throughout his interview, Gowan's commitment to being forthright and honest was palpable. He is a man who accepts responsibility for the many crimes for which he was imprisoned (beginning in his teens through to his life sentence) and continues to wrestle with the consequences of his actions. In spite of his openness, he is conflicted about how much of his past to share with his children. Now in his late forties, Gowan works full time and does a significant amount of volunteer work, both of which are rewarding and sources of pride. Despite these accomplishments, he is not boastful and is careful to share credit for any of his success. He would like his story of survival to offer hope to similarly situated others.

Gord, whose resettlement has been fraught with both major and minor setbacks, also wanted his story to be shared in order to help others. He has spent the majority of his life in prison (twenty-five years) or on parole (five years), and this experience continues to influence his day-to-day life. For example, Gord has not had an intimate relationship since his release, explaining: "I don't allow myself to get involved in those types of things. There's too much anger inside me still, there's too much frustration, there's too much decompression going on. I spent a lifetime in penitentiaries and I'm a person who feels things a little deeper than other people." His mindset, coupled with the deaths of most of his family members, means that Gord is profoundly socially isolated. Gord sustained a brain injury in an accident, and during the interview his train of thought was sometimes difficult to follow – he went off on disjointed, rambling tangents and often struggled to find the words to express his thoughts. These times were interspersed with moments of absolute eloquence when he captured the complexity of an issue and made the interviewer, and the reader of the transcripts, experience the texture, the smell, or the look of what he described.

Marcus, who was a teenager when he started his federal sentence, also describes his jail time as difficult, and the emotional implications of this experience have continued to reverberate in his life. Despite only being in his early thirties, Marcus had already served ten years and been out for five. While incarcerated, he had limited contact with his parents, and this separation stems from what he described as an abusive home life. After release, however, his family rallied to provide financial and some emotional support. Marcus credits the birth of his daughter with changing his outlook after prison: "I was angry, bitter, I had a lot of hate and resentment. What I felt inside was pretty anti-social, anti-establishment but the second she was born ... It's the coolest thing and from that moment on, I just knew that everything that everybody ever told me about having a child was there, like, the love." As a result of the birth of his daughter and the support from family, Marcus says his transition to the community was mostly smooth.

In sharp contrast to Marcus is Doc, who found re-entry difficult. He spoke at length about post-carceral challenges at the same time as he expressed pride at having surmounted them. Out now for over five years, he has undergone significant personal transformation. He fought to maintain his pre-prison social and personal identities as a biker and Northerner but, ultimately, relinquished these in order to get out, and stay out, of prison. Doc sees himself as fundamentally working class, and while he worried that he would not be articulate enough, his openness, forthrightness, and deep contemplation of daily life made his narrative powerful. He recalled details, such as his girlfriend's chiffon blouse, which made his stories come to life and pushed us to see the complexity in the everyday. In particular, his attention to the minutiae helped us to appreciate the gendered nature of release, re-entry, and resettlement (see Chapters 7 and 11 for some of his thoughts). Ultimately, he felt that he had been successful in his post-prison life, which was a perception that he shared with Dave.

Dave had served twenty years in prison on a life sentence and had been out for fourteen years when we spoke with him. Now in his early sixties, he is retired and sees himself as successful. In fact, the first time he met the interviewer he handed her his 'business' card that identified him as a full-time volunteer. He is a man who wants to feel needed and be seen as being 'okay.' Throughout his interview, he spoke of being an active member of his congregation and was enthusiastic about his faith, which he felt had saved him from what he considers to be an immoral past. Part of what Dave believes is morally reprehensible is his sexual attraction to men. At one point, he deliberately violated his parole so that he could atone for having had a same-sex relationship. For Dave, his ability to live as a heterosexual man is a marker of his success: "I wasn't born like that. I just got bad habits ... I have to learn, okay, I got rid of that bad habit, and that bad habit, and that bad habit ... but I have to be able to replace those bad habits with good habits. So if you got good habits going, you know, you've got a greater chance of success." Dave married after prison and immersed himself in his female partner's large family, and these relationships help him maintain his freedom.

Unlike Dave, Gerry, who passed away before this book was published, was a life long bachelor who had no contact with his family – a trend that started during his thirty plus years in prison. In many ways, Gerry was the type of guy who the public thinks of when they talk about someone with a criminal career. He served several sentences in various prisons in Canada and abroad and was unapologetic for a past he neither glorified nor negated. A senior citizen at the time of the interview, his warrant expired eleven years after his release and just months before we met. It was hard to reconcile the diminutive man in the interview with the hard time he had served – he was polite, avoided profanity, and was disconcertingly matter-of-fact – even when discussing things that were difficult or emotional for him. Gerry's pragmatism was evident in how he spoke about release, re-entry, and resettlement, and he was methodical in his efforts towards freedom. His tenacity served him well, and despite an extremely limited work history, he found employment in the service industry and earned enough to maintain a very simple lifestyle. He was content with this achievement.

Similarly, Fred, an Aboriginal man who despite not yet turning forty, has served fifteen years on a life sentence and has been out for nearly a decade, aspires to a simple life filled with lots of laughter. It is important for Fred to conceal his past from his children, who do not know about his conviction or that he is on parole. It is not surprising that, having spent most of his life in institutions under the control of various state authorities, he would want to protect his children from the implications of this stigma. He credits the birth of his first child (which occurred while he was still in prison) with motivating him to change his behaviour in order to get out, and stay out, of prison: "Of course you do it for yourself, but how would they [his children] feel if I was thrown back in jail again. They'd be devastated." He wrestles with helping his children understand their Aboriginal heritage while protecting them from what he considers to be negative influences in his community. He has also faced other challenges since his release, including difficulty finding steady employment, racism, and stigmatization.

Puzzle, an Irishmen and self-professed "red-neck," has also confronted many challenges, including one that he had not anticipated – being a stay-at-home father. Due to an injury, Puzzle left the paid labour market and now takes pride in maintaining a good home and being an attentive and involved parent. This is a major identity shift for this man, who in his early forties had already served over ten years on a life sentence and had been out for eleven years. Despite his relative youth, he presents as a very old-school type of convict, and clear role delineations are important to Puzzle. While he feels no qualms about essentializing others (see Chapter 7), it was important to him that he be seen as distinctive. During the interview, he would frequently suggest that his story was unlike the others we might hear: "So that's the key to understanding that if you want to get out, you have to play the game like that ... you haven't had that answer. I don't think you've had that one yet. Trust me, I don't think you have."[2] To his credit, his ability to frame his journey in unique ways helped to establish one of the main themes of this book – common experiences are always subjectively interpreted.

Another Irishman in the study is Barry, who served thirteen years and has been out for over twenty. He was the only man we interviewed who had received a state pardon for his crimes. Barry was very interested in helping us to understand the commonality of former long-term prisoners' experiences, and he answered every question in a direct and thorough way without straying from the point. Like several others, he spoke of a very abusive childhood, drug and alcohol addiction, the early onset of criminal behaviour, difficulties with health (physical and mental), and the challenges of adjusting to life outside of prison. Barry credits his ability to survive prison and to reintegrate to his own "Irish stubbornness," his intellect, his ability to get along with a wide variety of people, and his willingness to challenge the system. He served time in two distinct periods and, as such, offered considerable insight into the shifts in correctional approaches. He spoke of major transformations in himself as well – he went from being young and violent to being seasoned and thoughtful.

Jean also spoke at some length about transforming his identity. Prior to prison much of who he was revolved around his participation in a motorcycle club, and though this identity marker was no longer available, it was still important for him to be seen as 'tough' and 'in control.' This need was evident during the interview – he never lost sight of the fact that he was putting himself on the public record and was anxious to be seen in a positive light. That said, he was also willing to draw attention to his own contradictions in order to demonstrate the nuanced nature of human experience. For example, while Jean generally held a firm, and negative, view of workers within the penal system, he readily gave credit to those government employees who had had a positive influence on his life. Jean served twenty-two years of a life sentence inside and has been out for over ten. Perhaps more than anyone else in this research, he was emphatic that prisoners need to use their time to prepare for release. He even went as far as creating a list of things to accomplish while in prison: "[I wrote] out a list of the top ten things I always wanted to do in my life but never had a chance to do or never had the time to do it. Number 1 on the list was a college degree. Number 2 was play a guitar. And number 3 I can't remember, but I pretty well completed them all." Ultimately, Jean's actions in prison helped him to obtain meaningful employment (working with another disadvantaged group) after release.

Unlike Jean, who was hyper-prepared, Luc, by his own admission, had been naïvely optimistic. Despite having no work experience and spending thirty years of a life sentence (for robbery) in prison, he was surprised that it was difficult to secure employment. While Jean was careful to frame his story in terms of accomplishment, Luc was much more likely to point out the struggles he faced, and, ultimately, lost time and disappointment were predominant themes in his narrative. Despite being interviewed by a woman, Luc spoke frankly about his desires and sexual disappointments. He also provided valuable insights into the way gender manifests itself both in prison and on the street. While he is currently living with a common-law partner, he has found that his ability to foster healthy relationships has been undermined by the attitude and behaviours he cultivated in order to survive in prison (see Chapter 11).

Tom also helped us to better understand the gendered nature of the struggles men face when they return to the community. He was initially reluctant to participate in this research and only reversed his earlier refusal when he realized the potential he had to help other prisoners and those on parole. As you will see from the frequency with which we quote Tom, we are glad this gifted story-teller took the time to talk with us. Tom was candid about his strategies for finding work when he first left prison – he simply 'filled in' his twenty-year employment gap (due to incarceration) by 'creating' employment and enlisting the help of friends who would 'verify' the information if they were called for a reference. Tom has since died, but at the time of the interview had been out on parole for ten years, and though he was no longer employed, he was financially stable, as the result of a significant financial settlement that eased many of the pressures he had experienced in finding, and maintaining, work. Tom spoke often of coming to grips with being older and how that played out in his day-to-day life (see Chapter 11).

He went to prison as a young rebellious motorcycle club member and came out having grown children who had children of their own. He had changed in other ways as well – he had upgraded his education and was invested in legitimately acquiring the markers of middle-class success. Perhaps this is why, unlike most of the men we spoke with, Tom did not make even a passing reference to the crime for which he received his life sentence. Only one other man, Ernest, was similarly silent about his crime.

Ernest, a Maritimer, is a quiet, unassuming senior citizen who spends his days living in the country with his two cats. Like Gerry, Ernest has a lengthy criminal record, which started in his teens and finished with a life sentence of which he served fourteen years inside. He has two children with whom he has no contact, and this lack of relationship is reflective of his general social isolation. Although he occasionally gets together to play music with neighbours or share some conversation on the front porch, he maintains a relatively solitary existence. His interview covered all of the same areas as the others, but, in the end, we felt we knew little about him. We do know that he faced numerous obstacles (such as health and housing) after his release and that geography played a significant role in his resettlement. As we will see in Chapter 9, he used shifts in spaces to avoid some people and to find a place of belonging. At this point in time, he lives comfortably within his means on his old age pension, which was very similar to the situation of F.G.

F.G. is a senior citizen who has been out of prison for over five years after serving twenty-three years on a life sentence. Like Ernest, F.G. lives on a pension, but, unlike Ernest, he has almost no work history. His last paid job (outside of prison) was in the early 1970s. In many ways, F.G. represents the men who have been dependent on the state, by choice or by deed, for most of their lives. A life long bachelor, F.G. spoke often of the implications his long incarceration has had on his day-to-day life and on the strategies he has developed to deal with these consequences (see Chapters 6 and 11). Despite having only a primary school education, he is articulate and thoughtful about the experience of prison, release, and resettlement. F.G. is not boastful, and this characteristic is surprising, given the high regard others have for him. A number of the individuals with whom we spoke noted his guidance and his significant role as an advocate for prisoners inside. He refutes this assessment, asserting: "I hate when people say 'oh ya you were important.' I wasn't important." F.G. does not aspire to adoration – he simply wants to be 'okay.'

The Men as a Collective

The preceding vignettes were intended to bring each of the men 'to life,' to capture their individuality, and, in some cases, to highlight their peculiarities. They are also, however, part of a collective of predominantly white, mostly working, or underclass men who had shared a significant experience – ten or more years in prison followed by a long process of resettlement. Not surprisingly, there were a number of recurring, often intersecting, themes that warrant mention here, some of which will be teased out in greater detail in the coming chapters: class, masculinity, race, and the search for 'normalcy.' We begin with an additional theme – histories of childhood abuse.

Despite only being asked to briefly describe their childhood at the end of the interviews, many of the men spoke about their early years throughout the session, and descriptors such as horrific, suffering, and awful were frequently employed. Several of the men provided narratives of sexual, physical, and emotional abuse perpetrated by family members and others. Our familiarity with the literature around the victimization of children and the correlations to later criminalization meant that we were not surprised by their discussions of physical and emotional trauma, though, occasionally, the degree of abuse mentioned was disturbing. Their candour around sexual abuse, sometimes of an incestuous nature, was poignant and somewhat destabilizing. While well documented for criminalized women (Canada 1990; Eaton 1993), the sexual victimization of males is less acknowledged and often ignored entirely. While reliable Canadian statistics are not currently available, some data from the United States indicate that 14 percent of all men in prison were abused as children and nearly 8 percent of this abuse was of a sexual nature (Harlow 1999). Interestingly, the men did not use the abuse they had endured to explain or excuse their criminal actions, nor did they employ the language of 'victims' or 'victimization.' This reluctance may be the result of their preference to be seen as 'survivors' (which we discuss in Chapter 7) or it may simply be that, in light of our collective lack of acknowledgement of the molestation of boys and the link to later criminalization, this discourse was unavailable (Comack 2008).

The social class of the men's family of origin was a characteristic many shared. The majority of the men hailed from working-class backgrounds. Given Jeffrey Reiman and Paul Leighton's (2010) assertion that "the rich get richer and the poor get prison," this demographic is not surprising. Some of the men embraced the markers of working-class culture and celebrated its expressions. Other men, like many individuals living in societies in which the myth of meritocracy holds out the promise of intra- and inter-generational class mobility, sought to improve their positions within a stratified system. These men were endeavouring to become part of, or re-claim their belonging to, the middle class in a country in which income disparity is growing (Statistics Canada 2008) and the middle class is being increasingly squeezed out (Yalnizyan 2009, 2).

Gender was another prevalent (albeit often implicit) theme. Repeatedly, despite our direct questioning on the role of gender, the men engaged in a complicit masculinity in which they "neither explicitly support nor condemn the forms of masculinity that provide them with advantages" (Torres 2007, 78). While, they rarely acknowledged the privilege being male bestowed on them, they spoke to the pressures they felt in enacting various forms of masculinity in prison and afterwards as well as to their struggle to 'do gender' (Connell 1995; Messerschmitt 2001; West and Zimmerman 1987) at a time when gender scripts are being significantly revised.

The unwillingness or inability of the men to engage critically in regard to the role of race was even more evident. The most reflexive on this topic was the one Aboriginal man in our sample (Fred), who had a profound understanding of how race and racism conditioned his imprisonment, release, and resettlement. Interestingly, for the remaining men, the acknowledgement of racism was limited, almost exclusively, to their time in prison, and they would make statements such as Barry's: "When I look at it, there's definitely areas where I know that I was privileged because of course the majority of the officers in the institution were all white and yes there is racial prejudice in prison." Joel explained:

> There's white time and there's black time and black time is the worst
> time you can do ... I didn't have to overcome that. If they were going
> to say something to me, they would be, "You fucking convict," not
> "You fucking n**** convict! ... I think the people that had the worse
> time of it are the Aboriginals.

Most avoided racist comments during the interviews but exhibited a
certain kind of colour-blind racism wherein the impact of race was
minimized or their own white privilege ignored (Bonilla-Silva 2010).
For example, we asked the men about how race conditioned their resettlement, and the following excerpt exemplifies the tenor of their
responses:

> I imagine it would. I don't know really. I treat everybody the same. I
> don't know how other people treat other people. I imagine being a
> white guy is different than being a black man. I really can't answer.
> You'd have to ask one of those [guys]. I just went out for what I wanted
> to accomplish and I did. White or black or red, it didn't matter. (Jean)

In the end, unlike gender, the men gave us little material through which
we could explore the subjective impact of race on their own release and
re-entry.

Ultimately, the thread that most consistently ran through the fabric
of the men's stories was the desire for 'normalcy.' For the most part,
perhaps because of their criminalized pasts, these men did not want to
stand out, and in fact they strove, and sometimes struggled, to be 'average.' They endeavoured to conform to normative scripts and organized
their goals accordingly. As you will see, in many ways they and their
aspirations are profoundly 'ordinary' – they wanted to find love and
belonging, get good jobs, be respectable citizens, and move beyond
the moments that led to their lengthy incarcerations.

PART 1: INSIDE OUT

The journey onto the street begins in prison and we also start there. In this section we briefly examine the experience of prison and how it is institutionally structured, the process of release as the men prepare to leave the penal institution, and re-entry when the men are halfway in, and halfway out, of prison. There are really two stories in this section. One is of the management of federal prisoners by the Correctional Service of Canada through a system characterized by control and punishment and reinforced by the potential for increased privileges and the hope of eventual release. Accordingly, prisoners are able to earn (generally by demonstrating that they are less risky) degrees of liberty and 'cascade' through the system and (for the most part) out of the penitentiary and into the community.

The second story is the one that emerges when we integrate the perspectives of the men living under correctional authority. Seen through their eyes, cascading is allegorical to floating down a river. Rather than travelling in a smooth and controlled manner, the experience can more appropriately be likened to navigating an exceedingly slow-moving channel with periodic (and largely uncharted) currents, rocks, whirlpools and rapids. Not surprisingly, most prisoners find themselves caught in vortexes, unexpectedly (and sometimes expectedly) shooting backwards into higher security institutions, and periodically stranded midstream 'going nowhere.' In this section, our examination of the journey from the prison to the street is divided into three temporal chapters: being in, getting out, and starting out.

Being In: Negotiating Prison 3

Let me describe it to you like this: it was like a big psychopathic
nightmare. It was like a bad LSD trip that I had when I was younger.
You never knew when the thing would come to an end and finally
you're coming down, the hallucinations are stopping, you're coming
back to your normal senses. Thank God. Well, it was like a big, long
psychopathic nightmare. Maybe the last couple of years weren't
even like that, but as for the rest of it, it was just horrible. (Gord)

The prison experience has been the subject of many books written
from the perspectives of clinicians, workers, scholars, and prisoners.
This particular research project was not about incarceration but, rather,
about the transition to a successful life after prison. However, it is impossible to examine the latter period without addressing some of the
precursory carceral period. This chapter cannot, and should not, provide
the reader with a comprehensive sense of the deprivation of liberty.
Instead, we seek to contextualize former long-term prisoners' experiences in order to render visible the linkages between the prison regime
and the parole and post-parole apparatuses. To this end, we begin with
a brief overview of the penal system before tracing the ideological

trajectory of 'corrections' in order to demonstrate how these shifts are reflected (and resisted) in the men's lives.

Sitting, Sliding, and Security: An Overview of the Carceral System

The Canadian prison system is divided between provincial and federal jurisdiction. As of 31 March 2008, the provincial system managed the 23,858 convicted individuals who had received a sentence of two years or less, and the federal system absorbed the remaining 13,342 individuals.[1] On admission, all federally sentenced prisoners are sent to a maximum security receiving unit where they are assessed to determine their 'needs' and their risk to the institution.[2] At this location, they are subject to psychological testing and file reviews. It is also made clear to the prisoners that their time inside will not be easy. As Gord recalled, "[a prison guard] said, 'I'm going to tell you right now, you're going to face some of the toughest times of your life,' and boy, he was right."

After reception into custody, the individual begins a 'cascading' process in which he is moved through the system into lesser-security levels as his perceived threat and 'criminogenic' needs decrease. The *Corrections and Conditional Release Act (CCRA)* indicates that:

> Where a person is, or is to be, confined in a penitentiary, the Service shall take all reasonable steps to ensure that the penitentiary in which the person is confined is one that provides the least restrictive environment for that person, taking into account (a) the degree and kind of custody and control necessary for (i) the safety of the public, (ii) the safety of that person and other persons in the penitentiary, and (iii) the security of the penitentiary; (b) accessibility to (i) the person's home community and family, (ii) a compatible cultural environment, and (iii) a compatible linguistic environment; and (c) the availability of appropriate programs and services and the person's willingness to participate in those programs.[3]

Appropriate placement is important for the reasons noted earlier; however, the distribution of prisoners through the security levels has been identified as problematic (Solicitor General of Canada 1984). For example, the 1977 report by the Subcommittee on the Penitentiary System in Canada notes that medium- and maximum-security institutions were overcrowded, while minimum-security facilities were underutilized. At the time, the report acknowledges that the classification process "may not yet have fully adjusted itself to the innovations of medium and minimum security" (MacGuigan 1977, 132). While this committee predicted the increased use of lower-security levels as the system adjusted, current data from the Correctional Service of Canada (CSC) suggest that assessments of risk are very stringent, with "the number of offenders classified as maximum security at admission [increasing] by 50 percent since 1997" (Canada 2010a). This increase may be the result of an attempt by the CSC to maintain its goal of producing "an offender distribution of 15 percent minimum, 73 percent medium and 12 percent maximum-security." It may also be the result of Custody Rating Scales[4] that weigh a variety of factors so that a life-sentenced individual inevitably begins his sentence in maximum security[5] and stays there for at least two years, at which point he is eligible for his next review.

Two decades after the formal cascading process was introduced in 1979, the neat flowchart envisioned in correctional policy is not evident. In fact, "reverse cascading ... [which] is consistent with punishment/reward system" (Canada 1984, 37-38) may be just as prevalent and ultimately hinder prisoner release. As one of the men explained, "I got kicked out of ... Bath Institution [minimum security], so I went back to Collins Bay [medium security]. And from Collins Bay, over to Pittsburgh [minimum security] – with the recommendation from the Parole Board for ETAs [escorted temporary absences]. I sat for twenty-eight months, no ETAs" (Doc).

The men, who had been incarcerated in an earlier era characterized by less accountability, still believed that these involuntary transfers could occur at the whim of a warden and not be based on any proven disciplinary offence. Indeed, a previous warden of Joyceville Penitentiary referred to this approach as "greyhound therapy" wherein "you back up the bus, you throw five or six inmates in the bus, you drive them forty miles down the road to increased security and the whole tone of Joyceville, the medium security I work in, mellows" (cited in Canada 1983). While current transfers between institutions may demand more accountability, the Ashley Smith case has reminded us that the use of involuntary transfers to deal with 'problem prisoners' remains a contemporary issue. In his investigation of the death of Smith in custody, the correctional investigator concluded that there was a "long sequence of highly inappropriate, unnecessary and unlawful transfers between CSC facilities" (Sapers 2010).

While sections 28 and 29 of the *CCRA* declare that prisoners are to be incarcerated in "the least restrictive environment," transfers may be initiated for the benefit of the institution with little regard for the individual prisoner. This practice is significant because an institution's security rating has a profound influence on the prisoners. Many of the men told stories of the difficulties encountered at higher-security levels and how this experience was transformative. Rick, for one, commented: "Millhaven [maximum-security penitentiary] for 4 years – just 4 years ... [it] really damaged me that place. Emotionally. Psychologically. That damaged me. I lost innocence in that place. That small town innocence, I lost it there."

There are instances in which the effect of these transfers was to create a sense of displacement that can be seen as a "mode of desubjectification insofar as the bodies of the displaced are seen as objects operated on by outside hostile forces" (Delaney 2004, 848). This displacement affirmed the state's power over the men. The prisoners were forced to pack up their belongings and move to a different cell in a different building, and often this movement occurred with no warning and presented new challenges:

> It was hard to trust the other guys. It was like going from prison to prison ... or from range to block, from one block to another block. You know it takes a little while ... you just ... tippy toe, you know. You watch and you know pretty well who you can talk to and who you don't need to talk to. (Dave)

Research has shown that prison spaces are personalized by the individuals within them so that the blandness and uniformity of the environment become masked. Consequently, displacement can cause grief reactions such as anxiety, depression, and health problems (Fried 2000).[6]

Unwanted transfers can therefore be particularly rupturing since many of the men see their cells as their 'own' and as a 'safe' space within a block of people who are known to them.

Generally, given that greater control is exercised over the movement of prisoners at higher security, transfers to less secure institutions were welcomed. Medium- and minimum-security institutions allow increased access to programs, to community resources, and to decision making. As Joel, who had never served time before, explains:

> We'd all come from Millhaven. It's like you graduated. You went through something together that was bad and they even got me a fresh bed and mattress and everything. You could really facilitate movement around because it was really more open back then and I was at a group that night.

This cascading system is thought to better prepare prisoners for release, which is also true of the system of parole. The latter is premised on allowing prisoners to earn early release in order to "best facilitate the rehabilitation of offenders and their reintegration into the community as law-abiding citizens."[7] As illustrated in Figure 3.1, prisoners must serve a minimum of one-third of their sentence in prison before they can be considered for parole. Therefore, since every man in this study was sentenced to a minimum of ten years, they all had to serve over three years. In reality, all of the men were incarcerated for much longer – half spent more than seventeen years in prison. This statistic may have occurred because of the prevalence of life-sentenced individuals in this research. None of the lifers were even eligible to apply for day parole before the seven-year mark, and no one received full parole before ten years.

From "Good Intentions" to Discipline

The men were motivated to cascade through the system in order to access the resources and privileges that characterize lower-security institutions, and this movement also facilitated their eventual release on parole. In this way, the "cascading process is consistent with the

Figure 3.1 Conditional release eligibility

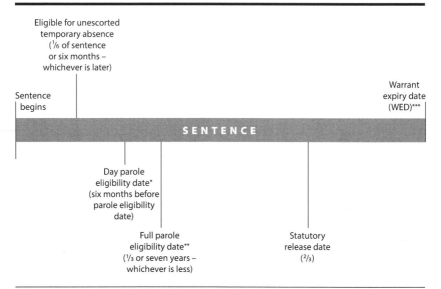

* Life-sentenced individuals are eligible for day parole three years before their full parole eligibility date.
** Eligibility for full parole for life-sentenced individuals is determined by the court. The minimum time before eligibility is ten years for second degree and twenty-five years for first degree.
*** Life-sentenced individuals do not receive a WED. Their sentence expires at their death.
Source: Adapted from Solicitor General of Canada (1998).

opportunities model. An inmate's reward for good behaviour is a transfer to a lower level of security" (Canada 1984, 37). However, the transitions were sometimes destabilizing, engendering confusion in the men over their roles and those of others:

> Yeah, as you get to the lower security, it gets worse. More intervention. I kind of liked that earlier stage at Millhaven when you were through the glass thing. Weren't really seen that much. You only see them [guards] when they locked up and they walked down the ranges, and they open the doors and let you out. Down into lower securities, they're sitting on a couch like this one. Talking to you all the time, wanting to know about you. Wanting to know this. Wanting to know that. I don't like cons being around me doing that let alone guards, right. So you just [say] "No disrespect or nothing but I want to be

alone here. Can you leave?" And they get all twisted. You don't want to talk to them and all this shit goes on your file. You're anti-social and this and that and you just want to be left alone. (Jean)

Jean's story exemplifies the period that Stanley Cohen (1985, 19) refers to as "good (but complicated) intentions – disastrous consequences." While initially characterized by hope and the idea that people could be rehabilitated, gaps between policy and practice became evident over time, leading to increased pessimism that these goals were realizable.[8] This doubt persists and echoes through the experiences of the men with whom we spoke. Fred shares his perspective:

> But they're not helpful, you know. Like, they don't come to you and say, "Oh this is what you have to do" ... We're just their pay cheque and I'm sure there's some of them that like to see you get out. But there's a lot of them that are, like, "Hey you're my pay cheque."

Cohen (1985, 44) contends that this disillusionment leads to a period of cynicism that he calls "discipline and mystification." Of course, in the 1980s (when these men were in prison), the social movements of the 1960s and 1970s had continued to resonate in vibrant social debates regarding the role of the state, capitalism, and self-perpetuating social stratifications. Like individuals on the outside, the men reiterated various critiques: "The system is corrupt anyway. Prisons are for the poor. The rich always get away with it" (Gord). In this context, efforts to change the criminal justice apparatus were critiqued as illusory, rhetoric was seen as empty, and real change was considered unlikely. The men indicated that even the optimistic correctional personnel who subscribed to the good intentions model were soon co-opted by a more negative approach:

> Prison staff, you know, they come in, they get some bright-eyed ideas and then boom, they fall quickly to the corruption. "I better hold on to my job here." You know blah, blah, blah and on down the tubes the horseshit goes and then they just become generally abusive assholes like the rest of them. (Doc)

While the earlier reform movement called for a more humane, inclusive, and community-driven response to crime, the practice was somewhat different. An expansionist trajectory gained momentum and focused on more punitive and repressive measures.[9]

Negotiating Risk and Responsibilization

By the 1990s, the men were beginning to feel the impact of two new, but symbiotic, discourses – responsibilization and risk management. The discourse of risk (borrowed from economic and medical disciplines) led the correctional system to a search for an algorithm to predict and control behaviour. The CSC had introduced the "Custody Rating Scale." Intended to establish "objective, standardized criteria for the initial classification of federal offenders" (Luciani, Motiuk, and Nafekh 1996, n.p.), this scale reflected the new "primacy given to the efficient control of internal system processes in place of the traditional objectives of rehabilitation and crime control" (Feeley and Simon 1992, 450). Bobby, who had served two long periods of incarceration, noticed this shift during his prison tenure (including the year that an automated version of the scale became available):

> This was definitely before the reformation that was done in '92. There wasn't anything anywhere near the scope, the detail and accountability that is done today. There wasn't any specific release plans. There wasn't case management ... It was just a very long slow lengthy process of "this year you'll be eligible for ETAs," "this year you'll be eligible for UTAs" and stuff like that. There wasn't any particular time spent looking at halfway houses and support structures. There wasn't – nothing there like that in the seventies. The second part [was] when I was suspended and revoked in '95. At first I thought it was way overboard but now I understand and completely agree with it. They tried to go back to pre-sentence reports, they tried to take a look at institutional behaviour and offences, and all those kind of stuff and criminogenic factors, and a number of sociological factors, and in my case mental health dispositions and stuff like that and tried to tie them all together.

In short, we see complex individuals reduced to a series of quantifiable measures so that elements can be removed or prophylactic measures added. To this end, new technologies (such as the Level of Service Inventory (revised), the Community Intervention Scale, or the reintegration of potential reassessment, computerized data banks, and drug testing capabilities) were developed with the goal of "provid[ing] a standard and tested risk criterion for decision-makers to employ under conditions of uncertainty" (Clear and Cadora 2001, 55).[10] In these technologies, we see the neo-liberal focus on management rather than on transformation (Feeley and Simon 1992). Fred echoed this focus when he stated: "We're just warehoused. That's all we are." In this context, it was no longer necessary for correctional personnel to engage with the multiple facets of a prisoner. This is in contrast to earlier eras when workers had discussions with the men in their caseload. As Jean recalled:

> I did eight years in Milhaven and they knew all about me. I didn't talk to any guards. They knew all about me. And it's because you got to see your classification officer every three months – sometimes every month.

Starting in the mid-1980s, reliance on the opinions of professionals in individual cases was not an acceptable strategy for managing risk. Case managers were no longer expected to exclusively use their professional judgment in determining a convict's readiness to be released from prison since this technique was subject to human error, manipulation by individuals, and, of course, some unpredictability. This shift in approach was potentially counter-productive because each man spoke about how one state-employed person (for example, a guard, psychologist, shop boss) who knew them and understood what they needed dramatically influenced their ability to succeed both in prison and afterwards (see Chapter 4). As Michel Foucault (1984/89, 82) argues, these non-scientific knowledges became "disqualified as inadequate to their task or insufficiently elaborated." They were now conceived of as "naive knowledges, [which are] located low down on the hierarchy, beneath the required level of cognition or scientificity" (ibid.).

Priority was thus afforded to certainty, non-randomness, and erring on the side of false positives (Clear and Cadora 2001). Bob, who without providing details of his index offence warned us of the high-profile nature of his crime, told us his release was delayed because workers were afraid of a false negative:

> Everybody was pretty nicely covering their butt and they said, "No, you have to have new psych. assessments" and everything else and nothing changed. And everybody said, "Let him go, let him go." But it was a case of getting it all done and making sure that there wasn't any heat caused.

The second major discourse that dominates is responsibilization, which, as John Pratt (1999, 141) points out, "has involved moving the general burden of risk management away from the state and its agencies and onto the self, in partnership with non-state forms of expertise and governance."[11] The men frequently engaged with this responsibilization discourse when they discussed life in prison and their preparation for release:

> As for the Parole Board, there's no point in giving her [girlfriend] any credit for anything. Because the only one that's going to make it or break it is me. Doesn't matter what she says or does, you know. I'm the one that's going to commit the crimes ... I think that families, you know, mothers and so on, are really influential, but again the bottom line is who makes the decision. I wanted to be able to show them that if you're releasing me, you're not releasing me into the care of a woman who's going to provide dah, dah, dah, dah, dah. You know, I'm capable of coming out here and making it on my own. That's what I wanted them to see. (Doc)

When prisoners refused to be 'responsibilized,' state workers were destabilized. For example, Bobby, who felt his conviction was not righteous and had appealed his case to the Supreme Court of Canada, categorically refused to engage with "technologies-of-the-self" (Foucault 1988):[12]

[They said] "Well we gotta get you out." I said, "No you don't gotta get me out. If we can devise a plan, which gets me down the river a notch, well, that's ok. Go for it. But I don't need to do that because I'm okay where I am right now." It can be very hard to explain that to a lot of people in case management because their whole agenda is to move you along. You know. One peg. This peg, that peg. He's gone. Ok. "Who is next?" This peg. This peg ... That's what they do. That's their mentality. So I see that. So I say, "Don't make me one of your pegs." So that's not really an act of resistance to them. It's just that I'm just not willing to participate in that whole scheme.

Up to this point in the chapter, we have traced shifting penal policies, practices, and discourses. We know that despite the state's current attempt to depersonalize the penal process through risk management strategies, prison is experienced in deeply personal ways. We now shift to an examination of the more general and transversal elements of the prison experience.

Living in Prison: Coping with Force

While not the focus of the interviews, the men did speak about their prison experiences and the process of "prisoning" (Comack 2008, 111), including the initial shock of the transition:

I was 17 years old, I had it all figured out, didn't I? I mean, I was going down the highway in a military convoy ... You know, getting ready to go out in the universe ... young and full of life! And a year later, I'm going down the same highway in a convict truck with a prescription to hell's heart. (Gord)

Once inside, the austere nature of the prisons in Canada allowed the men little sensory stimulation. The higher-security institutions are walled, and in the case of the facilities built in the 1800s, high stone fences make it impossible to see beyond the prison yard. Gord, who was very sensitive to his surroundings, describes his attempt to find stimulation:

I was in the old school penitentiary hall and it was on top of the building in BC Penitentiary and I would strain, just to see the flowers and the sun in front of the administration building. Just to see the flower because you could see it through a certain angle – the flower's bloom. Part of an eye, not even your whole eye, part of your eye could see through a little hole.

These impoverished environments can lead to depression because they limit the space for movement, restrict communication with others, induce extreme boredom, and deny sexuality (Gosselin 1982). Phil Scraton, Joe Sim, and Paula Skidmore (1991, 48) contend that the rigidity of the prison routine is designed to have a negative psychological effect, and they emphasize that prisoners "had relinquished the power to determine the direction of their lives. They were no longer autonomous individuals exercising personal responsibility ... they had become property of the state." Joel speaks to this issue:

It wasn't helpful being locked up every friggin' day. I mean the whole atmosphere is not helpful. Eighty percent of it is the loss of freedom, 80 percent, and the fact that your life is regulated. The regulation to the "nth" degree wasn't helpful. That wasn't helpful at all ... I'm a lesser person because I've had my freedom, I've lost all my responsibility, I can't exercise, I can't make decisions ... "Oh we had staff come through and tear your cell up." What can you do? Let it slide, water off the duck's back. Guy comes and searches my cell or whatever ... so what! I am in prison after all.

The imprisoned men endeavoured to mitigate the implications of the deprivation in a multitude of ways. One common approach was to use drugs and alcohol:

I test dirty for THC (tetrahydrocannabinol). Well. "Why are you smokin' up?" I said, "You know, I'm getting older here and you people talk about your retirement and I'm sitting here friggin' rotting away ... You want to know why I'm smoking up?" 'Cause it's friggin' insane. (Doc)

Others were able to break the monotony and gain a measure of control by upgrading their education or by participating in the vocational programs that prepared them to work in a trade once released. Gowan's story exemplifies this instrumentality:

> When I came into the system I couldn't read and write hardly. I had no trades, and I took advantage when I was in and went back to school and I went and got my grade 6, grade 7, 8, 9, 10, 11, 12 at Collins Bay. I ended up getting my welding licence and my apprenticeship in Collins Bay, and I ended up walking out of there with eighty-nine credits.

These programs have become increasingly rare over the past decade. As Tom, who had completed a year of university while in prison tells us, educational opportunities have been replaced by behaviouristically oriented programs:

> They took away all the trades and put in the programs. And, you know, everybody that was going up for parole, well they had you, you know, whatever programs they felt you needed, right. So I took a whole bunch. I didn't take them all. I can't say I took them all, but I took a few. I even took an alcohol one, and I didn't have that on my thing and the Parole Board said, "Why did you do that?" I said, "Well, just to upgrade myself in case, you know I get out there and do have a problem with it" ... They kind of liked that.

For the lifers, the ability to realize the (symbolic or concrete) benefits afforded by programs was difficult as access was limited, and those with indeterminate sentences were relegated to the bottom of the priority list. F.G., who throughout his interview demonstrated a very reasoned approach to matters, was proactive and found an unlikely ally in a warden:

> There was no such thing as programs for lifers although a lifer has to do all these programs. The problem is they ... have ten chairs for inmates being released ... I don't have a release date ... I talked to the

warden and I said, "If I can get eleven lifers that guarantee that they will stay the course for the whole [time], will you get us Anger Management?" He said, "Yeah" ... So I got him a list ... and that's how we got our Anger Management course.

While some saw the potential benefits of program participation, the men maintained a critical stance, especially in regard to instructor qualifications:

So I walked into the program and there's a lady there and I said, "Can I ask you a question?" She said, "Yeah." I said, "What do you know about drugs?" ... What do you know about me? Somebody using drugs? What do you know [about] the feeling I had when I do drugs? What's the difference between demerol and heroin? What happens to Heroin when you inject it into your system?" [She said,] "Well, I don't know." "Well, then, what qualifies you to stand up there and tell me about drugs?" (F.G.)

An even more skeptical attitude was evident when the men reflected on former guards adopting the 'teacher' role:

Then they turn around and just give a bunch of jobs to the guards 'cause that's who got the jobs. The guy was turning the key in your door the day before and actually now he's a cognitive skills teacher. I mean, come on man, you know. (Tom)

Some of the men made the link between this behaviouristic approach and the new penal preoccupation when they argued that these programs were merely a way for the correctional system to appear to manage risk. Mr. Flowers, who was perhaps the most cantankerous man in the study, did resist programming and was cynical about its purpose: "I've seen so many bullshit programs ... Programming in an institution is a cost-effective way of babysitting a large group of people ... I guess programming for me [was a] very devious, weak ... demoralizing, waste of fucking time."[13]

While the men spoke critically of the correctional approach to pro-gramming, a more pressing issue was the psychological harm engen-dered by incarceration itself. It is important to consider the prevalence of violence and aggression in prison (Comack 2008; Gosselin 1982; Haney 2004; Scraton, Sim, and Skidmore 1991; Zimbardo 1971). Indeed, Scraton, Sim, and Skidmore (1991, 61) have pointed out that "all forms of incarceration imply the use of force," and so violence is inherent to prisons. In Elizabeth Comack's (2008, 70) work, she finds that for former and current prisoners, "physical aggression was an important resource that they could draw on, for instance, to maintain a 'tough guy' image and thereby gain status and respect among their peers." The men we spoke to also told us that the penal system obliged them to adopt a hyper-masculinized persona. In order to survive, they had to be seen as strong and, at a minimum, potentially violent:

> You're inside and you live with people and we got 13,000 prisoners in Canada ... In order for you to function in that jail, you gotta be very severe. So, with this – and naturally arms and knives and baseball bats, whatever it takes – you establish a certain sphere of *you* which is called also respect, fear, and all that. (Luc)

The fact that the prison is a place of violence has long been acknowledged by the state. The 1977 House of Commons Subcommittee on the Penitentiary System in Canada explained the role of penal institutions in creating violence: "Most of those in prison are not dangerous. However, cruel lock ups, isolation, the injustices and harassment deliberately in-flicted on prisoners unable to fight back, make non-violent inmates violent, and those already dangerous more dangerous" (MacGuigan 1977, 16).

This statement, issued nearly forty years ago, clearly reflects the opti-mism of the earlier era about the rehabilitative approach. However, it is unlikely to be reiterated in the current climate in which the criminal-ized are conceptualized as 'inherently dangerous' and a risk to society. Nonetheless, the men that we interviewed still agree with the sentiments expressed by the Honourable Mark MacGuigan (1977). For example, even Marcus, who said he was not violent, found that he had to adopt a "hostile bravado" (Goffman 1963b, 17): "I think the front I presented was that which most other people did. I'm fine as long as you leave me be but if you screw with me, I'm going to have to kill you. I don't think I ever would've or maybe I would've. I don't know. But you had to present it" (Marcus).

Despite the men's concerted effort to appear 'tough' and enact a kind of "protest masculinity" (Connell 2004, 109) that projects an imagined powerfulness, most of the men in our sample indicated that they were at times afraid and insecure during their sentences. As a result, they experienced gender role strain as they tried to survive their imprisonment (Mahalik, Good, and Carlson 2003). Of course, care must be taken not to hyper-exceptionalize the prison. While the prison can be characterized as a place where long periods of monotony and boredom are punctuated with extreme violence, in many other ways it is merely a microcosm of the outside world. Indeed, Marc Maur and Meda Chesney-Lind (2002) contend that the very use of prisons is a reflection of a patriarchal approach to 'solving' social problems, which often explicitly demands aggressive tactics. Regardless, Barry's words effectively encapsulate the effect of the ever-present potential for violence: "Bloody scary would be the two words that I would use. It was frightening. It was very frightening. It was incredibly frightening."

Reflection

In this chapter, we have provided an overview of the correctional system in Canada. While a thorough examination of the experience of prison is beyond the scope of this work, it is important to ground the remaining chapters (which examine release, re-entry, and resettlement) in the predicating carceral world. The realities inside the prison mediate, for good and for bad, the men's lives outside the fence. The shifts between rehabilitation and risk/responsibilization that they first encountered during their incarceration do not get left behind but, rather, as we see in the second part of this book, continue to resonate in the 'free' world.

Getting Out: Finding a Way to the Street

4

> Everything seemed hopeless and pointless. Just why bother? I just
> desired to get out ... I felt I was obligated to get out for my family.
> I was obligated to move on because they cared about me. But per-
> sonally, I didn't feel worthy. I didn't feel like there was any point to it
> because I thought I'm not going to have – I've never even worked.
> I worked a summer job. I hadn't even done that since 1979. Now, I'd
> never had a job as an adult. I'd never owned a TV. I'd never owned a
> car. Never had my own apartment – it just seemed all so unattainable
> to me. (Joel)

In Canada, prisoners do not simply disappear behind bars only to
emerge as fully free citizens after a designated period of time.[1] Rather,
their release, re-entry, and resettlement are lengthy processes influenced
by both regulatory policy and practice as well as by the aims and actions of the convicted individuals themselves. In this chapter, we juxta-
pose the official release process with the experiences of the study's
participants.

Despite the prevalence of socially conservative rhetoric that espouses
the need for fixed sentencing and the abolition of parole, Canada's
criminal justice system is still largely premised on allowing prisoners

to earn early release in order to "best facilitate the rehabilitation of offenders and their reintegration into the community as law-abiding citizens."[2] Some of the men were cognizant of their eventual release and started the process of resettlement at the beginning of their sentence (see also Maruna, Immarigeon, and LeBel 2004). These prisoners started to plan for their releases as soon as they received their sentence from the court. For example, Dave, who began his life sentence in 1969, did his vocational training at the beginning of his imprisonment so that he would be qualified by the end and thereby would have used, rather than filled, his time.

However, most of the men who were serving life sentences did not have a sense that they would ever be released. There may be several reasons for their perception. First, the minimum eligibility for parole (ten years and twenty-five years) was implemented after the abolition of capital punishment in 1976. Therefore, many had no other similarly sentenced individuals from whom to get advice or on whose plans they could model their release. Second, many (and, especially, most of those who had never been incarcerated before) simply could not foresee surviving the potentially volatile prison environment for the many years ahead of them. Third, the lack of a temporal frame of reference may also have been an issue for those whose sentences were greater than the number of years they had been alive. Finally, the majority of long-term prisoners do not have previous federal incarcerations and, consequently, may be unfamiliar with the technicalities and processes that would allow them to serve part of their sentence in the community (Correctional Service of Canada 2009).[3] In this context, some of the men essentially 'gave up' and believed that they would spend the remainder of their lives in the penitentiary: "I was firmly convinced that I wasn't going to get out ... I figured well, this is it. These people are serious. And I had made the adjustment – and even the head psychologist said, 'You can live inside or out, can't you?' And I said, 'Yeah, I can'" (Ernest).

Ernest's acquiescence may also speak to the institutionalization that occurs when, as result of the psychological damage of incarceration, the individual demonstrates a dependency on the prison, is lethargic, and acts very passively (Marshall 1994).

Long-term prisoners have to accept the potential for release before they can begin the process. In other words, the first step in the 'pathway to the street' is a psychological adjustment. The catalyst for this perceptual shift was varied among the interviewees. For some, it was their belief that they were simply unable to do more time. Gord was on his twenty-fifth year of a ten-year life sentence when he "just hit the 'hole' [solitary confinement] for a few months and the psych ward and I knew I was losing it and I was dying. I'm in the hole and I said to somebody, 'I'm dying mentally, emotionally, psychologically, spiritually – I can't do this [prison] anymore.'" The catalyst for Tom was when he obtained 'new' information:

> None of us [lifers] thought we could be released ... So it never even dawned on me until ... I had a C.O. [correctional officer] and I'm in seeing him one day and he says "You know, you can be released someday." I said: "What?" He says: "Yeah man, probably in the next five years if you mellow out and stay out of shit. Out in five you go." So that settled it. That's what started me thinking about release.

Once the prisoners came to the understanding that they could be released, they engaged in two concurrent processes: technologies-of-the-self (working on themselves physically, mentally, and psychologically) and technologies-of-domination (navigating the state-imposed preparation process) (Foucault 1988).

Technologies-of-the-Self: "Get Your Head on the Street"

Earning release necessitated that the men 'get their head on the street' and envision themselves as future members of the community. Indeed, this self-work was a precondition to a mental/attitudinal shift to doing time. For Gerry, a senior citizen who did over thirty years in prison, this conceptual shift occurred after he had served the first fifteen years: "When the time comes that you feel you have to buckle down and be involved in programs, etc. in order to get out, you can't be taking chances on getting caught smoking dope and drinking brew and stuff and getting charged."

Some of the men were motivated by their families. Rick, whose "Mom and Dad were always there," explained that "part of wanting to succeed is trying to give them something to be proud of." Gowan demonstrated his humility when he credited his intimate partner for persuading him to develop a release plan: "I was one of those guys that if I didn't have a wife ... who knows where I would be today? ... 'cause I didn't care."[4] For others, prison visitors allowed them to conceive of the possibility of re-entry and also acted as a source of inspiration: "The fact that people are coming in to see you, gives you that symptom of hope that I should be out there and re-living with these people" (Doc). According to Dave, who often struggled with making what he considered appropriate social connections: "The volunteers from the community, they're so important. They make you feel like a human being. They accept me."

For several of the men, it was specific individuals within the system who helped them envision 'life after prison.' In Ziggy's case, support came in the form of an encouraging shop boss who took time to mentor him in his trade. For others, it was the staff psychologist or psychiatrist who helped them to gain perspective. In some instances, it was a case-worker who had faith in them and perceived them as individuals rather than as files. Joel summarized a sentiment shared by many: "It's not the system that makes any difference but the people in the system can make a real positive difference."

For some of the men, these technologies-of-the-self necessitated adjusting not only attitudes and behaviour but also their self-image and presentation-of-self. Doc gave away his prisoner activist and biker clothes, shaved his beard, and reduced his physical size (by ceasing to lift weights) in order to present himself as 'average' to the Parole Board of Canada (PBC). This process necessitated that Doc 'do' gender differently and engage in the ongoing process of adapting to the social setting (Messerschmidt 2001). He was aware that the muscular body that was so valued in the prison could be 'read' negatively outside the penitentiary walls. Moreover, Doc knew that "tidiness and personal dress functioned also as proxy measures of risk and compliance" (Crewe 2007, 264). He was therefore surprised when his efforts at transformation went unnoticed by a PBC member who seemed oblivious to his compliance with the normative expectations of appearance:

There was a report written about me one time about how dishevelled I used to keep myself ... The day I went up for parole ... I shaved my beard off. [The] woman is talking for like forty minutes – didn't even notice. I said to my wife, "See how observant this lady is. This is the one that's, you know, making decisions on my life and I'm standing right in front of her for forty friggin' minutes and she hasn't even recognized that my dishevelled look has become clean."

In short, the crucial psychological preparation required that these men engage with technologies-of-the-self and manipulate both their subject position and their actions. Concurrent with these preparations, they engaged with technologies-of-domination encapsulated in the formal process of release designated by the criminal justice system.

Technologies-of-Domination: State-Structured Preparation

The *Corrections and Conditional Release Act (CCRA)* outlines a series of concrete, tangible steps to prepare prisoners for release.[5] It would appear that this process has become considerably more structured in the context of neo-liberalism's 'new' penology, under which accountability and risk management, as discussed in this book's introduction, dominate the correctional agenda (Simon and Feeley 1995). The need for a calculable, objectively defined strategy has replaced the looser, more subjective process previously used. In short, while the overall structure (temporary absences, day parole, and full parole) of conditional release has generally remained the same, the underlying rationale, and hence how those elements are implemented and experienced, is different (see Chapter 5). The small sub-group of men in our sample who had been imprisoned more than once demonstrated this shift. Barry, who began serving time in his youth, refers to the conditional release during the rehabilitative rationality era as being "by guess and by gosh." He explained: "The release plans back in those days were not anywhere near as structured as they are now. There was no thought that went into it. It was just grab whatever you think and go." There is now considerably more structure with a clearly delineated process of graduated release, which starts with temporary absences, followed by day parole, and eventually full parole.

Temporary Absences

Under sections 116 and 117 of the *CCRA*, the Correctional Service of Canada operates a Temporary Absence Program (TAP), which is divided into supervised and unsupervised leaves from prison. An escorted temporary absence (ETA) is a short-term release immediately available to allow prisoners to attend court or counselling, perform community service work, address parental obligations, or receive medical treatment. In the official state discourse and in the men's assessment, the TAP helps prisoners prepare for release and enables them to have contact with the community without the pressures of day parole.[6] Some prisoners used the TAP strategically. For example, Puzzle, who wanted to be seen as being in control, obtained his car and motorcycle licences while on passes: "When I needed my licences, I phoned the guy in charge of the licensing bureau ... and said, 'This is who I am, I need a bike licence and I need a car licence ... the only way I can do it is on an ETA. The waiting list at that time was over a year. And he said, 'When's your next pass?'"

However, participation in this program requires that an individual approved by the Correctional Service of Canada escort the prisoner at all times. Not surprisingly, the time and date restrictions, coupled with fiscal restraints, make these passes not only hard to arrange but also subject to cancellation without much notice. Gowan, who wanted to maintain face-to-face connections with his wife, was discouraged: "When I started my escorted passes I was given 16 hours a year. It was hard. I couldn't even go to a movie." Under the correctional model, the ultimate authority to grant (or refuse) an ETA rests with the institutional head.[7] In an emotional moment, Dave recalled:

> My first pass with escort was sitting on a probation officer's desk when I got news that my grandmother passed away. My grandmother raised me until I was 7 ... and I loved her dearly ... Two guards had volunteered to pay out of their pocket, their own transportation to escort me to Hamilton to go to the funeral and back ... all of the executives at Joyceville [Penitentiary] at the time where I was said "yes" except one person – the Acting Deputy Warden ... And he told me, "Dude, I don't want you to take this wrong way but I know that you would not be able to handle that pass 'cause you've been in so

long. Emotionally, you would not be able to handle it" ... And I walked back to my cell and I felt aloneness.

In order to facilitate their participation in the ETA program, prisoners sometimes cultivated a relationship with a correctional worker. For individuals for whom the line between 'guard' and 'convict' was firmly drawn, this reliance on the former engendered a disconcerting 'greying' of the black-and-white division:

> I had fifteen [years] in and ... I got the one [ETA] ... Ironically I had to find a guard to take me out – and I didn't know any guards. I never talked to any of them. So a woman volunteered to take me out. And I was taken out on my very first pass after fifteen years by a female guard. I thought she had a lot of balls to take out a lifer. (Tom)

However, the frustrations around the bureaucratic delays that often characterized the ETA process largely dissipated once an individual became eligible for unescorted temporary absences (UTA). UTAs are available to those serving more than three years after one-sixth of their sentence has expired, unless the person has received a life sentence, in which case passes are not available until three years before their parole eligibility date.[8] At such time, it is possible for the prisoner to work at a paid or voluntary job during the day and return to the institution in the evening. Temporary absences also afforded the men the opportunity to organize for their eventual return to the community. For Ernest, who was not particularly outgoing, this meant readapting to the outside world:

> [I had] high anxiety levels. Not knowing where to go. Not having to be somewhere. Not knowing where it is and whether I'm going to be late ... Am I on the right bus? Where is this place? How do I get off, right? ... All the different coloured clothing and everything. It was like a multi-colour coming at me all the time. And the very fast [pace].

After being confronted with such sensory overload, their return to the familiarity of the prison after a pass gave them time to reflect on, and therefore adapt to, a changed world:

There's a big adjustment but when you get little bits of culture shock, you can go back [to the prison] and think about it. You know, if I get a six hour pass or an eight hour pass, go out and experience it, and go back – I can't sleep. You could never sleep after a pass. You always get this, like toothpicks in your eyes. And all I was doing was going over every minute of the pass and what transpired, and what I'd seen, and what I felt I should change in myself or do something differently. (Jean)

Yet, not all of Jean's experiences were so positive; indeed, on at least one occasion his pass serves to confirm sovereign power:

My first UTA [unescorted temporary absence] was a Christmas Pass to London and I went there [and I] had to sign in at a police station when I got there and I had to sign in when I left ... I walked in and they were nice and pleasant to me and my mother and I handed them my parole papers and everything changed ... It went from pleasant to friggin' nasty in seconds ... They didn't want me in London ... He [the police officer] made me sit on a chair for about forty-five minutes and they were calling all these cops in off the street and – cops and detectives coming down from different floors and pointing at me ... [Later that day] around one o'clock in the morning, I hear pounding on the door of my mother's house so the door opens, [to] a cop. [I said] "What do you want?" [He says] "Well, I was just checking to see if you were home, you know. You're not drinking" and he had his flashlight in my eyes. There was no privacy ... They were following me all over the place. They parked out in front of the house.

While Jean's story speaks to hyper-vigilant risk management, in other cases, the frustrations are linked to bureacratic rigidity:

After I was on the work release there [in prison] for a bit, I had permission to have my own vehicle ... So I drove my car to the halfway house [on a UTA]. But the rules of the halfway house are you're not allowed to drive ... I was almost being forced into being a prisoner in the community as opposed to being released on a release ... It was a whole new set of rules that were tying me up and I hated the UTAs. It was just something that I thought I would really look forward to. I didn't. (Rick)

While the technical distinction between a UTA and day parole is obvious, in practice, many of the respondents found the separation ambiguous. In the next section of this chapter, we first define day parole before moving on to examine the strategies used by the men to achieve this status and their experiences thereof.

Earning Day Parole

Day parole, which is granted under subsection 122(1) or (2) of the *CCRA*, is similar to a UTA except that the individual returns to either a community correctional centre (CCC) (operated by the government) or a community residential facility (CRF)/ halfway house (operated by a community agency) instead of the prison. A prisoner is eligible for day parole once he has served either one-third of his sentence or seven years – whichever is less.[9] If an individual is sentenced to life for second-degree murder, a minimum of seven years must elapse before he is eligibile for day parole; if convicted of first-degree murder, twenty-two years must pass before he can apply. The decision to grant day or full parole is made by the PBC, and it is based on the release plan developed by the individual as well as on the documents submitted by the case managers, parole officers, therapists, elders, community supports, and others.[10] In reaching its decision, the board is directed by section 102 of the *CCRA* to contemplate whether:

> (a) the offender will not, by reoffending, present an undue risk to society before the expiration according to law of the sentence the offender is serving; and (b) the release of the offender will contribute to the protection of society by facilitating the reintegration of the offender into society as a law-abiding citizen.

Parole is not a right but, rather, a privilege bestowed at the discretion of the PBC; therefore, the prisoner is responsible for developing a plan that will be positively received. Since all but two of the men in this study were released on day parole to a CRF/CCC, they had evidently success-fully navigated the process and received a favourable decision.[11] In order to do so they drew on a number of strategies, including: becoming in-formed, 'playing the game,' participating in programs, subverting the file, attempting open and honest engagement, and finding support. Many of the prisoners, having spent long periods of time 'inside,' found it impossible to envision their lives beyond their immediate carceral environment: "Trying to see past what was happening in there, I couldn't really see the future. In fact, that was the hardest thing about the parole hearing. I couldn't make plans. I couldn't think of anything concrete" (Joel). Yet, the state process of release requires that the prisoner have a 'flowchart of options' in his mind. In order to resolve this tension, the men sought out information. For some, this data came from community support people, family, and friends; for many others, knowledge came from fellow prisoners. Tom credits the Lifers' Group inside the prison for disseminating information:

> The Lifers' Group was a blessing for us ... We realized that we didn't know a lot about what would happen if we ever got released ... The Lifers' Group got us to invite in people from St. Leonard's ... Life Line ... We had no information when we started. Well, certainly the government didn't offer it.

Other men endeavoured to 'play the game' and to that end they carefully educated themselves about the system in order to identify expectations and tailor their correctional plan accordingly: "I was careful to make my [release] plans in such a way that they would be able to agree" (Joel). Fred manipulated the dominant discourses and employed a specific lexicon to his advantage:

> I was just working to get out. Just following their steps, using their words, that's what I do – that's how I've gotten everything. I read a lot. I've read everything that they have. Like cascading, reintegration, everything, and you use all their words. And then they go, "Ah, this guy is rehabilitated."

Others took instrumentality a step further. They attended programs, whether they perceived themselves to need them or not, in order to learn the language and to be seen to be engaging with the process. They referred to this practice as 'playing the game.' According to Mr. Flowers, who had the intellectual and social capital to 'win the hand': "It is all a game until your warrant expiry."

Participation in programs was not always a 'game.' Some of the men agreed with the Correctional Service of Canada that participation in programs is an essential component that demonstrates their readiness for conditional release. Indeed, most of them had taken part in at least one program and often in several. While resenting the compulsory nature of their participation, they also appreciated that programs could be helpful in some ways. The men understood that the completion of programs improved their placement on the Level of Service Inventory (Revised) scale (LSI-R) and also sometimes augmented their cultural capital, making them more competitive in the labour market.[12] At times, the men also gained skills they could apply in their day-to-day lives: "I was [so young] when I was incarcerated that I need[ed] some life skills ... So, I went into those ... you know, the money marketing management, cooking and baking. I just felt that eventually there's going to be a need for me to cook or bake" (Marcus).

The fourth strategy the men employed was to 'subvert the file' by putting the subject into focus. These men were aware that when rendering a decision, the PBC relies on statistical tests of risk (such as the LSI-R) and the individual opinions of caseworkers and PBC members – a subjectively mediated 'objective' process in which the prisoner's institutional file is a significant factor. Illustrating Michel Foucault's (1977, 194) assertion that "power produces; it produces reality; it produces domains of objects and rituals of truth," the file creates a "textual truth" on which further decisions are based. Since convicted persons have very little control over what this file contains, or how it is used, some seek to undermine the PBC's reliance on their dossier by putting themselves, as multi-dimensional human beings, into focus. F.G. applied for parole before he was eligible so that he would have an opportunity to meet with the board and establish a relationship:

I walked in and they said, "Well, you haven't got enough time ... Denied" and I said, "That's okay." I sat down and I talked to them. They looked at me as if I was nuts. But once we got the conversation going, I wasn't a file anymore ... Then you cease to be a piece of paper and you become a person.

Fifth, some of the men, aware of a significant 'problem' in their release plan or file that no amount of humanizing would neutralize, elected to address the issue in a forthright manner through open and honest engagement. For example, Doc eschewed deception (which, of course, carried the possibility of greater penalty later):

Even at the last [PBC] hearing, [they asked:] "Why are you making a stance [about THC]?" [I said:] "I'm letting you know this for a reason. I don't want to be released on a full parole, you give me a urinalysis, it comes back dirty. Now I got to start all over ... If you do me next month, I'll guarantee that it'll be dirty. I'm not stopping for nobody. It's not to be defiant. It's to say, this is me."

In Doc's case, his engagement can best be understood within its particular context. At the time of his full parole hearing, the *Report of the Special Senate Committee on Illegal Drugs* had recommended that marijuana legislation be modified to treat the substance more like alcohol or tobacco (Canada 2002b). This opinion was supported later that year when the *House of Commons Special Committee on the Non-Medical Use of Drugs* argued that the penalties for marijuana possession were too strict (Canada 2002a). Doc's strategy was effective, in part, because his argument concurred with the broader social and legal discussion. However, since it is rare for the interests and perspectives of criminalized individuals to coincide with popular social movements, this strategy is 'risky.' In a neo-liberal and law-and-order era, PBC members are not only responsibilized for risk management, but they are also surveilled. They must therefore be vigilant in their decisions. As a result, few prisoners are prepared to flag a 'problem' that can result in parole's being delayed or denied.

Finally, the men endeavoured to develop support networks, which could be a challenge since, by design, imprisonment is a very isolating process based not only on the deprivation of liberty but also on the separation and removal of individuals from the social body (Zimbardo 1971). Even though the structural restrictions on visitation in prison (such as physical barriers and time limits) reduce the benefits of this support, it is still favourably considered by the PBC (Breese, Ra'el, and Grant 2000). Those who did not have familial or other support in place faced the challenge of developing networks that the PBC would judge to be solid and acceptable. Some forged connections to individuals and groups during their UTAs and ETAs, while others made strategic use of in-reach volunteers:

> We started bringing groups in ... We invited them in, into our world ... And they'd get to know us. And then, "Oh, uh, you need somebody to do carpentry work? This guy's a good carpenter." So they'd take a chance and they'd take one guy down and he does good ... and that's how you do it – one at a time ... It was getting people out. So they were out in society. They were learning to live in society and society was learning to live with them. (F.G.)

Bobby, who was outgoing and personable, was emphatic that meeting people from outside support agencies was a useful strategy: "Anytime there was any kind of seminar, John Howard, you know, or whoever, St. Leonard's comes into the joint when they're promoting their halfway houses and stuff like that. I was always around glad-handing and shaking hands ... So I knew a lot of people." Indeed, according to Christy Visher, Nancy LaVigne, and Jeremy Travis (2004), most jobs obtained by ex-prisoners were found through personal connections. Joel was less confident about the utility of this approach. He recognized that the individuals voluntarily coming into the prison were not necessarily those people they would meet when they got out:

> You had the left-wing students and the right-wing old Christian geezers 'cause they're mostly older people ... We had a really good

group of Christian students one time came in. They were a pretty lively bunch but mostly older people – retired people and the left-wing students ... "Where the hell is the middle class here?" "Where are the people in the middle who are the majority who we're going to have to go out and live with?" ... The extremes come to prison because it's an extreme environment.

Resisting the Process

Before concluding this chapter, we need to speak about those prisoners who could choose not to engage with the gradual release program, knowing that regardless of their behaviour they would eventually be released. Perhaps reflecting the fatalism of (some) youth, Marcus explained: "I knew that there wasn't going to be any gradual release for me. The only date I was looking forward to was my eventual release date. I knew that was the date they had to let me out and I knew I wasn't getting out before that." Although not relishing the thought of remaining incarcerated until their statutory release or warrant expiry dates, those men with definite sentences retained a sense of control over their situation and could reject programming, for example, in order to deal with identified risk areas:

I made the decision that I'm going to do what I want ... I got high when I wanted to. I didn't work like I used to ... Every month for fifteen months, they [urinalysis] were dirty. Eventually, I told them, "I don't care. Stop wasting your money. There's nothing you can do or say to make me change" ... It was coming up to my release date for my statutory release, they had to let me out. There was nothing they could do.[13]

Reflection

While the men all participated in the process of release, it is obvious that their experiences were quite varied. For most, the TAP was extremely useful, while some found the associated bureaucracy frustrating. The majority of respondents were released on day parole, and they used various strategies to achieve this privilege, including inserting the subject into an 'objective' process, co-opting the state's discourses, participating in programs, and developing support networks. While we have discussed the general experience of preparing for release and day parole, we have not yet explored the specific challenges of day parole, and it is towards this topic that the next chapter on 'starting out' turns.

Starting Out: Halfway There   **5**

[Can you remember the day you were released from prison?] Sure – yes I do – I remember. Yes, I do ... A former Life Line worker came and picked me up at 8:00 o'clock in the Institution and I had my stuff packed and I had approximately twelve boxes. My worldly possessions in twelve cardboard boxes, and he packed them into a mini-truck and I came down here with another lifer ... It was sunny. It was a day very similar to this only it was warmer. It was in June, and we stopped a couple of times to eat and, uh, the feeling was that we went in somewhere to eat and, I remember ... I said, "Oh, I've got to go to the washroom." "Well, then go." He says "You're on parole. You know, you don't answer to anybody anymore, you're on parole." And there was a couple of those things happened and we got down here at approximately ... 4:30 in the afternoon and, um, Jill and a couple of the people were sitting outside [the community residential facility] and a couple of guys that I knew, lifers, who were down here were waiting outside for me, which was nice and they, uh, helped me carry my stuff in and, uh, they made me feel really welcome. And it was a good day. (Bob)

Having negotiated release from prison, the men found themselves adjusting to life on day parole. While incarceration, release, and re-entry are often conceived of as a linear process, we will argue in this chapter that, like the experience of imprisonment and release, there is considerable ebb and flow in the process. That is, while the men not only embraced a new degree of liberty they also vacillated between feeling 'free' and feeling constrained. They experienced trepidation and exuberance and, sometimes, a pervasive sense of malaise. Progress was made, and then they 'slipped up' and were either returned to prison or faced increased regulation. While the to-and-fro experiences were common, it was obvious that three major tasks needed to be accomplished in the period immediately after prison: re-acclimatizing, settling in, and moving on. For this group of former long-term prisoners, there was considerable fluidity as they figured out how to live in a highly changed world, adapt to a less restrictive environment, and prepare for life in their own spaces.

Re-acclimatizing

> I mean, how could I be prepared after all of those tough years. Twenty years before I even saw any daylight. I wasn't too prepared. It was a little shocking in some ways. (Gord)

During the ten, fifteen, or even twenty-five years that they were locked behind prison walls, the men had acclimatized to a very small world – one that was spatially and socially confined. On release, they found that "everything's totally different. We see it on TV and that when we're in prison over the years, but it's not the same when you see it on TV and doing it" (Dave). Luc explains: "I had to change in my mind here; 'Luc it's not like it was thirty years ago. Things have changed. People are different. They don't think the same way. They don't operate the same way.'"

Contemplation of the many 'big things' that would have to be accomplished (such as getting a job, finding a place to live, and so on) occurred while they were incarcerated, but the new parolees were unprepared for the many small tasks that would manifest during the re-acclimation period. As a result, completing these tasks was a source of stress. For example, Bob recalled having to get new identification cards or, as he put it, "piece my wallet together" in order to access services.

Even going to the doctor required a health care number, which necessitated the acquisition of another piece of government-issued identification.[1] Navigating the various agencies and bureaucracies to obtain these documents obliged the men to travel to unfamiliar places and speak with non-correctional personnel – things that they may not have done for over a decade.

The men also had to adapt to altered gender roles, changed folkways and mores, and the frenetic pace of contemporary society. In the midst of this culture shock, the men found that even mundane activities evoked fear and confusion:

> I can go where I want to go and do what I want to do, but I was kind of nervous ... You know, if I was going to walk down the road, get run over by a car, or ... I think I was really nervous to ... how I would react to people ... I grew up in jail ... so that's the only life I knew ... You do this, you do that, you do this, and you hope you don't get killed ... It's how you live in there. And then when I got out ... it was different. (Fred)

The destabilization experienced was further exacerbated by their "hyper-responsivity to external stimuli" (Grassin 1983, 1451). Following years of confinement, the men were highly attentive to the plethora of sights to which they were exposed: "The Rideau is beautiful. I know it's polluted and everything but the scenery of the Rideau, it's really nice – really nice. People take this for granted who live here ... The people who live here don't even notice it ... I've appreciated it from the day I got here" (Tom). The men positioned themselves almost as tourists who see sites as topographically unique, while the locals (insiders) pass by without notice. This intense awareness of space can be seen as a natural extension of Erving Goffman's (1963b, 14) claim that the discreditable will become hyper-aware in social interactions. Since spatial elements are an integral part of social dynamics, greater attentiveness in areas where these encounters occur is to be expected (see Chapter 9 for more discussion of this phenomenon).

This increased responsivity is, of course, influenced by the limits on what the men could see while they were in prison. In these carceral spaces, they were only allowed in their cells, the solitary confinement units, the yard, or the common areas (such as the weight room). Over time, these sites became monotonous. Several of the men spent considerable time in solitary confinement (formally referred to as administrative and disciplinary segregation) – a place where, as Michael Jackson (2002, 291) has noted, "the humiliation and degradation, the frustration, the despair, the loneliness ... [is] intensified." The deprivation of sensory variation is an issue that most people experience at different points in their lives. For example, when the lights come up in a darkened movie theatre, our eyes must adjust to the brightness while we are suddenly reminded that others around us are beginning to move. The difference for these men is the intensity and duration of the deprivation and, relatedly, the amount of time it takes to readjust.[2]

The men's dis-ease was further exacerbated by the fact that while their world had gotten smaller, society was undergoing transformation at an unprecedented rate. As a result, they faced a multitude of choices: "The challenge I had when I first got out ... was ... everything changed and ... there's so much more, like, to choose from than before" (Fred). They also confronted exponential changes in technology. The men went to prison excited about their high fidelity stereos and the eight-track cassette decks in their cars and came out to compact disc players and sophisticated portable music devices. For those whose lives are uninterrupted by major temporal or spatial breaks, such technological innovations are incremental, whereas, for these men, the changes were experienced instantaneously. As a consequence, Luc felt temporally out of sync:

> I didn't know how to function in society. The simple things that you take for granted every day, well they're brand new to me. I didn't really know how to work a TV ... I didn't know how to use a [bank] card. I didn't know how to use a phone properly ... Like I was 1960 coming out. It's as simple as that.

The challenges posed by these 'new' technologies may be more extreme because the recently paroled men had little opportunity to familiarize themselves with new mechanisms or apparatuses while they were incarcerated. For example, the prison canteens operated on a pen-and-paper system decades after barcode scanning had become common-place. Further, they had not been privy to the earlier changes that made things such as television remotes and bank cards possible, and therefore they had a limited frame of reference through which they could understand how things worked. Those who used their time to improve their education or learn a trade may have been better able to adapt to new technologies after prison because they had been exercising their brains and had refined their ability to reason:

> Learning is cumulative, and learning performance is greatest when the object of learning is related to what is already known. As a result, learning is more difficult in novel domains ... In a setting in which there is uncertainty about the knowledge domains from which potentially useful information may emerge, a diverse background provides a more robust basis for learning because it increases the prospect that incoming information will relate to what is already known. (Cohen and Levinthal 1990, 131)

Coping with newness after years of stagnation can be frightening and anxiety inducing:

> The first time that I had a pay cheque and I had to put it in 'cause the bank was closed. And I'm standing there with the cheque in my hand. I didn't sign it. No signature, nothing on it – and I still don't know how to use this machine so I'm trying to figure this out and I hit a button – and I guess – I was just holding my cheque, I guess it was close enough and whoosh all of a sudden, it's gone. I went into a panic. (Ernest)

During the countless hours the men spent imagining their lives outside of prison and envisioning how they would establish themselves as contributing members of society, these technological and social disjunctures were not part of the scenario. Neither did they expect to encounter persistent reaffirmations of their 'outsider' status: in the media's frequent articles documenting recidivism, in the discourse of 'law-and-order' politicians, and in the calls to disallow the dangerous back into the community.[3] In this context, they quickly came to appreciate that they were transgressing simply by having left the prison environment.[4] For Barry, who had naively assumed that he would be embraced by the community, this reaction came as a shock:

> I guess my biggest problem coming back into the community was a misunderstanding in that I thought the people in the community wanted me to come back, and I guess the first time that I ran cold into the wet fish slap in the face where they didn't want me back, I was hurt. I was really hurt. I admit I did the crime. I served the time. I paid my penalty but I was not welcomed back to the community with open arms. I had to fight for and establish my place. (Barry)

Confronted with such unwantedness, the men sought a place of belonging where they could connect with someone (or some group). For a number of them, this place was the Kingston area. It is a city in which the support networks the men had cultivated while in prison were still relevant and where the residents were not surprised by, or unfamiliar with, those who had been incarcerated. Whereas in other areas, the official sense of place may be about protecting their community from outsiders, in Kingston, the presence of former prisoners and their families is expected given the number of prisons in the area. Consequently, the often unanticipated dis-ease of the unfamiliar was partially mitigated, and this normativity made the other task of settling in easier.

(Not) Settling In

> I didn't need a halfway house. It was just an impediment. That's all it was for me. (Puzzle)

> [The halfway house is] calm against the storm. You know, to get your shit together. Get a job. Clothing. Car. Because you are basically homeless right ... At that time it was helpful, I have to admit ... I do believe in the halfway houses. I think they are necessary, especially for lifers and long-term offenders. (Mr. Flowers)

I saw that as doing time. And so it was more difficult for me being there than it was for me being in jail where I could do alone time. (Rick)

I was ready [to go to a halfway house] then, because I, it was one of those things when you do everything you have to do. And then you say, "Well, I can't do anything else here [in prison]. I'm not gonna learn to live. I'm not gonna learn to budget. I'm not going to learn this and I'm not going to learn that. So I have to move on." (F.G.)

Some people need that structure and those programs ... I'm pretty sure I went from day parole to full parole very quickly, you know, because I ... was minimal [risk] as to re-offending. (Gerry)

Some of the acclimation to the 'outside world' occurs during the process of escorted temporary absences and unescorted temporary absences while the individual is still a prisoner, but it is while he is residing at a community residential facility (CRF) or community correctional centre (CCC) that most of this adaptation occurs (see Chapter 4). Halfway houses were designed to provide an opportunity for paroled individuals to adjust in a supportive environment at the same time that they facilitate the monitoring and control of this 'risky' population. These twin goals of support and control exist in tension and, as we see in the comments above, the men experienced the halfway house as either liberating or confining – more often, they vacillated between these two emotions. It is this tension that is at the root of their often-contradictory experiences of settling into life on day parole.

For some of the men, the time in a CRF or CCC was merely an extension of their incarceration – just another type of prison. Some were frustrated: "I am paying you room and board so you can keep me in jail. It's a halfway house, but it's still a jail, right?" (Fred). That said, only four of the men felt that their time in the halfway house was an unnecessary step in their reintegration. Rick was one of these:

I was only on day parole for six months, but it was the longest six months I did in my incarceration, because I didn't feel I needed that because I had a home already set up. I got a job the second day I was out ... I didn't feel that, for me, that the halfway house was a support environment. I saw that as another obstacle for me to experience and put behind me.

Mirroring the penitentiary system, halfway houses also employ a type of cascading – as the individual adjusts to the CRF/CCC and is deemed less 'risky' by caseworkers, he is granted progressively greater privileges and freedom. At the beginning of day parole, early curfews and frequent 'sign-ins' at the office are to be expected. Jean, who had become accustomed to the differing degrees of freedom during his twenty-two years of incarceration at various security levels, explains:

> Yeah, it was kind of a trip going to the halfway house. You had a curfew – an 11 o'clock curfew. I mean, first they give you a 7 o'clock curfew, and then after the second week, it's 8 o'clock, and the third week, it's 9 o'clock, and the fourth week it goes until 11. And then after the first month in a halfway house, then you're entitled to leave for a weekend, for one weekend. After the third month, it's two weekends; and the fourth month, it's three weekends; in the fifth month, it's four weekends out.

According to Stanley Cohen (1985, 50), halfway houses "reproduce regimes and sets of rules very close to the institutions themselves: about security, curfew, passes, drugs, alcohol, permitted visitors, required behaviour and surveillance. Indeed it becomes very difficult to distinguish a very 'open' prison ... from a very 'closed' halfway house." Bob, who was generally very accepting of his punishment and of state policy and practice, initially tolerated the halfway house regime, but, as time passed, he resented the persistent monitoring in which his actual behaviour seemed irrelevant:

> I would start to get some resentment, urinalysis testing towards the end while I'm still living in the house. You know, "why do you continue to do this? Because you tell me I'm a model inmate if you will and all this sort of stuff." And so, yeah, I started to resent that stuff and I started to get a little vocal about it. Like, this is unnecessary.

The men were most frustrated by the mandatory programming in the CRF/CCCs that echoed their experience in prison: "I told them when I got out here, 'If you're going to program me anymore out here, screw me, send me back. That's it in a nutshell. I'll just go back and be punished. You're not punishing me out here with programs anymore'" (Gord). By contrast, the government is firmly committed to all parolees, participating in programs: "Research shows that supervision alone does not help offenders change. Supervision combined with good programming does work. Each offender on community release is expected to participate in programs tailored to his or her needs" (Canada 2010a). Some of the men alerted us that this 'tailoring' did not manifest in practice. Rick's experience illustrates how the bureaucratic 'one-size-fits-all' approach, based on risk group aggregates, plays out in logic-defying ways:

> [The staff at the CRF said:] "You've gotta be here for the employment training." I said, "Okay, but I'm working." They said, "It's during the day" and I said, "I'm working during the day." And they said, "Well you know we can't make allowances. Everybody has to. If we let you out of it, other people will want to get out of it." And I said, "What is it that I need to learn. I know how to write a resumé. The resumé is already written. I'm working full time ... it just doesn't make sense to me to quit a job to learn how to find a job – to do interview skills."

Mobility is a further area in which the state exercises strict control and asserts authority over the paroled men. Many of the men resented this geographic regulation of their freedom while they were attempting to settle into the community. Individuals on parole are allowed in certain places and disallowed in others, and they are assigned a radius in which they can circulate – any step outside of this invisible fence without pre-approval by state agents can (in principle) return them to prison.[5] In practice, since it is impossible for agents of the criminal justice apparatus to monitor a parolee twenty-four hours a day, these mobility radii are largely symbolic. That said, the implications of being caught in violation loom in the minds of the men, and this awareness ensures self-governance. Rick, who often challenged the dominant discourses and practices of the penal apparatus, illustrated how the parolee is responsibilized in relation to these shifting regulations:

> The rules would change, were always changing, and it became problematic for me. So, for example, we were just north of Baseline Avenue. The one time I went ... home for the weekend – to our house, me and Susan, and I left – went to work at 6 in the morning and I didn't have to be back to the halfway house until Sunday night ... Sometime during that day, Corrections changed the rule that you could no longer go below Baseline Avenue, which was only a couple of hundred yards from the halfway house, and you couldn't go into Nepean which was – all of this area was out of the 40 kilometre radius. So I came back and was asked what I did. So I said, "Well we went to the Home Show. It was in Nepean." [They said] "So that's in the Corel Centre. Oh, you're out of your parole jurisdiction – that's a violation of your parole." And I said, "You know, no it's within the 40 kilometres," and they said, "No, there was a memo during the day that told everybody they were no longer allowed to go below Baseline Avenue, no longer allowed to go into these other parole jurisdictions without a travel permit." I tried to explain that I was not aware of that because I left at 6 o'clock in the morning, and they said, "That's your responsibility to know these things" and, you know, "We're not going to penalize you at this point but you know that's a technical violation of your parole."

Another interesting aspect that created tension in the way the men saw the halfway house was the very nature of the facility. Despite being set up to minimize risk for those on parole, some men found the institution itself to be a potential threat to their freedom. While the CRF and the CCC offer a readily available micro-community, some men avoided forming relationships with other residents:

> There were people there that I didn't want to associate with. Like, other prisoners – other parolees, I guess, but you were forced to ... I didn't want to associate with these people but you had to build some kind of relationship with them ... A lot of guys at the house wanted

to hang around with me and I didn't want to hang around with them. And while they're looking at me like "here's a guy who was solid in jail" and you know, "he was a biker," and so they're bringing those issues to me. "Oh, I know so and so" and I'm trying to get away from that. 'Cause I don't know these people. So I saw those people as a threat to my freedom. (Rick)

Tom, who often reflected on the importance of solidarity in prison, went to some length to explain the potential 'riskiness' of these post-carceral relations:

A long term guy comes out. He's got a knot about himself with these guys coming out of there that just did three years, four years, two years, whatever. You gotta stay clear of these people because most of these people have not come to the point where you're at, where you really do want to stay out and you really do want to just be part of society now. Their head is not there. So you got to avoid these people. And not to the point that you think there's anything wrong with them or you don't want to talk to them, but just don't go out with them anywhere – because the bottom line is, yeah, they can go back for another six months. You're not going back for six years – You might never get out again.

While almost all of the ex-prisoners did find aspects of the day parole experience to be overly controlling, settling in to life in a halfway house was not problematic for most, and their experiences ranged from benign to very positive. Some did not invest the facility with meaning – for them, it was simply a place to be used to their advantage. They just did what was required and neither challenged nor 'bought into' the process: "I just did my own thing ... I didn't deal with anybody from the house, staff or residents, or whatever they call me ... I would come in, I'd sign in, and I'd go to my room. And I'd get up in the morning, have a shower and everything, sign out and gone" (Fred).

Mr. Flowers employed a variation on this approach by clinging to his personal "salty-mother-fucker" identity while presenting a different persona to the staff at the halfway house. In what Peter Fleming and

Graham Sewell (2002, 864) refer to as organizational disengagement, Mr. Flowers was able "to comply without conforming": "I ignored them. Made my curfew. Cleaned my shit and followed the fucking rules and never whined about it. Put them to sleep. That's all." As this example suggests, presentations of compliance often "masked backstage resistance of various forms" (Crewe 2007, 272).[6]

For some, who thought they might never be released from prison, the expectations of the halfway house did not seem particularly onerous:

> This is an opportunity here. I'm out. I'm on my way. They put me in this halfway house. That means I'm on my way ... I didn't find that to be aggravation at all really. I thought this is minor, I can deal with this. And even a guy that is irritating me there – I just totally ignored him. It's not a big deal. Because my point of view was there wasn't a lot they're asking. They're asking, at least this halfway house ... basically they want you to get employment, and don't cause any problems in the place and I didn't find it difficult. I thought, you know, hey they let me in here. I was kind of grateful. (Tom)

Even when faced with restrictions, many of the men appreciated being halfway out of prison. For Ernest, who has detached from his prison cohort, it was a 'fresh start':

> I think there was eight or nine guys [in the house] so there was a fair-sized house. It was more like a family there than anything else ... I didn't feel that – authority figure with these people ... And it was in a nice area ... There was a park down through there. I used to go down to the park and I would go down there and ao my work out because I would – I took some Tai Chi and stuff like that. And I loved the park. I used to go there and fish.

In this excerpt, Ernest draws our attention to the way that spatiality, social interactions, and power relations meld together to inform his experience in a positive way. At a more pragmatic level, most of the men recognized that their time in the halfway house was needed in order to allow them to adjust to society and its many major sources of stress (for example, employment, and shelter):

> I believe the most beneficial thing I got out of it was that it would give me an opportunity to take a slow pace and look at things ... and it let me pick out a job and if things didn't work out, I had the place [CRF] going there. And it gave me time to say "Okay, Gowan, you're not ready to move out." (Gowan)

As it was in prison, the ability of the men to settle in was heavily influenced by the individual employees and the philosophical approach of the facility. For example, Ernest states that one of the positive aspects of the CRF was the staff's welcoming attitude:

> They just treated you as [if] ... they met you for the first time and that's it. Take it from there, right. So that went a long way with me. [He continues later] ... This halfway house usually was dealing with long term offenders and usually taking those that would have never gotten out to begin with, so they were ... always there for you and ... it helped.

While Bob was anxious to 'get going' and re-establish himself in the community, the workers and the general approach of his CRF encouraged a slower transition that made it easier to settle in to life on day parole:

> We'd get up in the morning and I'd have a bite to eat, get a coffee, and we'd go sit in the backyard – a couple of guys, and just talk. And just sort of, oh boy, look around and be out in the sunshine and it was nice, and ... they said, "Bob do this for a couple of weeks, just take it easy." (Bob)

A number of the men appreciated that the day parole process, which was intended to mitigate risk to the community, did reduce the likelihood that they would re-offend. As such, it was a 'safe' space:

[If] they [Parole Board of Canada] just said, "okay, you got your parole, go to Toronto, go to Leamington." I'd be back in prison. Because if I go there ... I go to what I know ... and then I'm back into the drugs, guns and all that foolishness. So, the halfway house was what I needed, because then I became accustomed to this and this became my home. This became my life. I would say the halfway house – it saved me. I can't guarantee it saved anybody else, but, it saved me. (F.G.)

In short, some of the men were delighted to find themselves halfway out of prison, while some were frustrated with still being halfway in. Others were profoundly ambivalent and used the place instrumentally to ensure greater success once they were on full parole.

Moving On

The final phase of the "starting out" period was the preparation for full parole. Full parole means that individuals will finish his or her sentence under supervision in the community. Once achieved, parolees must report to their parole officers as directed and abide by other conditions stipulated by the Parole Board of Canada, but they are able to live outside of the correctional institution or CRF/CCC.[7] The men did not simply stop being on day parole but, rather, as with their transition out of prison, they prepared in practical and psychological ways for eventual full parole. We have seen that their experience on day parole was one of contradictory sensations, and this tension was also evident when it came time to 'move on' and leave the halfway house behind. For many, the day was too long in coming, while for others, the thought of not living in an institution was daunting.

As previously discussed, the current correctional-political system has become increasingly concerned with managing risk, and, as a result, individuals are spending longer periods of time on day parole. As Table 5.1 demonstrates, the men in our study who had been released first (Rick, Gowan, Gerry, Barry, and Luc) sometimes spent only a few months on day parole, while those most recently released (Ziggy, Gord, Fred, Bobby, and Doc) spent years in the CRF/CCC. Overall, for those in the sample who were most recently paroled (within the past five to

Table 5.1   Time served in CCC/CRF by respondents

Time since prison release	14+ years	11-13 years	8-10 years	5-7 years
Time in CRF/CCC (N = 18)	x̄ = 13.8	x̄ = 14.3	x̄ = 19.6	x̄ = 24.2
x̄ = 17.8 months	months (n = 5)	months (n = 3)	months (n = 5)	months (n = 5)

Note: This table only includes the eighteen men released on day parole; two men did not live in a CRF or CCC and are not included in these calculations.

seven years), there was a general increase in the amount of time lived in the halfway house as none of those five men had spent less than a year there and the average time in residence was twenty-four months.

While most of the men with whom we spoke acknowledged the usefulness of the transition period and found it personally beneficial, some felt that most of the adaptation was accomplished well before they were released: "They kept me back too long ... [When] you pick a fruit – you don't wait till the goddamn thing's rotten, you pick it while it's ripe. When you got a man that's ripe, don't wait till he's rotten 'cause he'll only scream at you" (Doc). That said, two of the men who only served six months at the CRF/CCC reflected that the brevity of time spent in the house compromised their resettlement:

> I left the halfway house only to find myself having to provide for my rent and my food and – major mistake, eh? I went from $100.00 a month for housekeeping at the halfway house to paying rent, buying food, and earning minimum salary. Quite a wake-up, eh? And this has become the difficult part of my life, where I was left alone without any resource really and at a dead-end job. And nothing. (Luc)

As Luc's quote illustrates, one of the most useful aspects of day parole is the financial subsidization that affords the men the opportunity to secure assets for eventual full parole: "I came out of prison with very little money. I lost everything when I went to prison. But living at [the halfway house] was one of the reasons that I was able to get on my feet 'cause I could save a lot of money there" (Bob).

The institutionalization that was discussed in Chapter 3 was evident as the transition to full parole loomed. The years in a total institution and the learned dependency were only partly mitigated by the men's time in the halfway house: "You have to become reliant on yourself and it's not easy when you've had people telling you what to do for x amount of years" (F.G.). What Mary Eaton (1993, 56) describes as "bringing the prison out ... and continuing to be imprisoned [by insecurity]" played out in the men's anxiety about moving on:

> One of the big issues for me was also the transformation ... the transformation of leaving St. Leonard's [CRF] and moving into the community on my own and there was probably more anxiety about that than there was about getting out of prison and making the transition from Frontenac [minimum security prison] to the halfway house because I thought, "Where am I going to live?" You know, I'm going to be living on my own. "Where am I going to live?" "Where do I want to live?" "Where can I afford to live?" All these sorts of things. (Bob)

In order to lessen their anxiety about independence, some of the men maintained contact with the CRF/CCC. The halfway house had become a fixture in their lives, and they periodically sought it out when they felt vulnerable while on full parole:

> It wasn't even that long ago that I said to hell with it and I got out of the building [where he was living] and I came here [to the halfway house]. "I just, I need a room. I need a place to go." I came here ... Alright let's go sit where I've got a nice place, instead of leaving me alone and I didn't particularly want to be alone during that particular time of instability so I came here. The structure of this ... the whole availability. My comfortableness with it for having been here for three years was easy to do. (Bobby)

Reflection

The period immediately after release was a tumultuous one for many of the men and universally confusing. The lives they envisioned establishing while in prison were in reality constrained by the discourses and practices within their communities, by the changed social landscape, and by both the regulatory and interpersonal aspects of day parole. They found themselves having to re-acclimatize to a much-changed social milieu, needing to negotiate day parole, and, finally, preparing for life outside the constraints of an institution. In spite of their acknowledgement of the readjustment challenges, not all were enthusiastic supporters of the halfway house process. Some appreciated their 'halfway-out-ness' and were relieved and exuberant to have this degree of freedom, while others were disappointed to find themselves still halfway in.

The experience of day parole was diverse and not easily amenable to blanket statements of efficacy or hindrance. The elements of risk management approaches that impeded some of the men made it possible for others not to slip back into behaviour that would have jeopardized their parole. The length of time needed by one individual was seen as much too long by another. The responsibilization that some embraced was resented by others. In the end, the transitory period of re-entry was more complicated than either release or resettlement, and perhaps this is why Elizabeth White (2002) notes that previous studies have concluded that "halfway houses are neutral at best in terms of effectiveness," but that this is in part the result of "CRFs ... develop[ing] over time in response to needs identified by local communities. Therefore, there is a great deal of diversity in the approaches used in providing services to offenders across Canada." Ultimately, this chapter on starting out has reaffirmed a theme that runs throughout this book and one that is succinctly stated by Gerry: "It's an individual thing really."

PART 2: OUTSIDE IN

The first part of this book was about imprisonment, release, and re-entry. In the second part, we turn to the process of resettlement – the period that commences when the men leave the halfway house – and, to some extent, never finishes. To return to the metaphor introduced in the previous section, during their cascade to freedom the men accumulate assorted bumps and bruises. Sometimes the physical and psychological wounds do not heal well, and, as we see in the coming chapters, they continue to have a significant and enduring impact. These echoes and reverberations, along with the men's 'lost' time, are the recurring themes in this section.

The chapters in Part 2 are divided into key challenges that were revealed in our conversations with the men. While we are committed to an integrated theoretical approach, we foreground a specific conceptual framework in each chapter to structure the narratives. We start with the insights of governmentality theory to explore the challenges posed by 'freedom.' In the two subsequent chapters, we draw heavily on symbolic interactionism to examine the men's negotiation of personal and social identity and their experience (and management) of stigma. We then examine home and homelessness primarily through the lens of critical human geography before turning to labour theory to aid in our reflections about the challenges posed by work and finances. The final chapter incorporates the insights of dramaturgical theory to consider the substantial challenge that social interaction poses for men who have been incarcerated for a decade or more. We conclude by reflecting on how different regulatory threads tie together and sometimes create tangles in the journey to success.

Negotiating 'Freedom': Echoes and Reverberations 6

Lifers are fucked ... For a lifer, the easy part is doing the time ... Once they got ten or fifteen years out on the street, they'll start agreeing. They come to the realization of the hopelessness of their position. A long-term offender feels the same pain but they can finally one day – try to wash the dirt off, the filth off their soul. It's like being a rape victim. You can wash but you never get that dirt off you. Prison is like that ... You've been violated. You've got emotional scars. They'll never leave. Ever. (Mr. Flowers)

After more than a decade in prison, the formerly incarcerated individual is 'free' to re-establish his life. In practice, however, as the stories of the men clearly illustrate, their post-release experiences are not as simple as picking up the pieces. To extend the metaphor, pieces from the puzzle that formed the full picture of their pre-carceral lives are removed, and new, differently shaped pieces are added. On release, the former long-term prisoner must find a way to reassemble those pieces in a cohesive manner while negotiating (sometimes unanticipated) challenges. In this chapter, we reflect on the journey to 'freedom' and attend to how the many years these men spent incarcerated in disciplinary institutions conditioned their experiences and influenced how they (re)defined liberty. We will also be drawing on the work of Michel Foucault and governmentality theorists to shed light on the porousness of freedom in neo-liberal societies characterized by "regimes of government through freedom" (Rose 1999, 273).

The Damaged 'Corrected' Soul

In *Discipline and Punish*, Foucault (1977) traces the emergence of prisons in the eighteenth century, arguing that they reflect a shift in penal intervention from the body of the offender (who, under sovereign power, was subject to torture, mutilation, and execution) to the soul of the individual. The goal of the prison was, and remains, to incarcerate individuals so that they "may be subjected, used, transformed and improved" (136). This process can hardly avoid scarring the souls of those it seeks to 'correct':

> Anybody who hasn't spent twenty or thirty years or a lot of big time wouldn't understand it. Some of them who have done two or three years would have a very vague understanding of it ... because the longer you're there ... the more chances of screwing up and going offside or [getting] stir craziness. (Gord)

All of the men with whom we spoke had spent at least seven years locked behind prison walls and, in some cases, considerably longer – indeed, the median was seventeen years. The duration of time lived in an inherently violent institution meant that they were unable to avoid witnessing disturbing and traumatizing events (see Chapter 3). In contrast to Frank Porporino's (2004) contention that long-term imprisonment is not detrimental to mental or emotional functioning, intellectual or cognitive abilities, physical condition, or social and interpersonal competencies, these men emerged with emotional and psychological scars. Despite the gender scripts that dictate that men should suppress their emotions, many of the interviewees did speak openly about the trauma of incarceration and its lasting impact: "I went to jail and I've seen things that nobody else will ever see unless you've been there and, like, I have a lot of disturbing memories from a lot of things I've seen" (Marcus).

Their experience can be likened to that of veterans – the men had nightmares and what they often referred to as "baggage." Throughout their interviews, they described symptoms suggestive of post-traumatic stress disorder, including not responding to happiness or sadness, irritability, depression, suicidal thoughts, insomnia, loss of memory, headaches, stomach pain, and flashbacks.[1] Ten years after leaving prison, Rick's symptoms persist: "Sometimes I wake up – I'm having a nightmare – that I was back inside and – it keeps you in jail." The challenge Rick faces in psychologically leaving the prison behind also speaks to the plethora of losses inherent in the deprivation of liberty:

> Going to jail had such an impact on me 'cause I lost everything. I lost my identity. I lost my place in my family. I lost my place in my community. I lost everything. And so, if something big impacts me now it doesn't have the same effect on me ... The worst thing that could possibly happen to me, happened to me. So I expect bad things to happen to me. (Rick)

While Rick's experience alerts us to the potential for imprisonment to undermine an individual's ability to feel free, a number of the men found ways to transcend the psychological impact of captivity:

> The challenges on the outside are minuscule compared to the challenges on the inside ... Seeing a guy killed on the range. Like, you know, how are you going to cope with that? How are you going to deal with that? What do you do as a human being versus what you're supposed to do as a solid inmate? Like, they're *real* challenges. (Bobby)

In the narratives recounted earlier, our attention is drawn to the extreme nature of the environment in which the men lived and the lasting implications thereof. The effect of this experience is that the formerly incarcerated man now has a relational position through which all others can be assessed:

> I can remember one guy saying to me that your worst day outside is better than your best day inside. And the freedom to walk out, you

know? You go buy a cup of coffee. When the world pisses you off, I got a spot that I go that's about twenty minutes from here and – most people here have no concept of what it's like. I mean ... there's wildlife, there's, uh, almost anything you can think of. But there's serenity and peace where there's no people. And that's, that's basically what's kept my sanity. (Puzzle)

In Puzzle's narrative, the concept of freedom figures prominently. However, what freedom means, and how it is lived, is neither straight-forward nor evident.

Reconceptualizing Freedom

In practice, freedom is a nebulous concept. While the *Oxford English Dictionary* (2010) defines "freedom" as "the power or right to act, speak, or think as one wants," the men quickly came up against the practical limits of freedom. None of them was able to fully re-embrace their taken-for-granted, pre-prison conceptualization of liberty. Instead, all of the men found themselves negotiating a new personal definition of freedom. For example, Marcus recalls his anticipation of freedom and what it meant to him in the post-carceral period:

All I want[ed] was to get out. I just want[ed] to be a free man. I'm not going to commit any crimes. I just want to live my life. All I wanted to do was walk through the park. I didn't want to get high or drunk, you know, have sex or do whatever. I just wanted to walk through a park and see a tree with leaves on it and listen to a bird and knowing that, if I'm walking somewhere, it doesn't lead back to the same point of origin.

At times, freedom is juxtaposed against captivity, and, thus, to experience the former is to focus on the elements that were missing in the latter. For F.G., who had spent only a few years of his adult life not incarcer-ated, looking at freedom this way meant:

I was free. When you're in prison you can only walk to here, to there and you're always bumping into people ... so you're never alone.

You're up on the range, you're never alone. You're in your cell, you're alone, but as soon as you come out the cell, you got twenty-eight other people. So, you're never alone. And I got out of the parole [office], the police station and ... I was alone. I could walk wherever I wanted to and I didn't bump into anybody. I was alone. I had my space to walk in. And it's what I had to get used to. Because without that space, I was back in prison. So I had to find space and that's what my walking did.

Some of the men drew on their lengthy incarceration in order to create a fulcrum on which they could balance their expectations with reality and find some resolution to contradictory sensations. As a result, a particular subjective definition and appreciation of freedom emerged:

It was total freedom ... I still gotta see a parole officer once a month. I can't leave the city but what I had *felt* like total freedom. After you've spent eight years in a maximum security institution and then nine in another maximum security institution which is supposed to be medium, then five at a minimum security institution, then two at a halfway house ... gaining full parole is great. It felt like a big weight was off my back and I could be where I want to be – within reason. (Jean)

No matter their subjective definitions, real deprivation of liberty loomed for most of the formerly incarcerated men. As Jean explains, they were still required to manage their behaviour in a way that permitted their bodies to remain in the community, and it was this self-regulation and responsibilization that influenced much of their day-to-day experience.

Responsibilized Freedom

It is profoundly ironic that disciplinary regimes, such as the prison, endeavour to produce "self-managing citizens capable of conducting themselves in freedom [and proficient at] shaping their newly acquired 'private lives' according to the norms of civility," (Rose 1999, 242) while keeping them in institutions that not only deprive those individuals of their physical liberty but also limit their ability to make choices (Rose 1999, 242). As a result, some of the men were unprepared for the responsibilities that accompanied their freedom in the community (Munn 2011). For many years, these men had little control over how their time was organized and had even fewer obligations. Sometimes the experience was akin to that of a teenager who is anxious to be liberated from parental control; desperate for freedom, he confronts stark realities and struggles with the economic constraints on realizing his freedom:

> When I first got out, I was totally discombobulated because I had to buy my own food. "What do you mean I got to buy my own food? What am I going to buy?" Now I got to cook it. "What do you mean I got to cook food." People have been cooking my meals for twenty-two years and all of a sudden I gotta cook my breakfast. I gotta go out and buy my groceries? Wait a minute now, there's something wrong here. "What am I going to buy?" I can't go and buy steaks because I buy two steaks and I'm broke so I go out and buy a can of beans. So I go out and buy some soup. I gotta buy bread and I need bread. I need milk. Jesus Christ! I gotta have cereal. "Holy shit, what's going on here?" I want to buy fresh fruit. I want to buy this and I want to buy that. You start adding it up. Wait a minute. I'm spending $90 here. "What's going on?" I can't spend $90 on food so that's what you get confused with and eventually you accept it and learn about it. (F.G.)

F.G. is drawing our attention to the "other side of the obligations of self-realization through choice" (Rose 1999, 273). Social actors are free to choose (albeit within rarely acknowledged constraints) at the same time as they are burdened with the responsibility of those choices. Many of the men found life in the community to be overwhelming. On occasion, despite the traumas they had experienced inside, some longed for the familiarity and contemplated going back to prison just to alleviate the pressure. Marcus summarized it in this way: "Jail is comfortable. Out here it's a jungle."[2] A few maintain prison-based routines even in their post-carceral lives. In some cases, this continuation of the temporality of prison life is a matter of habit; in other cases, it is just a way to eliminate at least one of the decisions they confront. For example, F.G. continues to shower at 4:00 pm because that is what he did during his over twenty years of incarceration and he is profoundly habituated to the routine.

In order to mediate the tensions inherent to life 'outside,' the men with whom we spoke employ a number of other strategies, including: relying on a support network; reminding themselves to have patience; seeing a psychologist; smoking marijuana; finding places of peace; trusting in a higher power or spiritual faith; playing music; and, most commonly, taking time to gain perspective on the situation. Somewhat expectedly, given his previous occupation as a counsellor, Barry's approach closely mirrored the cognitive skills developed in corrections programming when he advised others to "stop, think, assess, and then respond." Others, such as Mr. Flowers, endeavoured to be proactive and address the potential problems as they emerge: "You know when you drive you can be defensive because you are aware of everything around you and you can respond – be a defensive driver ... I'm like that in life. I'm a defensive 'live-er' It's like chess. Being three steps ahead of everybody" (Mr. Flowers).

Constrained and Fragile 'Freedom'

Restrictions on liberty can be conceived of as a manifestation of sovereign power over the individual. For those imprisoned or on parole, regulations and restrictions are lessened (or removed completely) with the passage of time. However, for the men serving life sentences, liberty is always tenuous – a condition that is not forgotten:

> I'm never going to feel that I'm really free because they can always come and grab me for whatever they want to grab me for. If it's made up, or if it's real, it doesn't matter. If they want me back in, they can come and say, "Okay, come with us. You done this." And I'm like, "What are you talking about?" And they say, "You know what we're talk[ing about]." You know, they can do whatever they want to do, whenever they want to do it, to me or to the lifers. It's always in the back of your mind. (Fred)

Aware that they are being surveilled created a pervasive sense of omniopticism (being watched by multiple others). This sensation led many to experience a persistent uneasiness and fear of being returned to prison. Cognizant of the restrictions, the men internalized the expectations and became responsible, self-regulating subjects:

> You're never allowed to be free ... You're ... perpetually ... on a string. You're never able to completely break the umbilicus. You always have to justify yourself to someone else ... At some point, and at your peril, you forget 'cause that's when you ... if you forget, you'll end up doing something like drive out of your radius ... At some point, there's no more progress ... You're at the mercy ... of society ... you're always diminished as a person. (Joel)

Consistent with Madonna Maidment's (2006) findings on women who had served time, this sense of susceptibility to future punishment was often discussed in relation to the men's hyper-awareness of police officers: "When we were living in Cornwall, the police used to set up a speed trap right on our road. I'd walk out the door and I'd see a cop car sitting there and go, 'Oh-oh, what's going to happen. Am I going to get arrested? Are they watching me?'" (Rick). In this way, we see that the men considered even the most innocuous actions by state agents to be suspicious. As a result, the watched also becomes the vigilant watcher. More often, however, the men worry about the possibility of false accusations, and this anxiety is most evident with those serving life sentences. This fear is not an irrational one as two of the lifers were returned to prison based on suspicions that were later declared to be unfounded. As Ziggy explained, "I got pulled ... It took me two years to prove my innocence. But they certainly put me through the mill ... No one asked me anything. I'm a lifer so I must be guilty."

Contained Freedom

Power relations are most explicit in the creation of an invisible perimeter inside which the paroled individual is contained. The choice to move freely is a taken-for-granted aspect of our social world, especially for men who have traditionally been associated with the public sphere and labour outside the confines of the home. When movement is restricted, power is rendered visible. This issue draws our attention to the existence of a power geometry:

> Different social groups, and different individuals, are placed in very distinct ways to these flows and interconnections. This point is not merely the issue of who moves and who doesn't ... it is also about power in relation *to* the flows and movement. Different social groups have distinct relationships to this anyway differentiated mobility: some people are more in charge of it than others; some initiate flows and movement, others don't; some are more on the receiving-end of it than others; some are effectively imprisoned by it. (Massey 1993, 25)

Framed as risk management, mobility is an area in which the state exercises strict control and asserts authority over those on parole. For some, terrains of exclusion jeopardized their ability to resettle. For example, despite the knowledge that familial support is important in reintegration, the ability to travel to see kin is constricted (Ekland-Olson et al. 1983; Maruna 2001). Doc told of not being able to return to his home community to visit his mother and other family members. Despite the fact that it had been over fifteen years since he had been there, the police considered him a "rabble-rouser" and controlled his access. Further control is instituted since, in order to visit support people or family members who are outside of their mobility radius, the men who are on parole need to apply for a travel permit each time they want to go.

This spatiality is used to establish moral boundaries. If a person on parole wants to stay overnight with friends or family, he must have a community assessment done in which the individuals and their location and locale are evaluated as to their suitability. Whether this assessment is used to protect the men from 'unsuitable' environments or used by the state's agents to ensure that the visited individuals are aware of the 'sullied' identity of the men is unclear. In either case, it has a significant impact on identity management techniques (see Chapter 8). The effect of this pre-planning requirement is that the men may choose not to travel because of the surveillance of their activities and the inconvenience of the process – in effect, they self-regulate their mobility. This is not to say that individuals on parole never violate this requirement, but, if they are caught doing so, they could be returned to prison, even if the reason for travel is pro-social (for example, work related). It is important to note that as the paroled person becomes perceived as a lower risk to re-offend, parole officers tend to relax, or even remove, the restrictions on mobility. Nevertheless, the men remain acutely aware that this accommodation is conditional, and any suspicious action can result in the revoking of the waiver and/or a return to prison.

Reflection

For the most part, with the notable exception of the two men who felt they were wrongly convicted, the men considered their imprisonment to be a reasonable societal response to their crime. Perhaps naively, they had assumed they would be able to serve their sentence and then move on. They were neither prepared for the many constraints that conditioned their freedom, nor expecting that imprisonment would reverberate and echo through their lives as they resettled into society. While the action(s) of the men served to remove their freedom in the first place, it is clear that it could not be fully restored by their other actions. Moreover, the threat of being returned to prison created an ever-present dis-ease to which they had to adjust.

Identity: Fractured and Fragmented Selves
7

I always had that reputation as being trustworthy and as someone ... who could help you out ... Usually that would be in school work or something like that.

A lot of people have a hard time believing that's what I did ... I'm a ... killer.

I'm too nice, I'm too soft.

I'm a Christian ... I've been a Christian for a long time.

I was a big guy. I weighed 240 and they [other prisoners] thought I was crazy too. So, I was a big crazy murderer. (Joel)

Few identities receive more attention in the mainstream media than that of the 'criminal.' Prime-time television is filled with police dramas, crime scene investigations, crime news stories, true crime biographies, and series that profile specific 'dangerous' criminals. It is not surprising, then, that the idea of the kind of person who commits crime is ingrained into popular consciousness, and, though it does not determine public perception, it certainly conditions it (Jewkes 2005). The image of the criminal as male, as threatening, as risky, and as immoral reverberates throughout society. Before considering how the men negotiate their social identity (in the next chapter on stigma), we must first reflect on the criminalized individual's nuanced personal identity. Indeed, his sense of self proves to be contradictory – the men concurrently speak of themselves as scared and feared, as perpetrators and victims, and as bad and good. Like all social actors, their "fractured identities" (Bradley 1996) not only operate at both the private and public levels but also are contextually conditioned by power dynamics, social norms, geographic location, and the nature (quality and quantity) of interactions. In this chapter, we explore how the men experience, negotiate, and manage the tension between the stereotypical social identity ascribed to them and their own multiple, and often contradictory, personal identities. As we will see, issues of identity are particularly complex precisely because formerly incarcerated persons must engage with the persona attributed to them, wrestle with the contradictions (and confirmations) between this ascription and how they see themselves, and manage the implications.

Shifting Identities

Based on their criminal conviction, judgment has been passed not only on the actions of former prisoners but also on their character. The prisoner's public image becomes "constituted from a small selection of facts which may be true of him, which facts are inflated into a dramatic and newsworthy appearance and then used as a full picture of him" (Goffman 1963b, 71), and the ex-convict emerges as his ascribed master status – the characteristic deemed so important that, overriding all others, it defines who and what the individual is (Hughes 1945).[1] Through "status degradation ceremonies," prisoners are transformed from members of the general population to convicted persons (Garfinkle 1956, 420), their public identity spoiled (Goffman 1963b), and new attributes ascribed to them (Becker 1963). They are now understood as belonging to a particular assemblage of people – a social grouping of outsiders.

The men are acutely aware of this stereotyping and the fact that "some people see criminals as dirty individuals, dirty uneducated individuals. Very few people see [a] criminal as a normal human being with feelings, who can be educated, can be polite, can be clean" (Luc). They are also highly cognizant of the implications of these stereotypes. Mr. Flowers, who was always willing to be blunt, makes the link between stigma and the surveillance of those considered to be inherently dangerous: "Prisoners are not welcomed back in the community per se. You are stigmatized. You know, I mean, it's real. People don't like ex-convicts. It's not in your head ... You're not wanted. You're not liked. You are something to talk about or be watched."

The men's critical engagement notwithstanding, they too are social actors. Perhaps it is not surprising that they periodically drew on the same linguistic frames, describing themselves as scumbags, screwed-up kids, manipulators, petty criminals, loners, or as violent or rebellious. By using these terms, the men assumed, or at least reiterated, a subject position consistent with prevailing public and political discourses. For some of them, these descriptors apply to their present conception of self, as when Joel states: "Oh, by the way, you know I'm a scumbag ... [I am] apologizing for who I am." For others, who employ the past tense, this negative identification became the foundation on which they could later conceive of themselves as rehabilitated, redeemed, or different: "But at that age, I was immature. Highly explosive. Screwed up to boot, you know" (Ziggy).

Moreover, for many of the men, the crime they committed had a profound impact on their sense of self. For example, Ziggy struggles with reconciling having committed a homicide with his personal identity as someone who "never wanted to hurt anybody." These men wrestle with guilt and oscillate between feeling worthless and feeling 'decent.' As Joel, who of all the men in this sample had perhaps the most dramatic identity shift, told us: "I was ashamed of what brought me there [prison] but I wasn't ashamed to be a prisoner." Later in the interview, he noted: "I still feel guilt and also a certain sense of unworthiness and sometimes I resent society because no matter what I do, the world will not accept [me]." For the most part, the men were once just 'average guys' (in their own eyes and those of others), who employed the same normative discourses to distance themselves from the criminalized other. As such, they currently struggle not only with how others construct them but also with how they confront their own deeply held beliefs.

Layered over the men's keen awareness of their ascribed master status and the tension between their social and personal identities is a sense of disaffiliation engendered by spatial disjuncture. Men who had been respected in prison must contend with the loss of status. One man, the former chairman of several prison-based committees, was able to 'do gender' in prison and enact hegemonic masculinity in his authority over others. He was, however, unable to transfer this role, and the conferred credibility, over to his post-prison life. He wryly noted: "I was the chairman of the committee. I came out here, there is no committee. I can't be a chairman."[2] Others grapple with the loss of social relevance:

> Like I was a non-person ... You come out here and people look straight through you. You don't mean nothing to them. They got their own problems. They got their own lives. They're stuck with bills. Their old lady is mad at them and they're friendless ... So you don't mean nothing to them. You meet. You have a beer, and tomorrow they don't even – they don't know your name then. They've never known you. (Luc)

For the men who had been obliged to relocate, the post-prison location was one in which they often felt out of place. The corollary to this belief was that things were done differently in the men's hometown. This disconnect was particularly evident in those who identified as being Northerners. Doc recalls how in his northern community, people got drunk and fought on Friday nights and then "licked their wounds" on Saturday. Now residing in the southern part of the province, he feels that his Northerner identity and its accompanying values persist in marking him as being out of place. In other words, the men demonstrated a keen awareness of the spatial elements that affected their identity and sense of disaffiliation. This awareness may be influenced by the years of limited spatial stimuli and their current sensitivity to geography that further set them apart from the social body.[3]

Negotiating the Prisoner/Lifer/Convict Identity
Many of the men recognize the identity markers that had been placed on them as a result of their crimes and endeavour to redefine the terms employed to describe them.[4] While other groups attempt to modify the

lexicon in the public sphere by using the negatively connoted terms in positive ways (for example, queer or whore), the men's strategy is different. These individuals do not reject the subtext of the stigmatized identity *per se* but draw attention to why it does not apply to them or to a select sub-population of similarly situated others. Rather than trying to get the words transformed on a global level, the men re-conceived and re-defined the terms in order to separate themselves from others who they consider to have different values. In the process, they construct a personally validating relational identity. This strategy was particularly evident around the terms lifer/criminal and inmate/convict.

Lifer/Criminal Identity

For those men who had received life sentences, it was often the case that they made a distinction between being a criminal and being a lifer. Somewhat ironically, in light of the dominant discourse that conceptualizes lifers as being among the worst criminals, these men spoke of themselves as not having 'criminal values':

> I think most lifers are not of the criminal element ... They did something wrong which was a criminal act but they're not criminals. They didn't intentionally go out and hurt a bunch of people or break into a dozen homes to pay for their drug habits or anything like that. You know, they were "straight Johns" who were out in the community and something happened. (Ziggy)

This attempt to distinguish themselves from others may occur because, for the discreditable, the preservation of face becomes a way of distancing themselves from a stigmatized identity. However, as we see in the earlier quote, this strategy occurs at the expense of others who are also discriminated against. In her work on erotic dancers, Chris Bruckert (2002, 130) notes that "the judgements of these 'insiders' which replicate the dominant discourses and position their moral self-identity against that of the deviant 'other,' powerfully legitimate dominant understandings."

In signalling their membership in the 'lifer grouping,' we see what Ram Mahalingam (2003) refers to as a "transcendent essentialization," whereby the men embrace the unifying factors and offer an alternative view. Distancing themselves from others who are criminalized allows the 'liferness' to transcend previous social, economic, and cultural distinctions and to unify them as members of a group: "Because being a lifer ... it's more than any other diversity that you might have of any kind. It overrides everything else including education" (Joel). Of course, this strategy has limited applicability and value outside the prison. While their membership in this lifer group is partly ascribed and partly embraced, they may struggle with their self-concept and their ability to relate to others once they are released: "If you're not a lifer, you have no idea what it's like ... I'm toe-tagged. And as long as you know you're getting off parole in ten or twenty years, you've always got that in your mind. I'm buried with this FPS" (Doc).[5]

As we see in Doc's narrative, 'liferness' assumes a tension that scholars often explore in regard to ethnicity. In much the same way that being a member of a racial or cultural minority can lead to an internalization of an essentialized identity, being a lifer can create feelings of helplessness and depression (see Mahalingam 2003). On occasion, we see a sense of being overwhelmed and powerless, as Puzzle shares when talking about the magnitude of having a lifer identity: "You're fucked until the day you die." This type of sentiment underlies much of the life-sentenced men's post-prison experience and positions them similarly to racial minorities who cannot escape their stigmatized attributes. Unlike other minorities who can externalize the reactions as racist, the lifer is forced to accept that his actions brought about the reaction and that redefinition can provide only limited respite.

Interestingly, some of the other men recognize that lifers are a subgroup and feel that any misstep would be projected onto all similarly sentenced others. Thus, they feel a solidarity and obligation to those who share this part of their identity, and a few of the men suggested that this membership contributes to their staying out of prison. That is, many expressed the idea that they are committed to their own success so that others would not be judged negatively.

Inmate/Convict Identity

In another attempt at reframing their identity through reclamation of specific language, several of the men were careful to identify themselves as 'convicts' and eschewed the more behaviouristic term 'inmates.' When the men used the term convict, they made links to being 'old school' and not being co-opted by the system. They embraced the term as implying that they had served their time with honour and had not provided information to the correctional officers about other prisoners (Demello 1993) and, by doing so, were creating a kind of fratriarchy (Remy 1990) based on their collective interest and desire to be in control as a group. This refusal to be absorbed by the system had gendered implications. As Andrea Leverentz (2006, 318) argues, "honour is one of the most basic social codes for prompting and regulating men's competition for status."

According to the men, their adherence to a 'convict code' may have increased the amount of time they served or strained their relationships with the staff, in general, and with the correctional officers, in particular. Puzzle, who often reiterated binary divisions and placed himself in the 'righteous group,' explained in simple terms the implication of this role set: "If you're an inmate, there's help. If you're a convict, there's none." With only two exceptions, when the men used the word 'inmate' with regard to identity it was negative, and, thus, we see a rejection of the language used by the state and an adoption of the alternate term 'convict.' The latter of these identifiers implies a reaction to an act by the state (that is, to have been convicted) rather than the more psychologically based 'inmate.' In addition to creating a different subject position, the men's particular usage can be viewed as a form of resistance against an essentialized identity. Tangentially, we see that the men also chose to manage stigmatized identities by substituting, or drawing attention to, alternate subject-positions, and it is on these identities that we will now focus.

Refashioned Identities

In order to manage the tensions noted earlier, some of the men made a conscious attempt to mitigate the master status by foregrounding other gendered identities as, for example, fathers, husbands, and/or workers. Others seek simply to have their humanity recognized:

Somehow, you feel that the prison has their ideas of what a guy should be when you're on parole. You know you should look like you're on parole. Well, what does a guy look like on parole? Like he's from Harvard? Like, I came from a place where there are no Harvard students ... I'm not a scholar, you know. And that's how I wanted them to see it. You shouldn't be judging me by my tattoos and my hair, although I understand part of it, you know, it's taking time to, you know, tear it down, see what you got. 'Cause I used to market it as there's a person here, you know, that committed crimes but he still – he hurts and cries. He gets lonely, just like everybody else, you know. (Doc)

The men's re-fashioning of their identity sometimes proves to be a source of tension with those who want them to fulfil the expectations associated with their previous public persona. Fred, who spoke of returning to his childhood community and to those who knew him before and after his sentence, found that people wanted him to be the guy who was available to 'party.' They resented him when he did not conform:

When I first got there, I had people coming to my door like clockwork. Non-stop people at my door. "Come on, Let's go. Come on. Let's go" and I'm telling them "Hey, that's not my lifestyle anymore. I've got a family now and I'm a family person. I'm not that partying kid that was running around here fifteen to twenty years ago" ... They thought "Oh well, you're too – you think you're too good for us" and ... that was everywhere.

Like Fred, the other men offer various other public identities that they feel equally, or more aptly, represent who they are. These presentations move them away from a position of exclusion to one in which they see themselves as deserving of social inclusion (see also Deane, Bracken, and Morrissette 2007).

It is important to appreciate that while the literature sometimes speaks to alternate identities in relation to desistance from crime, most of this work positions these self-concepts as changed or new.[6] While it is possible that the men's alternative subject-positions are recently manifested (as in Fred's example cited earlier), we saw over and over again that the men had not previously seen themselves to be 'other' and in need of reformation. Despite the attempt of the total institution to create a "role dispossession" by stripping prisoners of their possessions, identity, social contacts, and autonomy (Goffman 1961a, 14), this divestment is not always complete and a sense of their pre-mortification selves remains (Goffman 1963a). By demonstrating the ability to maintain or create identities, the men provided examples of both old and new personas, the most common of which were 'normal' guy, worker, good/helpful citizen, and survivor.

'Normal' Guy

The quest for 'normalcy' was a preoccupation of the men and one that, as we have seen, was a recurring theme of their narratives. After many years of incarceration, the men, for the most part, did not strive to be exceptional but, rather, to be an indistinguishable part of the social fabric – an average guy who was not remarkable in a positive or a negative way. As Marcus describes it, "[I'm] just a regular member of society. I work. I pay my taxes. I make sure my family is safe at the end of the day. I look out for my neighbours and I don't infringe upon anybody's rights." Despite bragging that people noticed when he walked into a room, Doc also spoke to this unexceptionality: "I'm not going to be the guy that breaks the mould ... I'm no more different or unique than anybody else." The fact that the terms average and normal appear frequently in the men's narratives draws our attention to their internalization of the disciplinary rationality of governance (Foucault 1977). The men not only evaluate themselves in relation to some abstract average but they also regulate their actions and manage their public and personal identities accordingly. One of the ways this 'normalcy' is affirmed is by getting and keeping paid employment and thereby consolidating their identities as workers.

"Joe Worker"

Most of the men, especially those who were from working-class backgrounds, self-identify as workers. By positioning themselves as being able to labour, the men are 'normalizing' their positions within a capitalist society and within normative gender tropes (Callard 1998; McDowell and Court 1994). For members of the working class, their position is reinforced through social structures and, as Paul Willis (1981, 2) asserts in his study of working-class youth in the United Kingdom, "labour power is ... the main mode of *active* connection with the world: the way *par excellence* of articulating the innermost self with the external reality."

Many of the men had laboured before and during their imprisonment, and they draw on this previously established identity as a "Joe Worker" (Tom) on their return to the community. As such, some felt that the correctional 'employment skills' training (resume writing, job interview techniques, appropriate workplace dress, and behaviour) was superfluous. As Doc explained, "[they were] almost assuming that a guy had never worked. Well, I worked. I was 25 years old [when I went to prison]. That's young but I started working at age 16. So I already had some good experience." Drawing attention to their own identity as workers was also a way of affirming their manliness since "the workplace is an area which men have established as being a significant site for the social construction of masculinity, including masculine identity" (Drummond 2007, 10). The significance of the worker identity comes into sharp focus when we appreciate the implications of its absence: "I was really struggling with feelings of worthlessness – that I don't have an identity. I don't work" (Bob). Puzzle, who is now a stay-at-home dad, also spoke to this belief: "A large part of what I hold my value, my own self-worth is in working and doing a good job." When the men discussed their ability to work as making them feel like a contributing member of society and, by extension, good citizens, they were reiterating a very conventional discourse.

Good Citizen

The men's desire to be seen as 'average' does not, however, mean they are seeking merely to fulfil the minimum social expectations. As Ian Hacking's (1990) work has shown, while the norm is a concept through which we relationally position the abnormal, it is also a benchmark –

something to be improved on. In fact, eight of the men spoke about their desire to exceed normative requirements. For most, this ambition took the form of doing volunteer work in the community, including sharing their stories in classrooms, co-ordinating sporting events, and putting in unpaid time at work. While their efforts are personally rewarding, these actions also facilitate the construction of a socially valorized public persona:

> You see me at charitable events and working with handicapped people. Even on my days off I take them out and do stuff with them. I get respect not only from them but from their families, co-workers and people in the community who see me working at these various events ... I'm like a rock star here. (Jean)

In some cases, their volunteerism, especially speech giving, is a "redemption script," through which they are able to rewrite "a shameful past into a necessary prelude to a productive worthy life" (Maruna 2001, 87). In this way, the men can maintain a measure of cohesion in their self-identity and, rather than amputating their criminal past, these "heroes of adjustment" can acknowledge the mark of criminality and subvert the subtext of the master status (Goffman 1963b, 25). In the process, they affirm (perhaps inadvertently) the rehabilitation discourse by suggesting that they were corrected by corrections.

Others are less inclined to construct a redeemed identity but, instead, draw attention to the positive qualities that they retain, sometimes in spite of their long periods of incarceration. For example, the men often described themselves as helpful, explaining that they used their time in prison to assist others (either in groups or individually). Some of the behaviour that started in the prison continued over the long term and became a type of "generativity script," wherein the individual leaves a positive legacy or symbolic contribution for the next generation (McAdams 1993, 240):

> Every little bit that I do today will help some other guy down the road ... It's payback because ... there are other prisoners who fought

and died for stuff that I've benefited from. My personal belief is that if I can be counted among them in the final roll call ... then I will feel that I have accomplished something. (Barry)

Even when asked why they participated in our research, a number of the men explained that they were trying to help us or, more often, aid others: "It would be nice for a guy sitting in there that has maybe no hope, to read about someone like me" (Tom). Gord, who often struggled to find the words to convey his thoughts, made a link between being helpful and being a survivor, which was another dominant identity: "Surviving, staying alive and striving. That's my identity. That's it in a nutshell and trying to help somebody else survive a little here and there, when I can."

Survivor

That the men understand themselves to have surmounted a major obstacle was evident in the interviews: "I'm a survivor. I've gotten through piles and piles of shit. I've survived" (Bobby). For a number of the men, this self-concept was part of a lifelong identity. The frequency to which these men referred to their sexual, physical, and emotional abuse was striking, and the anguish was palatable: "I think that my job is not to end up like 'Slingblade' ... All the frustration. All the anguish. All the suffering. All the baggage. All the up-against-the-wind stuff. You know, I don't have to face that if I self-destruct and go after the abusive, 'no good son-of-a-bitch' and alcoholic" (Gord).

Feminist research on criminalized women has drawn attention to the difference between male and female prisoners and effectively reconstituted the latter population as "needy and victimized" (Snider 2006, 328). In the context of this power-knowledge nexus, criminalized men's history of abuse is not only invisible but also implicitly denied. Not surprisingly, since their victimization is not part of the public transcript, the men employ decidedly masculinized images of survival. For example, some of the men drew on a sense of self as a veteran of prison and employ the language of warfare: "It's like old war soldiers. Not somebody who did six months in Vietnam but the Second World War where you did the whole thing ... Somebody who has done seven, eight, nine years of hell, those experiences, they don't get rid of them" (Mr. Flowers).

Reflection

When we reflect on the men's engagement with identity, we see that self-concept is complex, fragmented and fractured, and operating at both the private and public levels (Hall 1990, 18). The fact that these multiple identities exist for each individual is a reflection of their conditional nature and of the complex social contingencies. As such, through role segregation, individuals are able to select which response and presentation to invoke in particular circumstances and locales (Goffman 1961b). In short, despite the dominant discourses and media representations of the criminal, the men were not crippled by their membership in a group with an essentialized public identity. Instead, many of the men were able to reconcile their ascribed status with their own self-concepts. While most felt that their crime warranted social condemnation, they offered alternate social identities in order to be judged in relation to these as well.

Stigma: Negative Expectations and Amazing Reversals

8

> And then the boss that I worked for found out about my background ... He found out and this guy made my life miserable. Every dirty job that there was after that, he gave me. And I told him, right to his face, I said, "You don't have the balls to break me," I said. "CSC tried for ten years. You don't have the balls and neither did they." (Puzzle)

> I went out and begged the auto wreckers [for a job] – but he had so many guys on work releases. It messed him around. And one guy stole something off him. And he goes, "I don't want to hire nobody." And I said, "You're judging everybody as a package instead of as individuals. And why are you not giving me a chance?" And I remember going right on his floor, and said, "Dave, just give me a chance." And I was walking away. And he called me back and he goes, "All right I'm going to give you a chance." (Gowan)

Erving Goffman (1963b), in his ground-breaking work *Stigma: Notes on the Management of Spoiled Identity*, drew attention to social interaction between 'normal' individuals and those who are tainted or 'marked.' He identified stigma as "an attribute that is deeply discrediting," that isolates an individual from society "so that he stands a discredited person facing an unaccepting world" (3, 19). At the root of this process is essentialization, whereby common characteristics shared by members of a particular group (race, class, gender, and so on) come to be understood as significantly differentiating them from others who do not have these qualities. Essentializing criminalized individuals has led to the creation of a stereotype (cognitive essentialism), which has allowed a particular treatment to manifest (social essentialism) (Mahalingam 2003). In this chapter, Everett Hughes' (1945) concept of master status is used as a point of entry into our examination of the men's experiences of stigma, which emerge as surprisingly complex, layered, and sometimes counterintuitive. In the second part of the chapter, we consider the stigma management techniques that have been employed.

Master Status

The men who participated in this study represent a unique subset of those convicted. Through their arrests, trials, convictions, and sanctions, individuals become marked and, hence, excluded from their previous identities through these degradation ceremonies (Castel 1995). Marked as serious criminals, they become members of a particularly vilified and despised population, unlike political prisoners, such as members of the Irish Republican Army or the African National Congress, who were ascribed an almost heroic status when they returned to their communities after lengthy imprisonment (Jamieson and Grounds 2002). There is no refuge – the men must own the crime for which they are responsible. That said, unlike some other stigmatized groups, formerly incarcerated persons are not readily identifiable and, therefore, not so much discredited (by virtue of, for example, physical characteristics) as discreditable (their concealable 'flaw' vulnerable to being uncovered).[1] As individuals who possess spoiled identities, they are aware of their "blemish," negotiate the meanings attached to the stigma, and manage information surrounding their attribute as they seek to mitigate the negative outcomes of its application. As Chris Bruckert (2002, 133) has noted in her work on stigmatization, "different individual responses may not alter stigmatic designations in public and private discourses, but they transform the dynamic from the experience of shame or embarrassment to the negotiation of consequences."

Master statuses are social ascriptions that speak to stratified positioning. Some master statuses can be valorizing (doctor, student), and others are decidedly not. Once an individual is criminalized, the label of (ex)-convict becomes their primary and dominant marker, especially in their interactions with post-stigma acquaintances (Uggen, Manza, and Behrens 2004). In part, this significance may be engendered by the tendency of social actors to disproportionately attend to that which brought about this master status (Maruna, Immarigeon, and LeBel 2004). That is, according to the negativity bias principle, a multitude of non-deviant acts may precede and follow one deviant act, but it is the single event that indefinitely stigmatizes the individual (Baumeister et al. 2001). This is most profoundly the case for persons who commit homicide. Whereas other crimes (for example, bank robbery) are something an individual does, committing murder is read as revealing the person to be of a particular kind – act and actor are permanently fused. Gayle Horii (2000, 104), who was sentenced to life imprisonment for second-degree murder, reflected that:

> Less than five minutes of my life dictated my punishment, but it need not wipe out the woman I was for forty-two years previous to my particular madness. Because of the crime I committed, it may be difficult to accept my assertions that I should be granted human rights, and that I could still maintain decent values. It is a most abstract conundrum, to wrap one's head around the fact that a killer and/or prisoner could also be a good person. These are definitely contrary pictures.

The men recognize, and to a degree accept, that their criminal act(s) justified the imposition of a new master status. Doc, who was formerly recognized as a 'tough guy' in his northern community, was aware of his primary identity: "When I am out here, I'm a parolee – all the time. I'm not a citizen out here." Joel was more explicit: "The fact is now I'm a lifer and I'm different and I'm going to be treated different and when people find out about it, they're going to treat me that way." Later in the interview, he spoke about the concept of master status: "If they find out you are a lifer and an ex-con, that's going to totally eradicate all that other stuff [volunteering]."

It was apparent that the men's intimates were also affected by their master status. Goffman (1963b, 30) notes that those who are "related through social structure to a stigmatized individual ... are all obliged to share some of the discredit," and a sense of responsibility for this "courtesy stigma" weighed on some of the men:

> I brought a lot of shame to the family ... when I was charged with murder ... My brothers and sister ... were just kids then. They were told "Your brother is a murderer," "I'm not hanging around with you" or "My parents won't let me hang around with you" ... They'd come home crying ... What did my mother have to face when she went downtown? What did my father have to face? (Dave)

Yet, as we will discuss next, for many the burden of stigma was not excessively heavy and they did not have to negotiate their stigmatization at all times and in all places. In short, like identity (which we examined in the previous chapter), stigmatic designations are both fragmented and complex, and so living with this ascribed status was not always what the men had anticipated.

Living with Stigma

The literature on stigma indicates that released prisoners will encounter discrimination (Clear and Dammer 2000; Funk 2004; Harding 2003; Petersilia 2001; and Travis and Petersilia 2001). While this was certainly the experience of some of the men with whom we spoke, examples of non-stigmatizing behaviour were surprisingly common. The men indicated that on many occasions, their expectations of stigmatization outweighed the reality. When discrimination was encountered, it largely emanated largely from representatives of the state or was the result of factors other than their criminal records.

Expectations and "Amazing Reversals"

Many of the men asserted that they did not feel personally stigmatized in the community based on their status as former prisoners. Arguably, this experience is partly related to their discreditable (rather than immediately discredited) status. Some of this ability to 'pass' may have been a function of white privilege (McIntosh 1988) in a society in which people of colour and Aboriginal people are more readily 'read' as potentially criminal (Bonilla-Silva 2010). As Marcus commented, "the community was blind to me. There was no public knowledge of who I was ... I walked through a whole crowd of people. You know, just a regular old white kid with short hair. Nobody even paid a second glance to me." Bobby echoed this sentiment and confirmed Goffman's (1963b) notion of hyper-awareness when he stated: "No. No. No. I've never had a negative, a negative stigma coming from anywhere. Anytime, it's mostly been my anxiety, my anticipation." Some of the men worried that the stigma would be physically discernible: "I had no idea what to expect. For all I knew, I was going to have this big sign on my head, 'Prisoner,' 'Convict.' So I had a lot of stress about that and then I was also worried because I didn't know what I was going to do for employment" (Marcus).

Marcus' concern about stigma jeopardizing his job chances may have some basis in fact. Research has identified employability as an area in which the negative implications of stigma against the ex-prisoner likely manifest.[2] However, many of the men were offered work despite their criminal records:

> I went for an interview ... They called me the next day at the halfway house. They said they liked me and ... "We want to do two things. We'll put you on the payroll and then we're going to do a criminal records check." [I said] "I got a criminal record" ... "We've hired people before with criminal records. Come on in, we'll talk about it" ... I go on in there ... I said, "I'm presently on parole, life parole, for murder." He said, "What?" I said, "You asked me. I'm telling you. You said you've hired people with criminal records before." [He said] "Yeah, but those were car thefts and purse snatchers and stuff like that. Not murder" ... I assured him I would be an asset to the association ... So, I left feeling dejected ... Two days after that, they called me and they

wanted me to come in for another interview. I went down there and the first thing they said to me was "Who works here who knows that you had a criminal record?" I knew I had the job as soon as he said that. (Jean)

Jean's narrative speaks to the ways that personal contact helps in "reducing the negative effects of a criminal record" (Pager 2007, 104). In order to receive this type of treatment, the men draw on their ability to present well and to leverage this skill into a type of capital. For example, Puzzle utilized his confidence and awareness of stigma when he approached the boss of a company directly: "I told him this is who I am. This is where I've come from. I'm asking you, 'I want a decent paying job ... I'm not here to cause you any grief.' 'All I'm here to do,' I said, 'is try and get back in the community. I'll be a damn good worker.'"

The men provided numerous examples in which it was clear that members of the public did not simply reiterate the dominant discourses regarding those who are criminalized. Rather, when confronted with the opportunity, social actors will draw on their own values, beliefs, and subjective assessment in deciding how to proceed. Individual citizens' ability to reject the essentialization of the 'ex-prisoner' and rely instead on their own judgement supported the assertion by Julian Roberts and his colleagues (2003, 105) that the "public endorses individual justice and wants to be merciful."

It would appear that some individuals go beyond just rejecting the stereotype and engage in challenging the dominant images and discourses. For example, Mr. Flowers told of having his employer defend him against a parole officer who did not think he was doing suitable work. According to Mr. Flowers, his supervisor contacted the Parole Board of Canada (PBC) and told them: "There is absolutely no way that we will let a parole board member, [or] the Parole Board, in any way censor our employees. Mr. Flowers works for us; he happens to be on parole. He is not a parolee that happens to be working for us."

This acceptance on the part of members of the community was experienced by several of the men who felt welcomed back. Gord referred to such experiences as "amazing reverses of stigmatization." Differentiating from the role set established in prison (discussed in Chapters 3 and 7) and reinforcing the importance of place, one man's neighbour (a prison guard) offered to write a letter supporting his application for full parole and then followed up by contacting the parole officer and the PBC to provide a reference. Bob provided another excellent example:

> I went over to the bank and I said, "I want to get a credit card" ... [This] lady sat me down and I was very nervous because I didn't want to reveal my past and she asked me my particular information and she checked my credit rating and she said, "You don't have a credit rating." So I had to tell her where I was. And her comment to me was "Well banking's our business, that's your business." And I really appreciated it. I never forgot that comment ... And there's no stigmatization, anything like that. And I'll always remember that, how sort of kind she was to me. And she got me a credit card.

Bob's story also highlights another common dynamic – the interpretation of everyday or mundane acts as great kindness. Actions that are unremarkable for those who are not discredited become seen as extensions of generosity and as extraordinary gestures by marked individuals who may be more "situation conscious" (Goffman 1963a, 111). That is to say, the discreditable individual in the interaction may be more aware of reactions and interactions than others. These acts may also be interpreted as exceptional because some of the men have internalized their unworthiness and are thus surprised when they encounter others who do not hold, or act on, this belief.

Affirming Power: Stigma from State Sources

Notably, when the men did speak of stigma, the stigmatizer was often an employee of the criminal justice system. While they may not be 'marked' or 'detected' by community members, they are definitely recognized by agents of the state who are cognizant of their past misdeeds. In this context, the structurally influenced stigma manifests itself, and convicted persons are reminded of the attributes ascribed to members of their out-group: "Lifers are looked at the worst. They're looked at worse than sexual offenders. Because the cop looks at a lifer as someone whose crossed the line and can never walk back. They don't think you can ever be rehabilitated" (Puzzle).

As Puzzle noted, the stigma from this source is especially directed at those who are serving life sentences. As a result of the different regulatory requirements placed on this group, agents of the state are empowered to act on the stigma with near impunity. The treatment that parolees receive on reporting to local police stations when visiting friends or family in other communities exemplifies the interplay between interpersonal and structural stigma (stigmatic assumptions that are embedded in social structures and reproduced in state policy under the guise of risk management) (Hannem and Bruckert 2012). Bob confirmed this dynamic:

> The only place that I felt stigmatized was when I went over to the Police Station ... 'cause they would play some games every once in a while. You'd go in [and] you're supposed to check in at the desk and you know they were very polite, courteous, until they found out you were a parolee. And then they'd say, "Go upstairs" and you'd go upstairs, and the guy would say "You don't come up here. You check in downstairs." So, it's just these little games they would play for themselves.

Given that most of the men in this study are serving life sentences, they are subject to extensive surveillance. This monitoring (often justified as risk management) is entangled with messages of unwantedness and the "unfitness of these subjects to be 'in society'" (O'Malley 2001, 94). Given the statistics indicating that the former long-term prisoner is a very low risk to re-offend, this reaction to the stigmatized other is arguably about imposing a morality script rather than about protecting the social body from imminent physical harm.[3] Rick, who maintained contact with all of his family throughout his lengthy incarceration, found his experience of a commonplace activity with them was jeopardized by extensive police surveillance:

> I went to visit my daughter on this Hallowe'en and take my grandson out – the first time I ever got to do that. So we're walking down the

street and all of a sudden a cruiser pulls up and a cop gets out and comes over and says "Rick can I talk to you for a minute. Your car is parked there. You registered in with the Parking Authority and are you going to be in town overnight?" And I remember Carmele, my daughter, looking at me and my grandson's looking at me and he was 4 at the time and he's aware of, you know, who a police officer is ... I had a travel permit so I was okay with it, you know. But it just made me realize how vulnerable you really are. How embarrassing that is. You know, I went through that whole anger thing again and then again I shouldn't be on parole and all that [because I am wrongfully convicted]. But at the same time I was on parole. But was I ever lucky that I had everything in place.

Some of the men experience a negativity bias that assumes they will fail. Gord noted that "if twenty years down the line, I happen to screw up, 'well, we've done told you he would.' You know, that's the way they are." Perhaps it is inevitable since, according to Roy Baumeister and his colleagues (2001, 323), "when equal measures of good and bad are present ...the psychological effect of bad ones outweigh those of the good ones." It follows that the negativity bias is the default position in regard to the stigmatized other: "Since employers, agents of social control and other community members have little confidence in their own ability to discern between legitimate and illegitimate claims to personal reform, the safest option, is to interpret any claim to going straight as 'phony, feigning, unbelievable or implausible'" (Lofland 1969, 210). In our study, this negativity bias was most evident in the men's interactions with state agents since employers and the general public were often willing to rely on their own judgment, reject the risk discourse, and allow individuals to earn new credibility.

Stigma Management

Goffman (1963b), Lee Jussim, and colleagues (2000), and Michelle Hebl, Jennifer Tickle, and Todd Heatherton (2000) have noted that managing stigma requires the targeted individual to engage in social interactions at an intensified level. As a result, the individual may endeavour to avoid or minimize negative labelling. Given the very real consequences of stigma, the men employ a number of techniques, including: rejecting, utilizing the stereotype to advantage, concealing, disclosing, and creating social or physical distance.

Rejecting the Stigma

A couple of the men adamantly refused to accept the stigmatized label ascribed to them. Barry was one of these men: "I feel that there are people who attempt to stigmatize me. Some who work in corrections who know who I am and know my track record, but I don't feel stigmatized because I don't allow it to occur." Goffman (1963b) notes that while rejecting the stigma may be a useful coping strategy, it can also create a disjuncture in the individual who speaks of refusing the stigma while at some level understanding it to be earned. For example, Jean, when asked about experiencing stigma, refered to his crime first, thus replicating and reifying the very discourse he sought to challenge:

> If they only knew ... I'm a murderer and all this stuff. [Question: Did you worry about stigma in those first couple of years? Did you worry about people finding out?] I don't really care, people got a problem with me then that's their problem. I don't have a problem with me ... If somebody else is going to have a problem with me because of my criminal past, that's their problem – not mine.

Utilizing Stigma to Advantage

Other men chose to utilize the stereotypes for their own benefit. Adopting a "hostile bravado" allowed at least one of the men to employ his stigmatized identity to advantage (Goffman 1963b, 17). Bobby is very aware of the fear and sense of danger the term 'lifer' conveys, and he uses this reaction at his workplace: "I've used it as an asset. If guys give me a hard time, [I] say, 'Look, don't screw me around. I've been in jail for a very long time and I'm not about to start playing games with you ... I'm a fucking lifer. Don't fuck with me.'" Fred, who as an Aboriginal man serving a life sentence is subject to layered stigmatization, also appreciates that the stigma that accompanies his cultural identity is contested within the current socio-political context (Canada 2007). Fred used this tension to his advantage when he participated in

Native Brotherhood activities and emphasized his heritage to gain favour: "When I went up for parole, it's like 'Oh, you're a Native offender and you're unique and ... so we'll give you the benefit of the doubt.'" This strategy, of course, can only be utilized in particular settings and with specific interactions and audiences. As a result, it is rarely employed by the men who are more likely to endeavour to remain discreditable.

Concealing the Stigma

Concealment of a criminal past was the most often-cited stigma management strategy. Tactics range from allowing people to make assumptions of 'normalcy' to actively strategizing to disguise the information that could potentially reveal the individual's previous conviction. Notably, even those men who reject the stigmatization hide their prison past in some social situations. For example, Jean and Barry, who both indicated that they are unconcerned with individuals' knowing about their histories, also engage in 'passing' behaviour. Jean, who prior to his incarceration enjoyed his biker persona and the status it brought, said: "I never told anybody that I had a criminal record, what I was in for, or anything like that. I just acted like I was a normal guy out having a beer with some friends. I knew I had to."

Individuals who have accumulated tattoos while in prison face particular challenges. In spite of the increased popularity and mainstream adoption of body art over the past decade, a number of the men noted that their tattoos mark them as 'convicts.'[4] Research indicates that there are various reasons that a prisoner gets tattooed, but most agree that the symbolic images are part of the individual's identity work (Demello 1993; Hunt and Phelan 1998). Some consider the markings to be acts of agency and of defiance that position the prisoner as a member of a respected in-group (McDonough 2001). However, once removed from the prison environment, the meaning of these tattoos is transformed, and they become stigmata that brand the individual as an outsider (Stiles and Kaplan 1996). In some instances, it is the theme of the images (for example, prison bars) that make their source obvious. At other times, the identification of the tatoo as prison-generated body modification requires a knowledgeable viewer who is aware of various inking techniques:

> I got tattoos and a lot of people know that they are jail tattoos from
> just the way they look ... and I went to one [yard sale] ... and I could
> see the guy's checking me out. He comes over ... and he goes, "You've
> done time before, eh?" And I'm like, "What do you mean?" [He says,]
> "I can tell by your tattoos." (Fred)

In either case (theme or technique), these markings can become visible
schema through which attributes and histories may be read. This cor-
poreal manifestation of the "convict body" requires that the men adjust
their presentation of self accordingly (Demello 1993, 12). Gowan, who
dressed in conservative, working-class clothes, was hesitant to show his
tattoos on the job site because of potential negative consequences:
"I'm a good worker, and I don't need to be fired over tattoos ... and he
[the boss] says 'I'm not going to fire you.' And I had my shirt off. The
next day he told me not to come in."

The men also communicated a fear that by showing their convict
bodies it could lead to "courtesy stigma" (Goffman 1963b, 30) for their
intimates, and therefore they use concealment as a way to minimize this
possibility. Gowan, for instance, shared that his young daughter appreciated that he kept a long-sleeved shirt with him to change into when he
was attending her school events. Some of the men who are 'unmarked'
by tattoos claim this absence as a dis-identifier and are cognizant that
it allows them to maintain their facade: "I was working with the senior
staff and doing a lot of office work and I mixed well with them. And,
of course, I don't have tattoos and everything" (Joel). This sense of being
'unmarked' was not restricted to the absence of body art: "If my tattoos
are covered and my earring isn't showing, there's nothing to hang me
to a group. I just look like a fairly middle-class white male and, therefore, I don't set any alarm bells off by visuals" (Barry).

Some of the men, without acknowledging their white privilege, spoke
of being able to 'pass' because people in the community have an image
of what 'criminals' look like: "I don't appear to be an ex-offender ...
whatever that is! But that's the comment that's been made many, many
times to me. 'Nobody would know you'd ever spent a day in jail'" (Bob).
Dave, who's personal appearance was relatively non-descript, explained
how stereotypes allowed him to remain undetected when it became

known that there was a criminalized person living in his apartment building:

> We had a couple that lived there and they were all up in arms about the fact that there were lifers living there, criminals living there. I never said a word. I'd meet them in the elevator and I'd say "Hi," you know, and talk and chat and all and everything. [Question: And so they never knew that you were a lifer?] No.

Being aware, even if not consciously so, that in public places one's manner of dress is a means of indicating one's commonality and signalling belonging, the men also try to emulate the behaviours of 'normal' people in the community by mimicking their clothing style or avoiding particular forms of attire. Doc opted not to wear black leather because it would be indicative of his past association with a motorcycle club, while Dave took great care to dress in "beautiful civilian clothes."

Another concealment approach is the creation of 'back stories' to account for the time spent in prison. This strategy may require the co-operation of intimates and others who are 'in the know' and sympathetic – the "wise" who can assist the person to "pass" (Goffman 1963a, 19): "I made up a resume that was eighteen years full of bullshit, but I had people to back it up. I had a buddy [who] owned a bike shop ... and I had it all lined up and if they called any of that, it would have all come out right" (Tom). This type of concealment becomes particularly complex when it is family from whom the men are trying to hide their past. Those individuals who elected to return to their home communities risk having their children informed by others:

> And they went and told him, said, "Oh, your dad, yeah, he was in jail." "My dad wasn't in jail." "Yeah, he killed somebody" ... I will never lie. And [when my son asked,] I just said, "Yes I did." And he goes "Oh dad, that's ba-a-ad." And he couldn't get over it for a week ... 'cause he knows it's bad.[5]

Once the concealment fails, additional negative attributes may be ascribed to the individual since the person is now not only a 'convict' but also a manipulator or liar. Mindful of this possible double-reaction, some of the men chose to disclose their backgrounds.

Disclosing the Stigma

For several of the men, "conditional disclosure" – the forthright admission of the stigmatized attribute at the appropriate moment – is used to manage the implications of stigma (Harding 2003, 79). Marcus was cognizant of the potential consequences of not revealing his criminal past:

> I told [the people at work] the first day – like one guy he says, "So, what have you been doing your whole life?" I said, "Well, I was in jail for ten years." He almost fell on the floor and he said, "Hey, listen, don't tell anybody that." So I told him, "Either I'm honest with you now and you find out or I tell you something else and you find out later and you don't want to work with me."

Doc, who primarily engages in concealing behaviour, was candid with intimates or potential intimates and said of a new romantic interest: "This woman had no idea who she was ending up with. I told her everything ... Why would you tell somebody a story? ... Tell them the truth, you know, then sift through it." Bobby tried a variety of approaches, and he understands that sometimes his forthright disclosure means that he does not get called back for a second interview or receive a job offer. However, because of the men's hyper-awareness of situations, it was perhaps impossible for them to detach the stigma from the event (Goffman 1963b). That is, the men may not have received a call-back simply because there was a more suitable candidate, but they automatically assume the rejection is a result of their ex-prisoner status, what Elizabeth Pinel (2004, 39) calls "stigma consciousness."

Some of the men utilized full disclosure in an effort to educate others, raise awareness, or prevent youth from engaging in criminal behaviour. Unlike other "professional ex's" (Brown 1991, 219) who can use their past experiences as a means of exiting a previous deviant status (that is, the 'drug addict' becomes the ex-addict) and reinvent themselves (that is, the substance-use counsellor who 'has been there'), there is no positive category of 'ex-murderer' that those individuals convicted of homicide can create or inhabit. The act that brought about their stigmatized status remains, and, while it can be nuanced, it is never eradicated. As such, sharing their stories in public has potentially negative consequences. Some of the men spoke of weighing the benefits of disclosing for the greater good versus concealing for their own personal gain. Rick appeared on a television show to debate a prison-related issue and felt he was subsequently treated like a "coffee table book" on prison by his co-workers. This type of reaction highlights an additional risk of this approach – the individual can be forced into representing all like-stigmatized individuals.

In addition, these acts of tertiary deviance, which necessitate confronting stigmatic assumptions, can exact a toll from the men (Kitsuse 1980).[6] Like members of the gay, lesbian, bisexual, and transgendered community, the convicted individual must confront fears of losing jobs, friends, and being physically or verbally attacked if he chooses to 'come out': "I had done talks for five hours; three different classes – a girl came up and just raked me over the coals. [She said,] 'I think it's terrible what you're doing,' this and that and everything else" (Joel).[7] While Joel made the decision to be public about his stigmatic attribute, he demonstrated how difficult this strategy can be to maintain when he was confronted by an individual who held firm to her opinion about people of his out-group. As a result, even an 'out' individual may try to create a safe physical and/or emotional space for himself.

Creating Distance

The act of disclosure opens the individual up to rejection or other negative reactions. In order to avoid this possibility, and the exhausting task of trying to conceal stigma (Smart and Wegner 2000), some of the men chose to maintain spatial, social, or emotional distance. In terms of physical detachment, this tactic may include avoidance of particular places where the chance of stigmatization is greater. Alternatively, the individual may elect to remain in "back places [where] ... persons of the individual's kind stand exposed and find they need not try to conceal their stigma, nor be overly concerned with cooperatively trying to disattend it" (Goffman 1963a, 81). In these places, they find acceptance.

Some of the men did not return to their pre-prison communities or the areas in which their major crime occurred in order to geographically manage the stigma by creating distance between their current life and their past.

Creating social or emotional distance as a management strategy refers to the practice of avoiding intimacy or closeness with others – even those who are similarly stigmatized. Several of the men isolate themselves and avoid having a broad group of friends. Timothy Flanagan (1981, 119) indicated that long-term prisoners often sever ties with "external relationships to avoid the stress or 'hard time' produced by the attenuation process." In our study, this strategy could apply to pre-prison friends who were rarely mentioned in the interviews. In these cases, gender may provide a partial explanation since we know men are less likely to seek replacements for lost friends and are more comfortable than women in having a limited social network (Thompson and Whearty 2004).

Distancing may also be appealing since "by declining or avoiding overtures of intimacy the individual can avoid the consequent obligation to divulge information" (Goffman 1963b, 99), and, in doing so, the men could evade further judgement. Others avoid former prisoners in an attempt to manage the stigma and to solidify their new identity:

> I tried to separate myself from them [former prisoners]. It was weird because everybody I would run into would call me Champ. Champ. Champ. Champ. And then when I went home ... everybody would call me Fred. Then when I'd come back again ... people say "Hey Champ." And I'd say "Well, that's not me anymore ... Just call me Fred." (Fred)

Reflection

The way stigma emerges, is applied, and then is managed is complex. For the men, stigma was experienced on a spectrum that ranged from not being stigmatized based on their criminal past to feeling rejected, discredited, and vulnerable because of it. Still, the men demonstrate personal agency by employing management strategies that were varied and, at times, competing or incongruous. Disclosure and distancing sometimes intersect and sometimes collide with their attempts to conceal. Rejection of stigma by some contrasts with the embracing of it by others. Through these processes, stigma emerges as robust and malleable while it simultaneously appears fixed and stable. Perhaps most importantly, this research indicates that we cannot assume that cognitive essentialism exists or that, where it does, it necessarily leads to social essentialism. Surprisingly, the men's stories demonstrate that the negative images so prevalent in the media do not always play out interpersonally.

Home and Homelessness: Being In and Out of Place

9

They asked me what it's like doing this job and I said, "I've been doing that six years and I eat lunch alone 'cause I don't fit in." Like I can't go to the dining hall to have a meal with the guys ... so I'm by myself and, you know, I come home and I don't have an office to go to, I don't have a support member to go and unload this stuff. I got to bring it home ... so it infringes on me and on my space and I don't like that ... I don't want that here. Then there's the safe zones where I can let myself down and I can go to my brother's house and get stupid with him – and that's okay. So I look for safe zones so each of those things that I do, I'm a different personality for them. I guess we all are to an extent. You know, I'm sure you're not the same person at home with your husband as you are at school, but it doesn't have the same impact on you if you get caught outside your zone.[1]

In the narrative above, this man speaks to the complex way in which geography is implicated in his life. In the course of a few sentences, he reflects on his sense of belonging, safe spaces, power and transgression, identity and vulnerability – all of which are influenced by the places in which he moves. His words affirm that geography is not merely a backdrop for social interactions but, rather, a profoundly meaningful part of the experiences. To structure this discussion, it is useful to draw on John Agnew (1987) who, recognizing that 'place' has both objective and subjective elements, considers it to have three components (location, sense of place, and locale). Each of these elements helps us to better understand an individual's subjective interpretation of events and experiences.

Location is the most objective of the three components and refers to the geographic area or setting for interactions. Certainly, the relevance of location is evident when we consider that the men have experienced spaces of expulsion (Castel 1995) that are seldom witnessed by the general public. Locale is defined by J. Nicholas Entrikin (1991, 52) as "the environment to which actors give meaning in defining particular social situations," and, as such, it creates a specific context for interaction. In different social spaces, different identities emerge and certain behaviours and actions become seen as being in-place, while others are viewed as being out-of-place (Cresswell 1996). By recognizing this place-ment, the link between geographic and symbolic interactionist scholars is evident, and an overlap between Cresswell's (1996) notion of out-of-place and Erving Goffman's (1963b, 81) idea of forbidden or out-of-bounds places is clear – both are spaces:

> Where persons of the kind he can be shown to be are forbidden to be, and where exposure means expulsion – an eventuality often so unpleasant to all parties that a tacit cooperation will sometimes forestall it, the interloper providing a thin disguise and the rightfully present accepting it, even though both know the other knows of the interloping.

The final and most subjective component that Agnew (1987) addresses pertains to the emotional connection (both positive and negative) to particular spaces, which he refers to as a sense of place. Sense of place does not rely on knowledge of the physical space but, rather, is bound up with feelings of what could be or what is. Emotions such as fear, disgust, attachment, contentment, and 'homeness' become associated with, or "expressed and concretized in[,] place" (Cosgrove 2000, 722). It should come as no surprise that the prison as a place evokes emotional responses from those who live within its walls, but it is critical that our analysis not be restricted to that particular location. The emotional connection to place continues into the community, and a predominant theme in the men's narratives was the impact of place on their experiences in the post-release period.

In the following sections, we consider how differing experiences of place emerged for these men, even within similar locations (spaces). More specifically, this chapter will focus on the spatially located senses of vulnerability and security and the way the men's agency mediated their post-carceral lives. We will see that these feelings relate to the dislocations they have experienced, to a certain type of homelessness, and to a sense of disconnection from particular locales. Ultimately, these sensations lead the men to encounter being both out-of-place and in-place after release.

Being Out of Place

Spatially oriented criminologists and geographers have demonstrated that individuals typically engage in criminal activity in locations near their primary residences (Brantingham and Brantingham 2000; Capone and Nichols 1975; Rengert 1996; Rossmo 1993; and Santtila, Laukkanen, and Zappalà 2007). Presumably, then, the crimes committed by the respondents occurred at or near their homes, and, as a result, many of the men were not permitted to live in their hometowns after their release from prison. As we saw in Chapter 7, sometimes this banishment is overt, as when representatives of the state deny a release plan to that area, and other times it is more indirect, when, for example, correctional agents (parole and police officers) make it explicit (through conversations or by harassment) that the individual is not wanted back in the community. For some of the men, this ban prohibiting their return to their hometowns resulted in profound feelings of displacement:

> I reclaimed my home when this [house] became my home. Because I can't go back to Napanee. Part of my condition was that "No you can't live back there." A lot of people don't understand that. "What do you mean you can't live back there?" They didn't want me to *drive* through that community. That was an issue for the Parole Board and

it was a way of making sure that they were looking at it as reduced risk ... I know I can't live back there. So when I talk about ... community being home, I lost that. (Rick)

In this way, the men encounter a vulnerability that is linked to their sense of not having a location to which they can return.

As a result, many of the men made the choice to seek new home spaces, and, as discussed in Chapter 8, they worried about being found to be out-of-place because of their convict identity. Marcus did not return to his hometown, and this decision was influenced in part by the community itself and in part by his intentions: "That was where my crime was committed and I didn't really want to go into an area that was resentful of me or that might not have made for a successful reintegration, so I stayed out here." In short, the men found themselves homeless – not in terms of a residence but in terms of a place of belonging (May 2000).

The formerly incarcerated man is left in a precarious position between a nostalgic yearning for home and a knowledge that the elements that would make this place impart a sense of security no longer exist. As Arafat Jamal (1998, 3) writes in his work on forced migrants,

> whereas those mourning a human loss are able to rely on well-established rituals to help ease their pain, there is no such clear-cut mechanism to deal with the loss of a homeland. A dead body is a cold, irrevocable fact; a lost homeland, even if changed beyond recognition, dangles the possibility of eventual return.

By choosing to relocate in new areas, the men consciously gave up home places that had some positive affiliations for them. At the same time, the earlier comments also suggest that these familiar places were emotionally contaminated and, therefore, potentially associated with unfavourable memories.

Place-Memory

The decision to avoid a particular location may also have been a way for the men to deal with negative place-memory, which permits the past to be brought into the present: "Place stays there to greet us or threaten us after we have been away from it for a while. Place keeps coming back to mind (that is, in recollection) or in body (for example, as we again find our way about in a place we once knew by means of habitual body memory)" (Casey 2001, 227). Bobby, who had moved to at least ten different areas within Toronto, used geographic spaces to create social and psychological change. His experience exemplifies how sense of place is linked to memory:

> Moving around and having so many different evolutionary stages happen in Toronto. Being there for fifteen years you know, there's not one place I could go in Toronto ... It was only occasionally when I could drive through a certain section of Toronto and not have it come to mind, so many geographic cues, you know, that would trigger something. Got to be a problem. Now Hamilton [is a] clean place. Geography is, in this case, a remedy. It's let's not screw up this corner. Let's not screw up that corner.

Evidently, places are not just about map co-ordinates, but they also encompass the people and type of interactions that occur within those physical locations. We can see that Bobby felt a sense of vulnerability in certain places, and he frequently relocated in order to assume a degree of control and avoid feeling emasculated. Importantly, he does not see the space as being causal to his behaviour but, rather, as being implicated in his actions and certainly in his ability to recall them.

By drawing on memory of place, the men were able to avoid previous criminal affiliations or associates in particular locations. Sometimes passes for unescorted temporary absences and escorted temporary absences were used to get a new sense of old areas:

> If I go back to Leamington ... I have to bump into everybody I know and I didn't want that. I'm finished with them all ... I went to Leamington on a pass ... and as we pulled in, I seen five people I was in jail with ... and I said, "Jesus Christ, just think if I lived here. And I'd be seeing these people all the time" ... I don't want that. (F.G.)

For some, avoiding particular places was a means of evading negative (although not necessarily criminal) influences that could jeopardize their successful resettlement. At times, this decision entailed avoiding kin, despite family members' desire to have their sons/fathers/brothers/ uncles in close proximity: "I'm just saying that I'm out now and I've just finished seventeen years of all my life inside the wall. And I come out and I said, 'You guys are worse than the day that I went to the foster home. I don't want no part of that'" (Gowan).

Fred, who wants his children to know their Aboriginal culture and language, also avoids family spaces because of his own negative place-memory and his fear of the impact that this locale could have on his children:

> I remember growing up ... I was going to my uncle's place because he let us drink. He let all these kids drink and ... I remember I was ten years old, right. I know what goes on there 'cause nothing has changed ... I don't want my kids to be getting involved with that ... [Instead, I say,] "Get your friends to come over here" ... Their friends would come to our place.

For Gowan and Fred, geography is simultaneously the locus of their problems and the solution to them. In both cases, while their families thought a return to their 'home' would be helpful, the men's prior experiences contradicted this sentiment. The fact that there are multiple (and often competing) sensations of place means that, even in those places designed to foster a sense of security or safety, individuals may feel otherwise. For some of the men, the opposite was true and they were able to establish a sense of being in place.

Being In Place

For most of the men released on parole, the urgent need to secure shelter after incarceration was negated by the presence of halfway houses and various other state supports. This safety net meant that they could attend to interpersonal needs (friendship, love, family, and acceptance) and find a place of welcome.[2] As discussed earlier, the men encountered difficulties that created a sense of out-of-placeness (Cresswell 1996) that disrupted their ability to integrate into a community. That said, even within some of the same locations, the predominant sense was one of in-placeness, and a certain psychological security was developed through the creation of home sites.

Creating Home

Within the dominant discourse, 'home' is a place of belonging or, as Gillian Rose (2003, 5) argues, "it is a haven in a heartless world." However, as some feminist geographers have pointed out, home may be an idealized, masculine notion of a place of safety and belonging, which fails to recognize that homes are often the site of violence and other forms of oppression (hooks 1990; Rose 2003). Certainly, for some of the men in this research, childhood homes represented anything but a warm, loving environment. Yet, they spoke of seeking out and creating a different home experience that contributes to their sense of being in-place. In this way, home is not necessarily a nostalgic yearning but, instead, a "dream that situates it firmly in the 'future tense'" (May 2000, 748). Home, then, "can be made, re-made, imagined, remembered or desired; it can refer as much to beliefs, customs or traditions as physical places or buildings ... It is something that is subject to constant reinterpretation and flux" (Black 2002, 126).

Some of the men found it difficult to transition into a home space because they had developed a sense of in-placeness in the prison, at the community residential facility (CRF), or at the community correctional centre (CCC):

> I never felt ready [to leave the halfway house]. Like, I never felt I had enough to step out on my own in the sense that – again, I guess, it's part of being institutionalized after all those years ... I got my apartment. I had to go get everything. I had to go get living room stuff and I had to go get a bedroom set, and all this ... And when I moved I kept coming back here [to the halfway house] because I kept coming back to visit the guys that I was working with ... That took a few months anyway, until that sort of started to wear away and then I felt okay in my own place on my own. (Bob)

As we examined in Chapter 5, the CRF/CCC can be seen as either half-way in or halfway out. Those who saw the day parole setting as another prison environment resisted the idea that it could have any home-like qualities:

> I remember, when they were saying to me, "You're not investing in the house, the halfway house, you don't have a TV here." "No I don't. Why don't we do this interview at my house. I would invest in a TV in my house. It's ten minutes from here. I'll bring you there. I'll show you my TV. I'll show you my space." (Rick)

Providing further nuance to his inability to feel in-place while still in custody, Rick goes on to speak about how his own space in the community morphed into something more meaningful:

> For the longest time this was just a house and then at some point it became a home. It became a home. I wasn't in transition anymore. This became my safe spot ... and I didn't like being invaded here. I can let my guard down here ... so that becomes my release. I was able to do that in a small town ... growing up, I was able to do that. And then I lost that when I went to jail, and I didn't have that coming out. In Ottawa, you know, at the halfway house, I didn't have that safe environment. You know, that whole thing was foreign to me. I was put into a place where I didn't want to be. I didn't really have a choice of where I wanted to be. That changed when this became a home.

While the individual may have the intention of creating a home place, his ability to do so is mediated by his history, current interactions, and political climate. At times, regulations (such as parole, travel restrictions, and monitoring) can undermine the men's efforts and leave them with a fear of being homeless despite having a place to live: "At one point I thought, I'll never have a girlfriend ... I'd never have a home. I'd never have anything. You know, life is pointless" (Joel). However, one of the ways that the men achieved a sense of 'home' was by assuming some authority over their residences. This control takes the forms of owner-ship and restricting who, or what, is in the space.

Ownership and Success

Bonny Lindstrom (1997, 20) argues that housing and community are "markers that situate individuals and establish social identity." Ownership of a house and its contents was how some of the men expressed a sense of home and membership in the 'normal' social body. For men who had spent over a decade in an environment in which material possessions were regulated and choice restricted, the sensation may be so intense that the ability to purchase a house becomes a particularly significant marker:

> The idea of buying a house was probably the last thing on my mind when I got released. Because all who I am is a biker. Tar paper shack, Harley Davidson, Rottweiler, that's all I need ... Buying a home really changes people – like it puts you in a different class of people automatically. And that's, I guess it was kind of welcoming, you know. (Doc)

Owning a home creates a sense of insiderness, and, for those who perceive themselves to be marked, this perception is significant (Cuba and Hummon 1993). The transformative nature of a home can also provide a sense of much-desired 'normalcy':

> When I first got out, I didn't feel I was part of it. I didn't feel that I was normal. I felt like I was an alien on this planet, so to speak ... I longed to be like you. I longed to have that little picket fence. And I did get to accomplish that dream of the white picket fence. I built one eight feet long ... two-sided ... and all it cost me was ... the cost of one two-by-four and a nail. I salvaged everything else from the dump. Painted it. It was sitting in a little eight-foot dividing tent between our property and our neighbour's property, but it beautified it and that was my white picket fence. So many people say, "I wish I had a white picket fence" ... but I had my white picket fence. (Dave)

As Dave's narrative illustrates, the men often employed a "middle-class measuring rod" (Cohen 1955, 87) in assessing their success, which is particularly evident when they spoke of possessing real estate. In expressing these ideas, the men associated class with income and home ownership as well as with a sense of belonging (see Clark 2003; Lacy 2007). As William Clark (2003, 63) notes:

> Middle-class status is a combination of both income level and housing status. It captures the notion that both the ability to buy the middle-class lifestyle and the commitment to and integration into the local community, represented by ownership, are essential parts of the middle-class status.

Owning a home is also a way for the men to restore themselves and overcome the loss of what Lee Cuba and David Hummon (1993, 550) refer to as "treasured domestic objects – which serve as personal and public signs of self [and] ... can be used to ritually transform a *new house* into an *old home.*" Those who are incarcerated for long prison terms rarely retain valued items, and, thus, the home space and their ownership of it may become particularly significant and take the form of a new item that is treasured.

Control and Privacy

Most of the men seek to exercise control over the home space and restrict or permit access to it in order to achieve a sense of security. While the majority of the men limit the people who come into their homes, Ziggy invited his psychologist into his home in order to give him a better understanding of his life. Others control their spaces by disallowing certain things in particular areas:

> I bought this house because of the friggin' garage for my Harley. It wasn't more than a year later that I said, "That's it, bike is going" ... Come home and said [to his girlfriend], "I want to give you back your living room," getting rid of the whole Harley garbage ... 'cause if you walk in, you don't think that you're walking in a friggin' little club house, you know. I want it to be a home, and I think that's what we were accomplishing slowly, just to be a part of society. Like, they keep saying this is what the goal is, to be part of society. (Doc)

For many, having control over their spaces gave them the opportunity to make it more home-like by achieving a level of privacy. This quest for seclusion is not surprising given that the prison environment is one in which men are rarely alone and where they are perpetually subjected to the gaze of the correctional workers and others. As George Kateb (2001, 275) argues:

> One is placed under constant suspicion just by being placed under constant watchfulness and subjected to the implicit interrogation that exists when the accumulated information on oneself is seen as a set of integrated answers that add up to a helpless, and unauthorized autobiography. Such a loss of innocence ... is so massive that the insult involved constitutes an assault on the personhood or human status of every individual.

It is no wonder that the men would counter this subjection by creating private spaces in order to feel more in place. This need for privacy led some men to find residence in rural areas. Census Canada data indicate that in 2006 less than 20 percent of Canadians lived in rural and small communities (Statistics Canada, 2006a), but more than a third of our sample (seven men) were currently residing "way the hell out" (Barry). The choice to be away from urban areas was a deliberate strategy employed by some of the men in order to avoid the 'prying eyes' of neighbours. They feel that the rural setting offers greater anonymity so their ex-prisoner identities would be less likely to be revealed as they can "restrict the tendency of others to build up a personal identification of [them] ... [and they can] introduce a disconnectedness in [their] biography" (Goffman 1963a, 99).

More frequently, however, the men perceive of these secluded spaces as giving them freedom to be themselves and to express emotions that they would not feel comfortable with others seeing. It is important to remember that these men had spent more than a decade living in a relatively unisex environment, and, in this setting, they had constructed rigid masculinities that hyper-conformed to gender norms and discouraged emotionality (see Chapters 4 and 11). After release, concern about showing emotion was retained, and they sought out spaces in which they are "free to perform their private selves, enacting their private behaviours and desires" (Gorman-Murray 2006, 56). Home becomes a place for emotional liberation:

> We're so isolated out here ... If I feel like crying – it's not the manly thing to do. If I want to cry, I can go out on the deck to cry ... I can act as crazy as I want and nobody can see me and I don't have to worry about the neighbours thinking that I'm – nuts. Or I don't have to worry about somebody reporting me. Oh, I'm acting pretty bizarre alright. That's what I need behind me. That release. And I can do that in my own space. (Rick)

It is clear that Rick is using private spaces as a "metaphorical closet" (Brown 2000), which is "a certain kind of place of secrecy and a place of autonomy and safety" (Cresswell 2004, 105). While this concept was developed to discuss the experiences of members of the homosexual community, it is equally apt for those who have been criminalized, institutionalized, and returned to the community and who feel a need to hide any identifiers (including actions) of their stigmatized self. In their actions, there is a convergence of the metaphorical and physical wherein the closet space of the home becomes a place where they are free to be themselves without judgment.

Clearly, the men's ability to feel secure is linked to the very real threat of having their parole revoked, and this worry led some of them to seek privacy. However, the effect of this strategy was double-edged. By avoiding others the men protect themselves from being judged, but this isolation perpetuates their 'otherness' by limiting engagement with the social body or with approved social supports. In some cases, this avoidance creates or reinforces a sense of disaffiliation or a feeling of being out-of-place, while, in other cases, it affirms their own agency and allows them to feel a sense of security and in-placeness.

Reflection

We started this chapter with one of the men eating alone and his sense of out of placeness, and we came to see how this sensation resonates with the stories of others. No matter their place of origin, all of these men experienced major geographic ruptures. They spent years living in a six-by-ten-foot cell and eventually returned to open spaces – both of these events led to geographically mediated culture shock. Despite the extreme variations in the locations that they experienced, the men were able to move forward in their quest for self-actualization and use place instrumentally. This spatialized tactic helps them to create and modify their identity and to find belonging. In short, place is not merely the screen onto which the story is projected but, rather, a surface that helps to create the script, symbols, and actor's identities.

Work and Finance: Navigating the New Economy

10

> My first job was working in a warehouse and driving truck for a textile company in downtown Ottawa. So there are some people who are absolutely obnoxious workers and an obnoxious boss, you know, 'cause they're driving everybody for, you know, like, $7.16 an hour. But it was my first job ... But as the years go by you get better and better jobs ... Uh, I was a junior editor at the *Star Record* in Wakefield for a while. And then, finally, you know, in the, in the 90s ... [I had] that installation job for Bell in Toronto. Great job. You know, but it was a very long slow development. (Bobby)

Most Canadians either have a job or want one. First and foremost, employment provides economic resources that are very prized in a consumer society: "You know, you got a job. People want to work. You got a pay cheque coming in, you're not worried about money and you're fitting in there, right?" (Tom). A job also offers non-economic benefits. Most importantly, it structures time and allows a greater appreciation of leisure periods (Rinehart 1996). In addition, work may provide other rewards that render labour force participation appealing. These secondary benefits include contacts and friendships (MacDonald and Connelly 1989), social recognition and affirmation (Reiter 1991), an identity, a sense of accomplishment, and gender role validation (Kimmel and Holler 2011).

Most of the men we interviewed expressed the desire to conform to the public script and participate in the wage economy. Not only did they want to work, but there was a sense of urgency as they sought, in an unselfconsciously gendered way, to achieve what they assumed an 'average' man of their age had: a credit rating, a house, a car, and the other markers of financial (and, implicitly, gender and social) success: "Get a job. Get a wife. Get a white picket fence" (Bobby). Acquiring this 'white picket fence' was not simply a matter of working hard. Indeed, the men had to learn about, adapt to, and then navigate within an economy and labour market that had undergone significant transformations in the 1980s and 1990s while they were 'inside.' This chapter begins by sketching these shifts in order to contextualize the men's experiences. It then reflects on the question of financial security before turning to consider those men who found paid work and attends to the meaning they ascribed to it. In the final part of the chapter, we examine the stories of those who decentred work in their lives.

Neo-Liberal and Neo-Conservative Fallout: Adapting to a Changed World

In the 1980s and into the 1990s, the emergent global economy, technological revolutions, and free trade agreements changed the way labour was organized and the types of jobs that were available (Phillips 1997). It was during this period that corporations in North America restructured and that manufacturing was increasingly displaced to newly industrialized nations in which labour was cheaper and regulation was minimal. Not only were manufacturing jobs disappearing, but those that remained were also no longer as lucrative or as secure because of assaults on unions and collective bargaining (ibid.). In Ontario, for example, the neo-conservative policies of the Mike Harris government (1995-2002) systematically eroded the power of unions in that province.

Second, the gender composition of the labour force was altered. The division of labour in prisons (women correctional officers and wardens notwithstanding) continues to be largely gendered – most female employees work as social program officers, office staff, nurses, and administrators – the pink ghetto of corrections (Munn 2012). On release, the men discovered not only that women had made significant (albeit incomplete) inroads into non-traditional labour sectors but that they had also become a much greater presence. For example, between 1976 and 2009, the labour force participation of common-law or married women aged twenty to sixty-four years of age increased from 47 to 76 percent (Statistics Canada 2010b). These men, with their dated frame of reference and commitment to traditional gender scripts, suddenly found themselves competing with women for 'men's' jobs.

Third, the men were also confronted, as are many Canadians, with the increasing income disparity and higher rates of poverty that characterize the new economy. According to Statistics Canada (2008), between 1980 and 2005, the earnings of Canada's bottom income group fell by 20.6 percent, while top incomes rose by 16.4 percent. At the same time, those aspects of the social welfare state that aid the most vulnerable Canadians (non-profit housing, subsidized child care, and welfare payments) were being dismantled, ensuring that greater segments of the population were forced below the poverty line (Ivanova and Klein 2012). As we have seen in the economic crises of 2009 and 2010, this trend has continued into the twenty-first century. Engendered by corporate greed and irresponsible banking practices, the disparity between rich and poor increased exponentially, at the same time as social services were being slashed in the name of fiscal responsibility.

Making It: Seeking Financial Security

The men were profoundly aware of "the pressure on men in our society to work, to be self-reliant, to secure the material resources that will enable them (and their families) to get by and make ends meet" (Comack 2008, 74). It follows that developing economic stability is a significant preoccupation for the majority of the men during resettlement, and it proves to be a persistent struggle as they seek to 'catch up' in a world in which the rules of the economic game have changed:

> Trying to get back to the point of where a normal thirty year old would be. I'm now in my fifties and I'm still not where a normal fifty

year old should've been. It's playing a catch-up game that you can't win at, and if you let yourself get caught in it, then it becomes a treadmill and a grind. (Barry)

Some, who read their (in)ability to realize credit as a significant indicator of their otherness, were frustrated:

> Today I have difficulty getting credit. This is serious now. This is ten years after and I still have difficulty getting credit even though I don't have a bad credit history. But I got really forty years of my life missing. Like, I'm nowhere in there. "Where have you been all that time?" "What have you done?" So today it's becoming a little easier because we look back five years. So to do a credit check on somebody, we look back three years, five years, and things are getting better. (Luc)

In this context, the ability to obtain credit in order to realize the outward symbols of success take on added significance. They become the visible and concrete markers of manhood in the face of the gendered fears of not measuring up and 'being real men' (Kimmel 1994):

> Since I've done this – buying the house – I'm able to say, now I'm working. So I'm above, you know, most of my peers, 'cause they don't own houses ... When I bought this house, you know, my credit rating shot right through the roof ... I walked into a bank with nothing – I bought that Harley with nothing, just a signature. (Doc)

Sometimes having access to credit created its own set of problems. Dave found he was simply not able to pay his bills, and, with his credit overextended, he took a critical stance against the rampant capitalist-inspired consumerism by readjusting his expectations in order to be content with a dramatically reduced standard of living:

> We had to sell the house because ... we were getting bi-weekly mortgage payments. Plus we had her Scotia credit card, other bills, plus all the utilities and things like that and – you know, upkeep of the

house and maintenance of the vehicles and that. So we sold the house. And we were able to pay a couple of other bills as well. And then we went and got a loan and consolidated certain bills, paid that off ... and we've come to the realization that we don't need all the channels on the cable. We just need basic cable ... you know, being able to learn to just think, "We don't need that," "We don't need this." (Dave)

Re-entering the Labour Market

For most of us, achieving a measure of economic success is contingent on participating in paid work. For the men, the prolonged time out of the labour market; lack of, or out-of-date, skills; limited vocational training; stigma; and legislative barriers undermined their efforts. In addition, over the course of the many years in prison, memories of the rhythms and expectations of the workplace fade. In recognition of this issue, the Correctional Service of Canada (2007b) established CORCAN – a business designed to aid "in the safe reintegration of offenders into Canadian society by providing employment and employability skills training to offenders incarcerated in federal penitentiaries and, for brief periods of time, after they are released into the community." A number of the men took advantage of this opportunity to put into practice the competencies they had learned in vocational training and education. As Ziggy remarked, "I was able to use a lot the stuff I learned in school and actually apply it." For many, CORCAN provided a segue to other jobs, allowed them to avoid falsifying resumés (which would require the assistance of others to 'verify') and assisted them in establishing contacts. Others were persistent and relied on their own tenacity, assuming the responsibility of good neo-liberal subjects:

I went out faithfully every day with resumés ... I would start up one side of the street and go down and when I got to the far end, turn over and go to the other side and come back up the other way ... I'd create a book, a log book, and every business that I went in was logged, what it was, who I talked to, their phone number, and within days, if I didn't return to check on is anything happening with my resumé, I would phone ... because it's not enough just to drop a resumé off somewhere and move on. (Gerry)

Regardless of their willingness to seek employment, there were limitations that bracketed the men's options and opportunities. Of particular significance is the question of health. We know that "prisoners in general experience poorer levels of physical and mental health compared with the general population" (Viggiani 2007, 72). This fact is hardly surprising. By definition, a disciplinary regime removes self-determinacy, autonomy, and authority from those it endeavours to correct/reform/change. Speaking to the effect of class location and racialization on health, experts in the social determinants of health have identified the lack of power and control and being in a state of perpetual vigilance (as one would presumably be in a violent and tension-filled prison) as significant stressors that, according to Dr. Leonard Syme, a renowned epidemiologist, "change biological markers and make people vulnerable to being sick" (Alderman 2008). In other words, toxic hormone levels brought about by chronic stress result in a changed physiology associated with a host of health risks, including a compromised immune system, hypertension, stroke, diabetes, and heart attack (ibid.). For some men, their health status meant they simply could not work: "I tried one more cleaning job at not Giant Tiger, but ... something like that. It was a store like that. Anyway it was cleaning and again at night. But it just didn't work out. There's no way I could work. So I had to walk ... because of my health" (Ernest).

Other men confront reduced employment options as a result of the aging process. Some who had been labourers before their incarceration find it hard to return to that type of work because their bodies are no longer as capable: "If a guy comes out, say at fifty-eight, he's not old. He's not old enough to get a pension, but he's got to work and the jobs that are available for someone that age are tough slugging ... I was forty-six or forty-seven and it almost killed me. 'Cause I'm doing a job of twenty year olds. I did it for a year but it was tough" (Tom).

Poor health intersecting with the age-related loss of corporal competence may be particularly important for men who had relied on their physicality to help establish their masculinity (Drummond 2007). In the process, they lose one of the ways in which they had previously defined their masculinity (Connell 2004). Luc, who had a slight build and grey hair, was frustrated that his aging body was a barrier to employment, but he was sympathetic to potential employers:

> "What's this guy offering me – some talk? I don't need talk. I need somebody's going to put doors on my wall." All right. "Has he ever done that? No. Can I train him? He's kind of old, eh. He's small, and he's old. So, no, I don't want him" ... I always kept saying to myself, "Luc, you shouldn't have any difficulty finding a job. You're able" ... I forget that by [that] time I was fifty years old. To me it didn't mean anything but to an employer it meant a lot. It meant a very dangerous person to hire. "Tomorrow he's going to get sick and we're going to pay for him. He's going to hurt himself, and we're going to pay for him."

Finding a "Good" Job

Given the significance of paid work in realizing economic security, the men seek employment in which they will be well compensated:

> Everybody gauges their success by how much money they make. I started off at $8 an hour. I make twenty bucks now for what I do. I like working. My body's not liking it anymore, but I like it ... In order to be a man, I got to work and make money, and buy things, like a house, and to me that's our Christmas – I never bought a house before. (Doc)

Many also seek self-validation through their labour force participation. That said, their conceptualization of 'meaningful work' is classed and gendered. Lacking access to the cultural capital enjoyed by middle-class white men, individuals who are socially disempowered on the basis of class or racialization endeavour to mediate this discrimination by drawing on their body competence and being validated in physically demanding occupations (such as sports and construction) (Katz 2006).

However, while the men were in prison, the traditional 'good' unionized, well-paid, and secure jobs in the manufacturing sector (to which working-class men traditionally aspire) disappeared and were replaced by service sector jobs (Statistics Canada 2006b). When the men entered prison, these 'McJobs' (Ritzer 2004) were not only more prevalent, but they were also 'women's work' – and, in the masculine hegemony of the time, not appropriate for a real man. Moreover, these jobs were often characterized by part-time, casual, and/or seasonal labour arrangements (Rinehart 1996).

Adapting to this new reality proved a challenge:

> [I wanted] meaningful employment and so on as opposed to 7-Eleven, Tim Hortons, things like that. 'Cause for me ... that's really a central issue, and I think that pertains to anybody. Your employment is real essential to the way you're going to live your life and what opportunities that provides for you, and if you can't find meaningful, sustainable employment, then you're going to have problems in a lot of other areas of your life. (Bob)

Consequently, some of the men endure periods of unemployment as they are unwilling to labour in the low-status service sector. Others are prepared to accept the opportunities that present themselves:

> [I was doing] maintenance, like cutting lawns and flowers and planting tulips and stuff like that, which fit me. I have a soft spot for all that. And then, I think it was three months, six months maybe, the [halfway] house asked me if I would be interested in taking a nighttime, full-time job, at the university as a cleaner. And I said, "Well, there's one thing I do know how to sling – and that's a mop." (Ernest)

For Luc, it is about the nature and the prospects of the job: "I'd already touched a few jobs but they were all menial jobs, that didn't mean anything, that weren't leading to anything." Whereas Doc revels in the fact that after his long period of confinement, his job allows him to move freely at the same time as it affirms his masculinity: "After sitting in jail as long as I did, I now have a five-ton truck and I'm driving to Hamilton, Toronto, Ottawa, places I never even been. I thought it was just so cool after all that time, you know. Here I was on the open road again. And I'm being treated like a trucker now."

A select few find meaning in employment by drawing on their own troubled histories and becoming 'professional ex's' and working with prisoners or, in the case of one man, with substance (mis)users: "A month after getting into the halfway house, I had my first volunteer shift at a job which then became a full time job for me, which I stayed in for close to ten years after my release ... I became an addictions counsellor. I did a lot of work there in a detox centre."[1]

Of course, such work can be rewarding, but it comes with its own set of challenges. For example, the professional ex-convict must relive a painful past, perpetually recount previous traumas, and reaffirm a positive sense of self while being continually confronted by a previous, less positive identity. A Life Line in-reach worker told us: "I never thought I'd say this but it's more difficult working in prisons than it is living in prisons in the sense that I go back to this willingly every day in order to try to find a way to get other people out of it."[2]

Interacting on the Job

In addition to providing financial security and self-validation, employment also has a social component. Research indicates that places of work are important sites for developing networks and for "the acquisition of a set of appropriate role-behaviours ... the development of work skills and abilities ... [and] adjustment to the work group's norms and values" (Feldman 1981, 309). Bob spoke of work as a mechanism for the development of social relations: "When I started working full time, that's when I started to build some confidence because people would invite me to their homes say for dinner and to go over to watch a football game and things like that, and I started to have a lot more confidence to be out of the house." Sometimes the specificity of the workplace facilitates an individual's ability to 'fit in' and be in-place:

> I went to work at Corrections Canada so I'm working in the place where it was a requirement to be who I was ... I mixed well with them

... We were really tightly bonded there ... So, when the big boss retired just this last year, and I've been away from CORCAN for almost six years, I was invited to that party and I felt like I was part of them ... I wasn't in a place where anyone was going to challenge me on who I was or I was going to get fired and I didn't have to feel in any way embarrassed and I worked with really, really good people. (Joel)

Others are not so fortunate and feel profoundly out-of-place in their work environments, particularly when they are expected to socialize during work hours or, more importantly, after hours. Parole conditions prohibit the kind of activities that are sometimes taken for granted. Simply going out for a drink after work may lead to the violation of a curfew, 'check in,' or abstinence condition. For men who have not disclosed their criminalized status, these restrictions can undermine their ability to develop affiliations with co-workers who may assume the individual is being anti-social. In short, the limitations placed on the men can cause conflict between their personal and professional lives and negatively impact on their ability to develop an insiderness:

[I told my co-workers,] "It's [drinking alcohol] not part of my lifestyle" ... I said to them, "You know what, the last time I got drunk, I fucking killed someone." [They said] "Holy fuck! Okay. Don't worry, never asking you to drink again." But it got to the point it was ... they were different. And, even then, you're judged by them ... A hillbilly is looking at you like you're worse than them because you're a lifer. And you gotta be ready for that, 'cause if you're not, fuck, you're in for a rude shock ... I was in for a shock. (Puzzle)

Reconfiguring Meaning without Work

Some men, for reasons of age, health, or disability, find themselves excluded from the wage economy. For these men, paid work is unattainable. As Gord put it, "I'm not very bloody employable." Five of these men access social services. In direct contrast to those men who are preoccupied with 'catching up' and aggressively pursuing good jobs to meet their goals, these individuals are content simply to pay their bills and hopefully have a few dollars left in their pockets:

As long as I'm staying in the [halfway] house, I really don't need any work. I'd had some other small jobs where I could make ... enough money to get by. And I still have a guy, who I am still fairly loyal to who gave me some small odd jobs and a pretty good amount of money for doing these small jobs, in order to get by ... But when the ODSP [Ontario Disability Support Program] came through, it was "I'll play music because I want to not because I need to make a hundred bucks. I'll go and cut grass because I want to – not because I need thirty bucks." (Bobby)

Bobby's pension is the result of a mental health designation. A few of the men, however, lack the inclination to work. They epitomize the dependent social welfare subject who is critiqued from the right and left of the political spectrum (Rose 1996). For them, reliance on social services is a lifelong pattern:

I was on a disability pension when I went in in 1977. So the chances are good that I didn't get any healthier in prison ... When I made day parole, I went to the Parole Office and the Welfare Office and said, "I need forms to fill out for my disability" and they said, "Here you go." And I filled them all out and gave them to them. The doctor sent his report in ... I got day parole in May and got my pension in August ... Then I became an old age pensioner and I got that and went down to housing and said, "I was on disability, permanent disability on your files ... I just became sixty-five years old" ... So about a month later I get a call that there's an apartment ... "because of the gear to income and you're an old age pensioner, it's $341 a month, everything included." (F.G.)

For most of this sub-group, accessing this social support is not problematic. Gord, whose brain injury meant he is not able to work, offered a fiscal rationale:

Now the media ... they're not looking at the success rate, let alone the money it's going to [cost] society. For someone like me, they're far better off giving me $1,000 bucks ... that's what I put on my disability papers. Now, if you want to, uh, you can either help me in my stand or kick me in my can. If you think that giving $1,000 a month as opposed to paying $75,000 a year to keep me inside [is better], you're crazier than you think I am. (Gord)

Those men who are unable or unwilling to participate in the wage labour economy are not only managing with limited fiscal resources but also denied the identity and status associated with one's work. Puzzle, who, due to an injury, was forced to cease manual labour, finds meaning in being the primary caregiver to his children. This new non-traditional gender role necessitated a re-ordering of his values and challenged his previous acceptance of the "ideological linkage of fathers with breadwinning" (Ranson 2007, 199):

[Being off work because of an injury] sucks because a large part of what I hold my value, my own self-worth, is in working and doing a good job ... And the other part is societal values ... A male staying home is, if anyone thinks it's easier than what it was twenty years ago, it's not. You are looked at, kind of like a 'house bitch' and that's kind of tough some days. I'll tell you what, you go raise kids and look after a house and maintain a home, so when they come in it's clean, there's meals cooked, the laundry's done, stuff like that ... It's nowhere near as easy as what somebody who's never done it thinks.

Some of the men mediate both the fiscal and self-validation issues by participating in the informal economy. This strategy ensures that these men, like those employed in the formal economy, are acknowledged for their skills: "I do people's tax returns for them ... It's almost a bit of, say, the underground economy. I do their tax returns and stuff and, you know, they do things for me" (Bob). Gord, who busks on the street, told the following story with evident pride:

I've done weddings for people out here ... and they were very, very grateful. They said, "You did a fantastic job," and they just picked me off the street. They heard me sing and play and they thought I did fairly well and they asked me how much I would charge and I said, "Whatever you want to give me." For an hour, they gave me $60; I think that's pretty good.

Reflection

For some of the men, the challenges of the new economy, their poor health, aging bodies, and sketchy work histories are significant obstacles to finding meaningful and rewarding work. Those men who are able to work in the wage economy find comfort in being integrated into the normative socio-economic order and take pride in demonstrating their puritan work ethic (Weber 1904). In so doing, they find much-desired status and new identity and revel in their acquisition of the material markers of success. In addition to giving them fiscal security to meet their economic obligations, work enables them to (sometimes problematically) gain access to credit. Ultimately, their ability to labour establishes them not only as contributing members of society but also as conforming to normative gender roles. Those who are unable or unwilling to fit into this public script need to first justify their non-participation by drawing attention to the challenges confronted due to their advanced age and/or ill health. Excluded from the personal and social validation afforded workers, these men negotiate positive self-identities outside the labour framework.

Interactions: **11**
Etiquette, Intimacy, and Fitting In

You must establish your area. Like the "King of Beasts," a male lion comes in and he establishes his pride because it's his area. Well, in prison we do the same thing. We establish what is ours and out here we try to do it and we realize we can't ... It doesn't work out here. It works in prison because you know what you have to do and there's no grey areas, it's either black or white. Out here there're grey areas and you have to learn to live in them and when you first get out, you can't see the grey areas. Like, you walk down the street and you hear some guy go, "Hey, you're a fucking goof." [If he] says that in prison, somebody's going to cave his head in. But you've got to get used to it ... So, therefore, you've got to become part of the people out here and that's the thing. You have to take your space that you've created in there; I mean, get rid of it and find a new one. So that you can walk down the street and somebody bumps into you and you bump into somebody and say, "Oh, excuse me" and they say, "Oh, it's okay" and you keep on walking ... So you see, you must learn all over again. (F.G.)

In his text, *Presentation of Self in Everyday Life*, Erving Goffman (1959) employed theatrical metaphors to reveal the process by which identity emerges out of interactions in which social actors give (verbal) and give off (non-verbal) signs that are then 'read' by the audience. His work continues to resonate, and in this chapter we draw on the insights and language of his dramaturgical theory to shed light on the men's negotiation of these new (for them) "grey areas" (F.G.). In social interactions, all individuals follow 'scripts' that "provide our routines and roles with significance and meaning, tell us how we should be acting and feeling at a particular moment, provide us with details of others whom we encounter in the situation and forecast the next move in the game, the next development in the play" (Cohen and Taylor 1972, 70). For most of us, our familiarity with the scripts and subtexts of our everyday performances enable us to make sense and affirm our own conceptual frameworks (Goffman 1959). The men have had to learn multiple scripts – the ones that apply to their pre-prison lives, those that emerge during their incarceration, and others that manifest on their return to the community. In practice, the men find themselves unknowingly skipping between the theatrical beats.

Casual Relationships

During incarceration, an individual undergoes a mortification process (Goffman 1963a)and is transformed into a 'prisoner.' However, a comparable re-socialization process does not characterize the journey back into 'free society.' As a result, the men released from prison stumbled as they sought to re-assume the role of citizen. Their discomfort is evident in the difficulty they have engaging in commonplace social interactions in which they feel they no longer know the language and lack a certain taken-for-granted cultural cachet. While the men were 'standing still' in prison, the social world (with which they had limited contact) had changed. A comparable experience can be found by looking at research on forced migrants: "The psychosocial difficulties of reintegration do not lie so much in the fact that the country of origin has changed during their protracted absence, but rather in the returnee's expectations that he/she and the home country have remained the same during the time spent in exile" (Ghanem 2003, 37). Like the forced migrant, these formerly incarcerated men are destabilized by "the discrepancy between past and present [as] was shown by uneasiness about 'not knowing how to act and react'" (Muggeridge and Doná 2006, 421):

They said I needed to see these people. I said, "Yeah, okay, you want me to see the psychologist; I'll go and see the psychologist." So, he said, "Come and see me at 8:00 tonight." I said, "Yeah, all right, no problem." So I come down here and go in there at 8:00 and we're there for an hour, an hour and fifteen minutes. It's got dark out. And I haven't been out at night when it's dark for a long time. And I cross the road here ... This kid walks up and taps me on the shoulder. I said, "Oh, gosh, lucky one of us didn't die." Because I almost had a heart attack and I was going to kill him because I don't know who he was [laughter], all he wanted was a dollar. He said, "You got any change?" I said, "Yeah, here," I gave him a dollar. But I had to get used to that. Because I had never been out at night and I never had anybody come up behind me and put their hand on my shoulder. (F.G.)

During imprisonment, convicted men have to learn how to adjust their behaviour in order to 'fit' into the prison milieu, a "*gendered* site and *gendering* experience" (Comack 2008, 110). After release, they must learn a new set of interactional styles and techniques that are often quite different from those they used prior to their incarceration. The interviewees are acutely aware of their lack of familiarity with the folkways and mores that govern contemporary social interaction:

Personal rudeness in the prison system is not tolerated under any circumstances, at least in the old days when I was there. You could not 'dis' somebody and get away with it. In our community now out here on the street, there's not a day that goes by that somebody on the street doesn't act disrespectfully towards me. And I let it go ... The bottom line is, I found it a shock that people in the community that I was aspiring to live in were so absolutely rude to each other, and they are rude every day, and I found that really frightening. There were times when I asked myself, "Do I even want to live in this society?" ... Now after twenty-one years in the community, I still see this and it still appalls me. (Barry)

As Barry's statement suggests, the adjustments required to assimilate may take years, and it is difficult to relinquish prison-related behaviours for ones that are more conducive to being in society. F.G., who started his federal prison time in the late 1970s, explained:

> When you go to prison, you've lived here and you've got these rules now. When you get to prison, you're here, you've got to forget them rules and live by these rules. Now, when you get out you've got to forget these rules and live by these rules. So it's, you have to learn to live all over again.

Even after they have figured out social etiquette, their years of imprisonment leave them with little to say during social interactions:

> [It was] very difficult. Very difficult. The night that we spent at the pub upstairs there eating peanuts and drinking, very difficult to fit in because every time I start a conversation and I return, well I'm either returning back X number of years or what experience do I have on the street three months, six months, nine months, you know. What am I going to say to you? What am I going to talk about? (Luc)

> Not surprisingly, the men feel more at ease in the company of others who have served time: "The discussions are different. I'm not sure how to articulate it but there's a real comfort and familiarity to the discussions whereas there are times when I'm in other social circles, I have to be careful what I refer to and how" (Bob).

Intimate Relationships

The men's social unease is particularly acute in terms of intimate relations. For some of them, this dis-ease is exacerbated by earlier experiences in their lives. For example, some of our respondents shared that they had been raped and molested as children, and this victimization had a profound impact on how they see themselves and on how they interact with their families and their partners. According to the National Clearing House on Family Violence's (2008, 4) guide for men who were sexually abused as children, male victims may "have difficulty with sexual relationships as a result of their abuse," and these issues may cause some to avoid these types of interactions. Others are likely handicapped by their time in prison where they "had to be especially vigilant around expressing emotions lest their actions be taken as a sign of masculine weakness" (Comack 2008, 126).

Some of the men, such as Gord, elect to avoid romantic entanglements: "I haven't enveloped myself in relationships. Why does somebody deserve that and the baggage that I'm dealing with – it's not fair on them, it's not fair on me." A few of the men are content to rely on "professional girls" for sexual relief. Most, however, are anxious to resume intimate relationships: "I came out [of prison], 'Luc you ain't gonna have no difficulty, all right.' Now I'm out, I'm going on six months, and excuse the language, I ain't got a fuck yet. Some fuckin' thing wrong man. This is wrong, wrong, wrong, wrong. I'm in the wrong ballpark" (Luc). Luc went on to explain that his desire for a connection goes beyond sexual gratification. For him, like many of the others, a relationship is about achieving a sense of belonging and 'normalcy' – both of which are themes throughout the men's narratives. By establishing a link to a female partner, they can forgo the possible homophobic stigma historically attached to being a bachelor and affirm their heterosexual masculinity (Snyder 2007). For the most part, the men unquestioningly subscribe to, and seek to realize, hetero-normative conventions of couple-hood:

> I basically don't know how to – how to communicate with the other gender, so I thought it would be a normal conversation like everybody has here. Everything had to be ... really important. And it wasn't important. But for me it was important for me. I needed the attention. I needed – uh – more than the attention. I needed recognition, attention – but recognition from what, I don't know ... I think I just needed somebody to be associated with, where I could – I don't know, get roots. I didn't have any roots. (Luc)

Evidently, considerable adjustment is required. First, establishing and maintaining intimate relationships are complicated by the men's previous contemplation of the life they would have on the outside. Their reliance on gendered scripts extends beyond the need to share their life with someone. Indeed, it includes a visual image of the appearance of the female partner, which is often one that is rooted in a cinematic male glaze (Mulvey 1975):

> I walk out of jail with a $1,500 car. Did I expect to get Marilyn Monroe? ... You're in there reading magazines for twenty odd years. Every time you friggin' flip the page, they don't show her [normal woman]. It's a playboy girl, you know, like, ideal girl ... Well, where the hell are you going to find her? And do you want that? (Doc)

Second, as Doc's quote vividly illustrates, the limited interactions with women during their incarceration (restricted, for the most part, to female correctional workers or volunteers) occurred at the same time as they were bombarded with media images of idealized women. For years, their visits (from family and partners) had been constrained by physical partitions or the supervised milieu in which they were held. So while the men had an established idea of what a couple should look like, they have few actual skills to employ in those relationships:

> I think that it [prison] skewed my development and my ability to have open and honest relationships with women because of the prison mentality and the objectifying of women in that environment ... Because all interactions with women were forced, strained, over-supervised. There was no natural ability to learn how to talk to women. (Barry)

Third, the men also need to come to terms with their biological age:

> I would go to the Haughton bars in downtown Peterborough 'cause I was allowed to drink, pull up on my bike and go in there, and I realized, you know, these kids all think that their Dad's looking for them. When that realization sunk into me it freaked me out a bit. (Tom)

While Jean was able to adjust his self-image from a "dashing young man" to that of a "grey old fox," others consciously engaged with "technologies-of-the-self" (Foucault 1988).[1] Tom walked us through his "self-talk":

> I went to jail [when I was] twenty-six, so my girlfriends were twenty, twenty-one. Alright, I get out at forty-six, and that's a huge adjustment to make 'cause mentally you're still looking at twenty, twenty-one-year-old women and, you know, intellectually, that that's not right. That you shouldn't be looking at them 'cause you wouldn't want one. Because if I had a younger girlfriend, I'd feel like an idiot, you know. So you don't really want one, but it takes you a while to adjust to go "Okay, I'm supposed to be with a woman this age, but I'm not attracted to a woman this age." It came with time. (Tom)

Interactive styles are the fourth challenge the men confront as they seek to establish intimate relations. Some of the men went to prison just as the second-wave women's movement was gaining momentum and before initiatives such as no-fault divorce, abortion on request, and employment equity were firmly entrenched into the social fabric. These transformations changed the way women saw themselves and how they expected to participate in a relationship. As a result, the men find themselves having to relearn social interaction techniques. They also find the skills they employed to survive in prison sometimes counterproductive afterwards:

> Having a companion under certain circumstances [is] very difficult. And having a companion for somebody that never lived with a companion for most of his life was an even greater challenge ... [While incarcerated] we pick up all kinds of masks that we put on to survive in jail and these masks work ... So it's very easy when you're out in the community and things don't work out the way you want them, to put back some of these masks again. It doesn't work. (Luc)

Lastly, because the men are deemed to be 'risky' individuals, they are subject to state regulation. In this context, they are not only morally, but also legally, obliged to disclose their past to potential intimate partners. It can be terrifying for individuals invested in stigma management to find themselves having to reveal their shameful acts:

One of the things that Father Pete and Sam had told me to do after I've been out for a coffee with her a few times, "David you have to sit down and you have to tell her who you are" ... A most frightful thing. Nevertheless, I did what I was told and I went out for a coffee. We sat in the parking lot in a car for about almost four hours and I just talked with her about everything that I've ever done in my life that was done to me – just like a book. And when I finished, she said, "Is there anything else?" and I said, "No" and she said, "Okay." So Gertrude knows anything and everything there is to know about me. (Dave)

"Risky" Intimate Relationships

In the context of state regulation, men who are involved in intimate relationships feel pressure to perform a script of (unrealistic) marital bliss. For example, Rick sought to maintain a facade of perfection after his release. He felt that if the state's representatives knew that he was experiencing obstacles, his placement on the risk assessment scales could be negatively impacted:

> I knew if I went and started complaining too much, I was going to be seen as a problem ... Not that I wasn't doing well, but how do you sit down with somebody and say "I'm having a hard time adjusting to the rules." Because they look at you as being problematic then and so they consider your risk is elevated.

Even Ziggy, who values the years of support from his psychologist, gives a careful performance in his therapeutic sessions:

> [In talking with my state-supplied psychologist,] I'd use the word 'fight' and then alarm bells would go off. But that is what you would say with your husband. Well, we had a fight or an argument or spat. But if I use any of those words ... everyone is terrified.

Others, cognizant of their master status and vulnerability to being read as dangerous and/or threatening, perceive the role of intimate partner to be, for all intents and purposes, unavailable to them. Joel, who had married and divorced after prison, feels fortunate that the marriage ended amicably because, had it not, his freedom could have been jeopardized. Joel spoke to his current situation:

> That's why I avoid relationships ... because you know what if she gets afraid of me or what if it breaks up or what if she's unstable or what if she _____? It isn't like you might call on your husband and the police say, "Well, there's nothing we can do ma'am." Well, boy, there is if it's me. There's plenty that can be done ... That's a part of being an ex-convict.

While the men recognize that participation in intimate relationships can increase their chances of re-incarceration if they go badly, most do choose to have partners after prison and are often grateful to the women who are prepared to overlook their 'spoiled identities':

> Being able to love her. And, you know, all the little things like sitting down and taking time to rub her neck when she wakes up in the morning because she's had her hair done. Tomorrow morning I know she's going to have a sore neck 'cause today she got her hair done and ... I'm going to have to massage her neck. But that's okay. Doing all kinds of little things at home for her, you know, and remembering what she went through for me also. (Dave)

"Risky" Social Relationships

While many of the men are unwilling to abandon intimate relationships, they are prepared to forgo social relationships with individuals defined by the criminal justice system (and sometimes by the men themselves) as negative influences. Cognizant of the potential implications of the "looking-glass self" (Cooley 1902) they worry that in the company of others who continue to envision them as criminally inclined, they will also begin to see themselves in that way, take on that role, and thereby jeopardize their success:

> Because I've always felt that, even though sometimes and it hurts, and I've had to do it, not have to – I've done it because of the need

that's been there. Sometimes in your life, as much as you may not want to, it's sometimes better to change your location, change your friends, period. Cut them right out of your life and move on. And if that's what you have to do, then do it. Get down and do it. And I would do it in a second if it was jeopardizing my safety, okay. I would say I would cut all strings and all attachments and I would just be gone, that's all, because nothing holds me, you know. (Gerry)

For these men, successful resettlement necessitates careful self-regulation and judicious policing of their own social interactions:

I've had many people pull over and go, "Gowan, here's my address, come on over." And, you know, they know that I'm still a solid guy and I just said, "Are you still partying? Are you still smoking heavy?" [They say,] "Yes I am." [I say,] "Then I can't come there" ... But that's part of that reintegration. You've got to keep focused. And watch your boundaries. (Gowan)

The natural extension of rejecting some social relations is the fostering of other (pro-social) ones. This process can be challenging for individuals whose history and presentation-of-self effectively denies them access to the 'costume' of middle-class respectability:

They didn't want me around anybody that, you know, rides a motorcycle, been in trouble with the law, blah blah blah. "Okay, fine," I said. "I accept that but who do I hang with?" "You people don't want me here alone. Maybe that guy that's never, ever going [to be in conflict with the] law doesn't want me in his home." I said, "That kind of leaves me isolated, doesn't it?" (Doc)

Their social isolation is exacerbated by institutional definitions of acceptable and appropriate support persons.[2] The state prohibition on having contact with their co-accused or others with criminal records leave some of the men to struggle with the after-effects of incarceration without support:

> I've got a lot of emotional scars and I've seen a lot of things and I've got nobody to talk to. Why can't I talk to someone who has similar experiences? Why can't I have a couple of people like that to talk to because that will help me work through it. (Mr. Flowers)

Self-regulation and state-regulation sometimes collide. Surprisingly (or perhaps not), it is those individuals who have been incarcerated who are attuned to the hidden risks precisely because they are sophisticated observers who 'see through' the performance of some social actors and recognize the inauthenticity of the roles assumed:

> I didn't want to go anywhere or do anything because of the fact that I'm on parole. I was asked to go to N.A. out here. I went to N.A. – two meetings – and I came back and told my P.O., I says, "I don't want to be there. Those are all the drug dealers in this city that I don't even know, but now I do. So by you guys asking me to go there I'm being introduced to drug dealers. I don't want to know who they are or where they live 'cause it makes it tempting." (Doc)

Professional Relationships

Perhaps the most significant and challenging professional relationship for the men to navigate is the one with their parole officer. In part, this difficulty is a result of the nebulous nature of the parole officer's role – the specific characteristics of which are far from being clear-cut. According to the Correctional Service of Canada (2007a), "the parole officer must be flexible, enforcing strict controls, in some cases, and acting as counsellors in others." In real terms, these standards mean that parole officers must foster a "professional relationship with each offender," ensure "that the offender follows his or her Correctional Plan," and "take disciplinary measures, which include sending the offender back to jail" (ibid.). Parole officers are also expected to "work together with many community agencies to help secure stable housing, employment, income and positive personal contacts" (ibid.).

Negotiating the complex supervised/supervisor relationship necessitates that both are sophisticated readers of social interactions who will respond appropriately to the actions of the other:

I made it very clear to her [parole officer] not to [call employers]. It's hard enough out here for me as it is, to get a job out here ... My argument is, well, you can't be going around and calling my employers saying, "Oh, this is so and so, and I'm calling to check on Fred just to make sure that everything's going good with him." And I said, "No, no. That doesn't happen." I said, "How am I supposed to have a normal life if you're going to be intruding in it?" ... She didn't really like it at first but I think she seen my point – after I talked [to] her a little more about it. (Fred)

Puzzle, who does not like ambiguity, finds that clearly articulated role parameters ease the strain inherent in the surveil/surveilled, helper/client relationship:

[My parole officer was] the first person I've ever, I've actually worked with. She said to me: "Don't ever give me any surprises and I won't give you any." And she's honoured that. That's the first person I've ever worked with in the system that actually kept their word.

As Puzzle's comment suggests, once both parties become accustomed to each other and are comfortable in their particular roles, tensions are eased considerably. This balance led some men to concede that their parole officers are not just doing their job but that they are doing their job well:

We were able to look at him [the parole officer] as a guest coming to our house to visit. And he quickly saw the accomplishments that were taking place and he recognized it. And he didn't treat me like a parolee. He really didn't. You know – it was, "You know what your conditions are. You know what you have to do and don't allow me to interfere with moving forward." (Rick)

Rick appreciates his parole officer and is able to look at him as a guest while still recognizing the regulatory script that conditions their relationship. Other men lose sight of the compulsory nature of the interactions:

I had a good parole officer in Toronto. And I had good parole officers here, very good ones. You know, like Mr. Jacobs – there's an exceptionally good one. And he went out to Sudbury. We kept in communication. And one time, me and Gertrude went out there to drop off my sister ... and I called him up. "You want to go for a coffee?" "Sure." And it was like two brothers. (Dave)

While Dave conceives of this relationship as being kin-like, the parole officer may simply have been doing his job. Dave, who seeks a family to which he can belong, may fail to appreciate that the intimacy of the relationship was authentic at the same time as it was confined and defined by the roles of the participants and the context of the relationship.[3]

Care must be taken not to assume that commoditized intimacy is therefore, by definition, somehow not real. As Kim Price (2000, 177) points out, 'pure' relationships (that is, outside of the market) are based on the "rational utilitarian calculation of costs and benefits," and, thus, for the parole officer, like the bartender and the psychologist, the creation of trusting relationships is essential for success. Establishing this connection may necessitate a "cynical performance" in which parole officers "act in a certain way solely in order to give the kind of impression to others this is likely to evoke from them a specific response he is concerned to obtain" (Goffman 1959, 6). This instrumentality is not duplicitous but simply professional. However, the significance of these boundary-maintaining strategies are brought into sharp focus when those parameters are breached:

[My psychologist and I] met once a week initially, and then it was twice a week because she felt there was more of a need and she wanted to get me away from things. We'd go to her cottage [and] we'd sit down and she'd let me drink a beer or two even though I wasn't supposed to. She'd just take me away from things and we'd talk. "So, how was today?" We wouldn't talk in the professional sense that I'm the patient, she's the doctor because we became friends in the institution and we became better friends out here. (Marcus)

In short, the narratives of Rick and Dave speak to authentic human relationships and the importance of the discretionary use of authority. However, Marcus's story draws our attention to the potential for slippage. In a supplementary interview conducted with a criminal justice professional, she too identified role breaches as a problem among her colleagues:

> I mean, I had one co-worker who helped a guy buy a car. He thought it was a really good thing to do but the problem was, the guy wasn't financially stable enough to buy a car. He didn't have his licence yet so he couldn't store the car anywhere. It was a bad decision. He did it because he thought, "Well, this guy should have a car." But I mean, there's this big picture so I tend to look at the big picture and see everybody's involvement and that all has to be part of the reintegration. Not just what the guy wants. (Madison)

Reflection

After prison the men must learn to navigate social relations in the community. Hindered by their lost time and the (dys)functional skills they acquired in prison, the men often struggle. Post-carceral interactions are both unique and mundane. Some aspects of their relationships are profoundly influenced by their previous incarceration, while others reflect the same difficulties encountered by the majority of the population. This realization demonstrates that the formerly incarcerated man is first and foremost a social actor who, like all other social actors, struggles to get by.

Final Thoughts: Understanding Life outside "the Rabbit Hole"

Life parole is life beset with perils, partly because things out here just simply would not stay the way they were. Obstinate time had done its worst and I stepped out on a January morning to a bending moving world where I had once only learned to walk upright. I felt so out of place. So visible, a kind of black-light beacon. And so wrong. So guilty. So unworthy ... Perpetually unsettled, as the shine wears thin from polishing my image for these fifteen years out on the street. I keep it up because I need that clarity when I venture near the edge ... I could go back. Oh, probably not for long. But whenever fear decides to rise up through the shape of accusations or small infractions, and mere behaviours could be used to land me back in jail, I know this horror, much worse than before. (Rives 2008, 2-3)

Throughout this book, we have highlighted the issues that arose in the lives of these former long-term prisoners. We have attempted to shed light on the complexity, commonality, and uniqueness of release, re-entry, and resettlement. We have spoken of their struggles with essentializations and with their conflicted senses of self; difficulties negotiating 'freedom'; and the challenge of finding a place in society. We have seen that resettlement was more arduous for some who were, for example, dealing with mental health issues, who had less cultural capital, or who found it difficult to navigate the ever-changing penal and social terrain. Beyond simply recounting their stories, we have tried to understand them within a socio-economic-political context. In this concluding chapter, we endeavour to weave together some of the recurring themes of the narratives – gender, class, and a sense of belonging – by thinking about them in relation to 'normalization' and governance.

Success and the Problem of 'Normal'

The men in this book are classified as being successful according to the criteria of the Correctional Service of Canada (1998). They themselves, however, resist this ascription. While pleased with the implicit recognition, many were nonetheless critical and questioned, refuted, or, at a minimum, nuanced this definition of success: "I question what a success is. I believe that I'm termed a success because I haven't been revoked or re-offended. Other than that, I'm not sure how I could be referred to as a success. I'm not back in jail, so I'm a success story. It's a bit of either/or and a little simplistic" (Bob). Puzzle also challenged the limits of defining success as the absence of new charges for five years or more and indicated that the parameters should be more encompassing: "That's what the system will teach – in order to succeed, you must be this. And their only success is recidivism. It's not when you get out how you'll be as a parent, how you'll be as a neighbour, how you'll be as a co-worker."

We see that, as is the case with freedom, the men impose their own definitions and ultimately want others, including the state, to do likewise. In short, they want (primarily) to be judged in a more normative way that decentres their 'otherness.' Indeed, the pursuit of 'normalcy' emerged in the men's aspirations for a 'normal life,' which are characterized by the accumulation of 'assets' (a house, a job, a wife) and by the management of their public and private identities (through their attire, language, presentation-of-self, labour force participation, and so on). Their narratives were peppered with phrases such as "a regular member of society," "an average Joe," and "a normal guy my age." Evidently, they are operating in relation to a normative measuring rod that they consider both significant and so self-evident that it does not require explanation. As Mary Louise Adams (2003, 95-96) points out,

> normalization draws our attention to discourses and practices that produce subjects who are "normal" who live "normality," and, most importantly, who find it difficult to imagine anything different. These discourses and practices work to delineate possible forms of expression, sexual or otherwise, as legitimate, while others are left to exist beyond the limits of acceptability ... normal is the point from which we deviate, for better or worse.

The norm, which is so embedded with social meaning, is of course, at its root, a statistical artifact – the middle range that emerges when a population is plotted on a graph. When people assess themselves and organize their behaviour in relation to a statistical average, they self-regulate. As Michel Foucault's (1977) work has shown, surveillance and 'normalizing' judgment are disciplinary tactics that operate both on and through individuals. However, their engagement with technologies-of-the-self notwithstanding, these men are, statistically speaking, not normal with respect to some variables. Despite mass incarceration in Canada, they are outliers on the edges of the bell curve – they have survived extensive time in prison and some will always be under the control of the penal justice apparatus. They are left with a profound sense of being abnormal, of being outside, of not belonging, despite their efforts to manage identity and accumulate assets. In their 'obsession' with the norm, we see the men's desire to be part of the social fabric, which is perhaps most evident in relation to class and gender.

In principle, because most of the men share a (working)-class location, one might assume that they would have found a sense of belonging through class solidarity based on similar relationships to the means of production. There was, however, little evidence of this commonality. Indeed, the men, like most Canadians, 'buy into' the dominant ideology and the myth of meritocracy that contends that a middle-class lifestyle and affluence is achievable if one works hard enough. While socio-economic stratifications are becoming increasingly entrenched in our neo-liberal world, class and the reality of oppression are obscured by a discourse of choice. As such, based on the illusion of a middle-class norm, being working class is not to be celebrated. Indeed, class stigma continues to operate as another "hidden injury of class" (Sennet and Cobb 1972, 119).

Despite the men's aspirations and attempts to 'pass' by emulating the normative middle class, their discreditable status as members of the working class manifest in their lack of access to fiscal and (middle-class) cultural capital. Their facade slips as they recount stories in which they relied on classed cultural expressions (for example, language, demeanour, values) to communicate the essence of their experience. That said, these cultural manifestations of class location are complicated by their range of inter-class differences. As is always the case, class does not function in isolation but, rather, in relation to, and combined with, other socio-economic, political, cultural, and personal dynamics, including gender and, more to the point here, normative masculinities. Judith Butler (1999, vi) argues that

> a *normative* account seeks to answer the question of which expressions of gender are acceptable, and which are not, supplying persuasive reasons to distinguish between such expressions in this way. The question, however, of what qualifies as "gender" is itself already a question that attests to a pervasively normative operation of power.

Given this insight, it is not surprising that the men's enactment of gender is, at its core, inextricably linked to their desire for 'normalcy.' They strive for a body that conforms to the locales and locations in which they operate; they seek out labour that corresponds to gender roles and, when they can not attain it, they have to confront their own understandings of what is acceptable and what is not; and they cling to a hetero-normative standard of couplehood and often reproduce and reify a somewhat dated archetype of the patriarch. They are destabilized when confronted with revised gender scripts that require them to give up some of their taken-for-granted masculine privilege. Not surprisingly, they find it difficult to reconceive of themselves in a positive way without relying on über-conformity to the masculinized roles used to survive lengthy incarceration.

Ultimately, outside the prison walls, their ability to see themselves as successful when they feel they have not achieved the classed and gendered average is difficult. This conundrum between feeling (marginally) successful and feeling they should accomplish and acquire more is a struggle. In these last pages, we want to reflect on how governance conditions the struggles that permeate their narratives.

Navigating Governance

In the poem that opened this chapter, John Rives (2008), a man currently on parole and serving a life sentence, demands that we attend to his perpetual dis-ease, his guilt, his worry – his struggles after prison. This poem reminds us "that striving and struggle precede success, even in the dictionary" (Ban Breathnach, n.d.) and, like all of us, the men's accomplishments must be evaluated in relation to the significant challenges and obstacles they have overcome. The *Oxford English Dictionary* (2008) defines struggle as making "great efforts in spite of difficulties; to contend resolutely with (a task, burden); to strive to do something difficult." This definition aptly captures the essence of the men's preparation for exiting the prison and their post-carceral experiences. The men navigated multiple obstacles in preparing to fall "out of the rabbit hole" (Rives 2008, 1). While some obstacles were self-inflicted, many others were structurally conditioned or state imposed.

Particularly evident in the experiences of these men is the unpredictability of their release, re-entry, and resettlement process, which often leaves them frustrated that things are not as straightforward as the policy and legislation suggest. They are willing to 'play the game,' but they have discovered that the rules are not always known, that they are open to multiple interpretations, and that they change frequently. From the outside and with the advantage of hindsight, this malleability in a seemingly stable process is not surprising. During the men's tenure as prisoners and parolees, they were witness to the "uneven progress" from inclusivity to exclusion, from "good intentions" to "discipline and mystification" (Cohen 1985, 15) and to risk and responsibilization. The men were (and are) caught by the overlapping interventions that emerged under the rhetoric of each approach.

The shifting ideological landscape obliges the men to employ a plethora of strategies to meet the challenges of release, re-entry, and resettlement. Variation in approaches also occur because they have differing degrees of social, educational, and financial capital on which they can rely. This fact reaffirms the idea that access to justice is not evenly distributed and that some individuals are positioned advantageously relative to others. Despite the evidence of unbalanced access to the conditional release process, individuals within these structures (both workers and the convicted) are able to exert considerable agency to sway the official mechanisms.[1] The ability to adapt to the perpetually changing social landscape and regulatory framework is a key variable in these men's ability to endure the prison experience and to survive, and sometimes thrive, in the outside community.

In addition to operating in different ideological eras, the men provided stories through which we could see that their struggles are mediated by the overlapping rationalities of governance that Foucault (1980a [1991]) refers to as governmentality. In the force exercised over the men during incarceration and in the restrictions imposed on their mobility once they are in the community, sovereign governance is evident. Disciplinary regimes, which focus on efficient management and transformation/ improvement of individuals so as to render them productive, is apparent in the programming in which the men, often begrudgingly, participate. Finally, the contemporary reliance on actuarial risk management speaks to the logic of population. This rationality of government plays out when risk assessment tools trump the actions of the individual. In short, the men's experience of release, reintegration, and resettlement provides a clear example of Foucault's assertion that "we need to see things not in terms of the replacement of a society of sovereignty by a disciplinary society and the subsequent replacement of a disciplinary society by a society of government; in reality one has a triangle, sovereignty-discipline-government" (102). It can be concluded that self-governing practices intersect with control over the individual to shape and mediate their experience. While the contemporary rhetoric speaks of inclusion and integration, the associated practices become those of compliance and self-regulation. Those who succeed are able to navigate the inter-sections in technologies-of-governance.

At the conclusion of this research, we realized that the absence of the stories of success that bothered us over twenty years ago actually spoke to something much more profound. We started out by wanting to challenge the dominant discourse of failure or the more behaviouristic ones of rehabilitation and redemption, but we found ourselves meticulously documenting challenges and struggles. At times, it was difficult to maintain the optimistic lens with which we began. Hope was incredibly elusive but increasingly important. Ultimately, we came to appreciate that if the men did not dwell on their struggles, nor could we. They were after all participating in this research to give hope. In the end, the men's stories helped us to see brightness beyond the grey of prison: "I had no hope ... There was no literature out or anything like that. There was no successful guy that you could read about. You heard about the odd guy ... but it would be nice if a guy could say ... 'There's not just one guy out here – there's tons of us'" (Tom).

Epilogue

More than twenty years after we were young undergraduate students sitting around Melissa's table wondering where the men we knew were in the discourse that focused so resolutely on failure and danger, we found ourselves puzzled by a different question all together. By now, our curiosity had been satisfied – we had collected the men's stories, pored over them endlessly, coded and recoded meticulously, and argued regularly about the 'best' conceptual framework to make sense of this or that narrative. We had also started to put these stories of success 'on the record' – we had given presentations at conferences, written chapters, and submitted a number of articles. Considerably older and greyer, we now once again sat at the dining room table snacking and drinking tea, trying to figure out how to make this research relevant for 'the guys.' It was not that we, two firmly university-embedded professors, did not value the academic process and production, but it was simply that we knew committed scholarship necessitated more than publishing peer-reviewed articles and writing a book. We needed to find a way to make the information resonate with current and former long-term prisoners. We hoped that we might emulate three of our role models, Liz Elliott, Ruth Morris, and Clare Culhane, by contributing in some small way to a broader process of penal transformation.

The first thing we had to do was share our preliminary analysis with the real experts. With knees knocking and carefully crafted PowerPoint slides in hand, we presented our findings to a group of Life Line in-reach workers from across Canada. We talked to them about the challenges 'our' men faced, the obstacles they surmounted, and the triumphs they enjoyed. For most of this presentation, these former long-term prisoners sat expressionless and silent, their arms firmly crossed over their chests – never a good sign, we thought. Occasionally, we would see them nod and look at each other – a better sign, we hoped. At the end, one of the men who had not known about the research told us: "You got it perfect." Despite our best intentions, we know that we could not possibly have gotten it 'perfectly,' but his words, and those of the others who spoke, gave us confidence that we had indeed heard the men's stories. The experience also reminded us of the importance of gender. We had read our audience through a profoundly gendered lens and were destabilized when we did not see the nods and smiles we had anticipated. That, along with the comments of the other Life Line men and the sole woman at the meeting, reminded us that, while our findings had linguistic and geographic resonance across Canada, much of what we had to say did not apply to formerly incarcerated women or, at any rate, did not correspond neatly.

This limitation notwithstanding, on the basis of the 'endorsement' from the Life Line workers, we decided to write a short, accessible booklet (*Getting Out. Staying Out: Words of Wisdom from Former Long-Term Prisoners*) for long-term prisoners and those starting their journey into the community. The objective was to provide information, hope, and perhaps even direction to this group and, more importantly, to affirm that there is life after prison. After writing the booklet and convincing our friend Gayle Short to donate her skills as a graphic artist, we had a text waiting to go into production. On hearing of our project, St. Leonard's Society of Windsor generously, and without prompting from us, covered the cost of the first printing. The booklet was distributed (at no cost) to the incarcerated and the freed, and we were giddy when the requests came pouring in – from parole officers, institutions, and individual men and women. Our initial thousand-copy print run was gone in no time, and St. Leonard's Society of Canada picked up the tab for the next thousand. Option Vie delighted us by having the booklet translated and published in French. Given our critical stance, we were pleasantly surprised when the booklet was adopted as an official part of the Lifers Resource Strategy by the Correctional Service of Canada in 2011.

We also believe that academics have an obligation to leave, at least periodically, their 'hallowed halls' and 'walk the walk.' While Chris is busy mobilizing for sex worker rights,[1] Melissa has continued to try to 'make a difference' with those currently or formerly incarcerated. To this end, in addition to providing one-on-one support, she has been meeting with prisoners and those on parole in cities across Canada to discuss strategies for getting out, starting out, and staying out. Melissa has also been conducting workshops for front-line halfway house workers to strategize on how they can better support men who have served extremely long prison sentences. The positive response she gets in these sessions is affirming, as are the queries she receives from past participants who are currently working with this population and want to 'do right' by their clients.

In the process, we have learned a great deal, and our understanding of the implication of geography on resettlement has become more nuanced. We have come to appreciate that while different locations have unique challenges, they simultaneously afford unique opportunities. For example, while individuals released to Calgary may benefit from an economic boom that has increased job prospects, they also face higher costs of living and a more overtly conservative social climate. Those released into the Maritime region may have difficulty accessing social services (mental health, choice in halfway houses, and so on), but they benefit from a slower pace of life and more affordable accommodation. In the end, regardless of province or territory of release, it seems that the individual's ability to maintain hope and forge social connections trumps these other factors.

In some ways, over these years we have felt a little like Alice in Wonderland ourselves. We had not fallen down the rabbit hole, but we have been at times bewildered. We have seen the men emerge – the same and changed, confused and certain, sad and elated. Over the course of the project, Bobby, Gerry, and Tom died and Doc became gravely ill. Each time we heard about their health struggles, we became recommitted to representing their narratives to the best of our ability and telling the 'story that is not told.' It is the least we can do – after all it was Tom, Gerry, Bobby, and Doc along with Joel, Rick, F.G., Bob, Fred, Gowan, Dave, Ziggy, Barry, Ernest, Mr. Flowers, Gord, Jean, Luc, Marcus, and Puzzle who were our tour guides, who helped us draw the picture, and who allowed us 'in' so we could find our way to an understanding. They, in turn, left us to show others; we are still working on that.

Appendix:
Methodological Considerations

The research that informed this book is part of a project funded by the Social Sciences and Humanities Research Council and entitled Release and Reintegration after Prison: Negotiating Gender, Culture and identity.[1] For this brief review of the methodology, we have organized the process into four stages: planning, sampling, interviewing, and coding/analysis. We conclude with some reflections on research ethics.

Planning

This research had two primary goals: to privilege and acknowledge the expertise of those who have lived resettlement by centring their perspectives and to contribute to the transformation of a flawed correctional system. In order to do so, we employed a "committed scholarship" approach, which involved the adoption of qualitative methods, a critical perspective, and attention to praxis (Kobayashi 2001, 58). Audrey Kobayashi (2001, 58) argues that it is morally imperative that a qualitative approach be used in order "to recognize that subjects' lives are multifaceted, interconnected, contextually situated, and deeply meaningful, in ways that cannot be conveyed easily by simple descriptions such as those achieved quantitatively." We agree with this statement and employed it as our litmus test in the consideration of various qualitative approaches.

To some extent, our decision to collect the data by conducting in-depth, semi-structured interviews emerged from a process of elimination. Ethnographic methods were not an option. Even though we had a history of walking alongside ex-prisoners, we had not done so as a technique of data collection and so had not been participant-observers *in situ*. We also ruled out the focus group approach. Not only would this strategy have been inconvenient for the men who were in different geographic areas, but we also wanted each man to have individual attention and not be subject to cohort pressures. Moreover, in-depth interviews allowed the narratives to emerge by affording time and space for reflection.

Recruiting

There were two criteria employed to determine whether an individual was eligible to participate in this research: length of prison sentence and time since release. The time frames adopted for this project were the same as those that are employed by the state to define long-term incarceration and successful reintegration (Perron 1991). Ten years is also a temporal distinction used by incarcerated persons. For example, in many penitentiaries in Canada, prisoners have established 10+ groups to support the men and women who receive these long sentences. By adopting the ten-year standard, this research focused exclusively on those individuals whose lives would be majorly disrupted by imprisonment. Other individuals could be charged, convicted, and imprisoned for a shorter period of time without significant impact on their day-to-day lives. Not only would they not be handicapped by such a long period of disengagement, but there would be less chance of others knowing about their criminalization (making it considerably easier to manage stigma and 'pick up the pieces').

We elected not to access our sample through referrals from state departments or employees. While requests that emanated from employees or representatives of the correctional apparatuses would not necessarily be perceived to be obligatory, we were nonetheless concerned that participants would take part in order to protect themselves from potentially negative consequences – the very opposite of free and informed consent. Moreover, we wanted the men to feel that they could criticize or praise the criminal justice system without thoughts of retribution or reward. Accordingly, we elected to access participants through other means.

We began by contacting our networks, which included a couple of men who we already knew fit the criteria. They, in turn, referred us to other men who were eligible – a method known as snowball sampling. Referrals were also received through prisoner advocates who passed our information on to men they knew. Life Line, a prison in-reach program staffed primarily by individuals who are serving life sentences, also provided referrals. This connection to Life Line had the unintended consequence of helping to establish legitimacy with the men to whom they referred us and created what Richard Tewksbury and Patricia Gagne (1996) call a knowledgeable insider working with a knowledgeable outsider. However, we were cognizant of a potential problem – that the men would see this research as part of Life Line. Accordingly, in order to ensure free and informed consent and to distinguish our research from Life Line, it was made clear to the participants, during the initial phone calls to set up the meeting and during the reading of the consent form, that Life Line was not officially associated with this project. We emphasized that the Life Line service and its employees would not have access to the data, nor would they know who had been interviewed.

Evidently, this method of sample generation had internal diversity limitations. Few individuals who had completely isolated themselves from their prison friends or the official post-prison supports were included in our sample. Also, by chance rather than by design, none of the men in this study was labelled as dangerous offenders or sex offenders and not being 'marked' in this way may have mitigated their experiences. It is possible that since snowball sampling was used, the men who were the first contacts referred us to others with whom they had served time. Since sex offenders were usually separated from the general prison population, these men would have had limited contact with this population. Given that the effect of these individuals' absence on the data is unknown and unpredictable, it would require unsupported assumptions and presumptions to hypothesize further. That said, the homogeneity of the sample does improve internal validity and may be why, as we will discuss later, data saturation was achieved earlier than originally anticipated.

Interviewing

Once each of the men agreed to participate, a mutually agreed on time and location was selected for their interview. Following some pre-talk, the men were given a copy of the consent form, it was read aloud, and any questions they had about the project and the way the interview data would be used were answered. Permission was granted by all of the men to tape-record their interviews, some of which exceeded three hours.

While every research method has its limitations, we chose to conduct interviews that would give the men an opportunity to speak of their experience. We understood that this structure imposed an unnatural formality and focused the discussion. The time-bounded interview format also limited the "intrinsic qualities" or depth of each interview by constraining the period allowed for reflection, re-evaluation, and reformulation of thoughts (Pires 1997, 172). We recognized that research participants were cognizant that they were part of a study, and this awareness may have mediated their responses. Martin Hammersley and Paul Atkinson (1983, 112) have addressed this issue:

> The problem of reactivity is merely one aspect of a more general phenomenon that cannot be eradicated: the effects of audience, and indeed the context generally, on what people say and do. All accounts must be interpreted in terms of the context in which they were produced.

To counter some of these limits, we designed an interview guide that gave us the freedom to ask about specific areas while providing space for the men to explore those facets of the experience that they prioritized. We used a semi-directive approach that contained "pre-structured partial probes concerning specific topics or issues" (Pires 2005, 34). Given the committed scholarship frame that we had adopted, we felt that we were "active participants" (Devault 1990, 100) in the process and so did not want to simply nod as they told their stories – this seemed all together too cold and clinical. We believed the men would be more comfortable if they were given some rope to grab onto throughout the process, especially for those who were timid and less verbose. As a result, we employed a retrospective/reformulation approach to the interviews whereby we started sections with general invitations to speak on a particular topic and then followed with specific probes designed to aid the individual in reflecting more deeply on their experiences (Pires 2005). One of the concerns of this technique is that themes are imposed rather than being allowed to emerge organically. However, it was clear from the transcripts that, where a topic did not resonate, the men were comfortable refuting the idea even when we probed further.

Though pleased that participants were comfortable challenging the embedded assumptions in our carefully constructed guide (culled from the literature, theory, and, inevitably, ourselves), it also led to frustration on the part of both interviewer and interviewee. This was most evident in relation to our many probes about the impact of gender and race. For example, towards the end of Joel's interview, he stated: "Well, you were pulling specifically at some of these ... gender and race issue ... This is Canada, we're pretty much the same." Over and over again, the men denied the relevance of certain factors. Later, we would find ourselves disappointed at the lack of depth in their contemplation, dutifully coding their non-responses. While these comments (and non-comments) were in themselves revealing, it sometimes made for thin analysis on these topics.

A copy of their anonymized transcript was made available to the participants in order to afford them the opportunity to remove any names, places, people, or stories that they felt might be identifying and/or that they did not wish to be part of the analysis. Seven of the men did take the time to review (and, in a few cases, offer minor corrections), but none made substantive deletions, nor did anyone request a follow-up interview despite its being offered.

Coding and Analysis

Before they could be coded, the interviews first had to be transformed from verbal speech into a textual product through transcription. During transcription, all pauses, hesitations, and "uhms" were included because these can represent "not-quite-articulated experience, where standard vocabulary is inadequate and where a respondent tries to speak from experience and finds language wanting" (Devault 1990, 103). These hesitations were part of the original transcripts, but they have been largely removed from the excerpts used in this book. While these "para-linguistic elements" (Gray 2003, 151) were important in 'hearing' the voice in the whole interview, they hampered the reading of the respondent's words once they had been cut from the interview and pasted into the text. Tangentially, juxtaposing the men's on-demand responses against our own carefully constructed and edited words seemed unfair (Bruckert 2000). That said, in some excerpts, their hesitations were critical in conveying the meaning, and, in those instances, they remain in the text.

A first level reading of each transcript was conducted to get a sense of the story the individual was telling (Hoggart, Lees, and Davies 2002). Focusing on the narrative allowed us to get a big picture of how the individual recounted his history and made sense of his experiences (Chase 1995). This approach, in turn, helped to sort out any incongruities and contradictions that emerged when the interviews were coded line by line. Following this process, a specific coding of each line of text was conducted, with codes being "interpretive tags to text (or other material) based on categories or themes that are relevant to the research" (Cope 2003, 445). Stephen LeCompte and Margaret Schensul (1999, 68) refer to this basic level of abstraction as coding "items," which are "discrete and concrete units of analysis or things." Using N-Vivo software, each interview was marked for both "*in vivo* codes" (terms used by informants) and "constructed codes" (more abstract and imposed by the researcher) (Jackson 2001, 202). These two types of codes were important since the men told their stories in ways that were not always how we, as researchers, would analyze them. For example, a man might describe his body during particular periods *(in vivo)*, and this description might be more abstractly understood in terms of geographic placement or identity (constructed).

When the coding process began, a few anticipated codes (< 10) were established, and additions to the code book were made as items and patterns emerged. Each additional code necessitated careful consideration

Figure A.1   Excerpt from Coding Manual

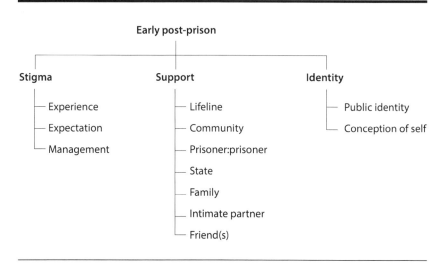

and operationalization (definition) to ensure coding consistency. Often a code would have a variety of sub-codes within it, and this system resulted in a total of 293 distinct codes being developed (Figure A.1 provides an illustration of how a very small portion of the coding manual looked). The amount of coding per interview varied dramatically as some men spoke at length and in great depth about their experiences, while others were more succinct. In addition, in some cases, a paragraph could be placed into multiple codes as the speaker addressed several themes concurrently (Figure A.2 provides an example of this overlap in coding from Ziggy's transcript).

The following statistics are provided to give a sense of the extensive coding done during this project. The least coded transcript had 121 items marked, while the most coded had 301. The mean number of passages coded per transcript was 168. Further, each transcript spoke to a multiplicity of themes, with the least variety occurring in one in which there were fifty-three different codes addressed and the greatest variety occurring in one where ninety-five different codes were marked. The mean number of codes per transcript was seventy-three.

Figure A.2   Excerpt from Ziggy's interview

Early post-prison

Cause I was at a halfway house, they had a right to tell me where to go. And they said well you forced our hands, we'll force your hands. You will go to Newmarket. I said 'I don't have a job there or anything.' Well, 'we'll get you work.' Which they didn't. I got myself work, right. I said well what if I just stay here and continue 'cause I was making money hands and fists. I had community support. They said no. If you refuse this, we will send you back to a medium because you are refusing a program. So that's how I ended up back in Newmarket. Which is good cause I met my wife and a lot of good people.

Excerpt coded as following nodes:
- Vulnerability to the state
- Geography
- Resistance
- Financial challenge
- Support

In the process of doing this line-by-line coding, conflicting sentiments emerged in the participants' interviews. For example, when directly asked whether they had ever been stigmatized, many of the men said they had not but then went on to give a number of examples of discrimination. This contradiction may speak to miscommunication (the men not understanding the words employed) or, alternately, it may be congruent with Sandra Harding's (1987) assertion that since an individual's experiences often exist in tension, the recounting can be disjointed. It is up to the researchers to make sense of the full story. Of course, such incongruence is to be expected in a time-limited, semi-structured interview setting since individuals are being asked to instantly recall and relate specific experiences based on the language used by the interviewer. Any one of these factors could have dramatically influenced the content of the interview.

Since the coding was conducted on the extant transcripts as they were available, we felt that data saturation had been reached after the seventeenth interview. However, three additional interviews were conducted to ensure that "a representative sampling of data reflecting the major sociological and/or psychological structures and processes inherent in a given phenomenon" had been attained (Maruna 1997, 70). We were surprised to have achieved data saturation at this point, but when we turned to the literature we found that our experience was not unique and that others had struggled with the imposition of numeric quotas as well (Mason 2010). As Judith Green and Nicki Thorogood (2009, 120) note, "the experience of most qualitative researchers is that in interview studies little that is 'new' comes out of transcripts after you have interviewed 20 or so people."

Once the coding of each interview was completed, a horizontal trans-interview analysis was conducted to examine points of convergence and disjuncture (Pires 1997). Peter Jackson (2001, 207) refers to this process as rendering themes into "discursive repertoires" that highlight commonalities within the group. From this horizontal read, an analytic framework emerged based on the identified phenomenon of significance (Entrikin 1991). At this point, it was necessary to move to a higher level of abstraction and attend to broader cultural phenomena. The challenge in conducting this constituent level analysis was to find a theoretical framework that made sense of all of the men's experiences. This process involved taking all of the coded items from each thematic grouping and organizing, reorganizing, conceptualizing, and reconceptualizing them until each was accounted for in the analysis. Once we arrived at this understanding of the experience, we then reviewed past and current government policy and regulation (such as the *Commissioner's Directive* (Canada 2010b) and the *Corrections and Conditional Release Act*) to inform our analysis.[2]

Reflections on Ethics

Throughout the research process, various ethical issues demanded our attention, and we will conclude by reflecting on a few of these here. First, we had a history of activism, and this background granted us some insiderness. We could therefore never know whether we received information because of our privileged position as known commodities or, conversely, whether information was withheld so that these men could maintain a particular presentation-of-self. Moreover, while an unknown researcher may not have had access to some of the men interviewed, those who participated may have disclosed different information to a previously unknown person, creating "different phenomenological realities" (Tewksbury and Gagne 1996, 80). This fractionality of knowledge and reactivity are important to acknowledge, but they do not nullify the findings. On the contrary, throughout the process of analysis, we recognized that we were getting distinct information in a specific interview setting and attributed value to this privilege.

In keeping with the committed scholarship frame, we decided to use our place of privilege to help emancipate these often-neglected voices. However, we wanted to make sure that we were not simply taking their voices and committing "epistemological violence" by coding, decoding, structuring, and theorizing them to our own ends (Raju 2002, 174). We were keenly aware that criminalized individuals are rarely given a venue in which to have their stories heard and, even more rarely, published, but we still questioned whether we should be presenting their stories. Ultimately, we agreed with Aihwa Ong (1995, 354) who states:

> Given our [researchers'] privileges, there is greater betrayal in allowing our personal doubts to stand in the way of representing their claims, interests and perspectives. The greater betrayal lies in refusing to recognize informants as active cultural producers in their own right, whose voices insist upon being heard and can make a difference in the way we think about their lives.

Notes

Chapter 1: Telling Tales

1 The discourse is predominantly about men, with the exception of some high-profile women such as Karla Homolka. While men comprise 95 percent of federally sentenced individuals, this gendering renders criminalized women invisible (Mahony 2011).

2 Cohen and Taylor (1972) and Johnson and Toch (1982) have established that incarceration is a psychologically scarring process, but they did not examine the effects of this trauma after prison.

3 This book is about male ex-prisoners. For research on women's release and reintegration in Canada, see the work of Schantz and Frigon (2009, 2010), Schantz, Kilty, and Frigon (2009), and Maidment (2006). See also Eaton's (1993) excellent book on women's experience of prison and release in the United Kingdom.

4 *Safe Streets and Communities Act*, which can be found online at http://www.csc-scc. gc.ca/text/pblct/lt/06-eng.shtml

5 *Criminal Code of Canada*, which can be found online at http://laws-lois.justice. gc.ca/eng/acts/C-46/.

6 According to Statistics Canada (2011), there were 26,641,500 adults over the age of nineteen residing in Canada in 2011. The one-in-seven figure is likely an underestimation since there is a two-year gap in the numbers.

7 The *Safer Streets and Communities Act, supra* note 4, which introduces mandatory minimum sentences for a range of offences, mandates harsher sentences for young offenders and restricts the use of "house arrest" (conditional sentences). It will certainly increase prison populations at the same time as prisons are being closed.

8   Neo-liberalism is a reconfiguration of liberalism, an economic model that shifts control from the public to the private sphere.

9   In 2009-10, 86.7 percent of day paroles were successfully completed (Public Safety Canada 2011).

10   These forms of conditional release will be defined and discussed in Chapter 4.

11   *United Nations Standard Minimum Rules for the Treatment of Prisoners*, 1975, online: http://www.csc-scc.gc.ca/text/pblct/rht-drt/07-eng.shtml.

12   A special thanks to one of the peer reviewers who flagged this issue and forced us to confront our lexiconic discomfort.

13   For ease of reading and because males are the subjects, in this book we have chosen to use masculine pronouns exclusively.

14   The concept of 'normal' is, as we note throughout this text, bound up with notions of what should and should not be. What is defined as normal and by extension, abnormal, speaks to relations of power – ascribing some things, people and actions with value while simultaneously framing that which falls outside of this definition as dismissable. As such, in this text we use single quotation marks to flag the problematic nature of this term.

Chapter 2: Introducing the Men

1   A bad beef would be a charge such as sexual assault or a crime against a child.

2   In fact, many men speak of "playing the game" (see Chapter 4).

Chapter 3: Being In

1   This number of federally sentenced people includes 4,774 life-sentenced individuals who will serve a minimum of ten years in prison.

2   When the men in this research started their prison sentences, there was not a designated reception unit and their assessment may have been done at the local jail prior to their entry into the federal penitentiary system. The level of detail and formality of their assessment varied considerably but does not approach the consistency or rigour currently employed.

3   *Corrections and Conditional Release Act*, SC 1992, c. 20, s. 28 *[CCRA]*. Corrections and Conditional Release Regulations, Doc. SOR/92-620 (1992).

4   The Custody Rating Scale includes items such as the prisoner's age, substance use, history of escape, street stability, sentence severity, and prior parole.

5   To be placed in maximum security, an individual must score 134 or greater on the security risk dimension of the Custody Rating Scale. According to the *Commissioner's Directive*, the severity of the current offence would be designated as extreme (sixty-nine points), and sentence length would receive maximum value (sixty-five points) (Canada 2010b). Previously, "offence severity [was] weighted to prevent the initial placement of an offender serving a life sentence in minimum-security" (Luciani, Motiuk, and Nafekh 1996, n.p.). This approach has a residual aspect of the earlier periods in corrections wherein the criminal was equated with his

criminal act (Gosselin 1982). Current standard operating procedures require that the life-sentenced individual spend two years in maximum-security facilities regardless of his or her individual characteristics (Correctional Service of Canada 2003, 700-14). This policy, which was not in place at the time the men we spoke with entered prison, has been called "contrary to the law, unreasonable, and improperly discriminatory to specified offender groups" by the Correctional Investigator (Canada 2001, 36).

6 Baer (2005) provided an interesting account of how visual imprints are made in the carceral environment. In his study, youth prisoners in the United Kingdom used a variety of personal hygiene and air freshening products to decorate their cells and, in doing so, created identifiers that signalled them as clean, wealthy, or connected. These items would get 'passed down' when the prisoner left the prison.

7 *CCRA, supra* note 3, s. 100.

8 For more on this period, see the *Stories Told* section of the introduction to this book.

9 Cohen (1985, 49) argues that, despite the rhetoric, the system actually became more interventionist. He states that "the use of community alternatives actually causes an overall system extension, which might not otherwise have occurred."

10 For example, "the LSI-R [Level of Service Inventory (revised)] is a quantitative survey of offender attributes and their situations relevant to level of supervision and treatment decisions ... the LSI-R helps predict parole outcome, success in correctional halfway houses, institutional misconducts, and recidivism. The 54 items are based on legal requirements and include relevant factors needed for making decisions about risk and treatment ... The LSI-R can be used ... to assist in the allocation of resources, help make decisions about probation and placement, make appropriate security level classifications, and assess treatment progress" (Andrews and Bonta 1995, n.p.). Similarly, the Correction Service of Canada states that "Reintegration Potential Reassessment is based on the Statistical Information on Recidivism – Revised 1 (SIR-R1) scale, the level of intervention based on static factors, the level of intervention based on dynamic factors, the security reclassification scale outcome and the level of motivation" (Cormier 1997, n.p.).

11 Silverstein (2001) notes that family members are included in these non-state forms of governance.

12 Technologies-of-the-self refers to the ways individuals work on their identity, consciousness, and behaviour in order to transform themselves.

13 The Task Force on Reintegration of Offenders also problematized programming as being overly relied on and argued that "core programs" should not be seen as the only valid techniques for risk management (Correctional Service of Canada 1997).

Chapter 4: Getting Out

1 Of course, the exception to this rule are those individuals who are wrongfully convicted and then exonerated. These indivuduals, who, after years of appeals and professing their innocence, are suddenly released and their record expunged.

2   *Corrections and Conditional Release Act*, SC 1992, c. 20, s. 100 *[CCRA]*. The National Parole Board came into existence in 1959 to support and supervise parolees. The name was changed in 2011 to the Parole Board of Canada.

3   Recognizing this issue, the government has recently introduced an informational video *(Your Guide to Parole)* that is shown to prisoners during their orientation. A copy of this video and a full transcript can be accessed on the Correctional Service of Canada website at http://pbc-clcc.gc.ca/vids/htm/csc-parole-eng.shtml.

4   Of the five men who were married or had a common-law partner before they began their prison time, only one (Gowan) was able to maintain that relationship through-out his sentence. That said, while their pre-prison intimate relationships often did not withstand the incarceration, many of the men developed new relationships, and sometimes married, while in prison.

5   *CCRA, supra* note 2.

6   As per the *CCRA, supra* note 2, s. 17, "the institutional head may grant these passes when: ... an inmate will not, by reoffending, present an undue risk to society during an absence authorized under this section ... the inmate's behaviour while under sentence does not preclude authorizing the absence, and ... a structured plan for the absence has been prepared."

7   Under section 17.3 and 17.4 of the *CCRA, supra* note 2, "the institutional head may cancel a temporary absence either before or after its commencement ... [and] the institutional head shall give the inmate written reasons for the authorizing, refusal or cancellation of a temporary absence."

8   *CCRA, supra* note 2, s. 115.

9   *Ibid.*, s. 119, in some cases, the sentencing judge may stipulate that the individual not be allowed to apply for parole until one-half of his sentence has expired.

10 According to the *CCRA, ibid.*, s. 126.2, "if the Board is satisfied that there are no reason-able grounds to believe that the offender, if released, is likely to commit an offence involving violence before the expiration of the offender's sentence according to law, it shall direct that the offender be released on full parole." For more information on this policy, see the Parole Board of Canada's policy manual, http://www.npb-cnlc.gc.ca/infocntr/policym/PolicyManual_vol1no13.pdf. Generally, if an individual has not been granted a form of parole, those with a definite sentence will be released on statu-tory release after serving two-thirds of their sentence. This was the case with Marcus.

11 Of the two remaining men, one was granted immediate full parole and the other was incarcerated until his statutory release date.

12 The Level of Service Inventory (Revised) scale is a quantitative risk/need assessment survey developed to predict risk of recidivism.

13 For more on this technique of resistance, see Munn and Bruckert (2010).

Chapter 5: Starting Out

1   The men were in possession of a parole identification card but were often hesitant to use it because of fear of stigmatization.

2 Jackson and Stewart (2009, xviii) have noted that "the time in administrative segregation can extend to months, even years. It represents the most powerful form of carceral authority. Because the conditions of confinement are the closest thing to solitary confinement, it is also the most intensive form of imprisonment. Segregation is perhaps the best documented example in Canada of the abuse of correctional power."

3 Reinforcing this rhetoric, and not statistical facts, was the support of the Correctional Service of Canada Review Panel (2007b, 228) for municipally created "no-go zones," which apply to parole offices and community correctional facilities in order to "protect potential vulnerable communities or areas."

4 For more discussion of stigma, see Chapter 7.

5 For more discussion of this issue from a geographic perspective, see Chapter 9.

6 For more on techniques of prisoner resistance, see Munn and Bruckert (2010).

7 According to the Parole Board of Canada's (2008, s. 7.1-7.3) *Policy Manual*, "under no circumstances will the Board relieve an offender from compliance with any of the following conditions: obey the law and keep the peace; report to the parole supervisor as instructed by the parole supervisor; and immediately report to the parole supervisor any change in the address of residence." Of course, since individuals in Canada who receive life sentences remain under judicial control for their lifetime, the monitoring for these ex-prisoners expires on their death.

Chapter 6: Negotiating "Freedom"

1 This is consistent with the findings of Irwin and Owen (2005), Jameison and Grounds (2005), McEvoy, Shirlow, and McElrath (2004), and Richie (2001).

2 This may be linked to Jewkes's (2005) idea that prisoners live in a liminal state in which they are disengaged from both past and future roles as the normal rules and struggles do not exist. See also the work of Richards and Jones (2004), who speak of shifts in structures as a major challenge in dealing with the changes in routine.

Chapter 7: Identity

1 Some master statuses remain even after one no longer participates in the activity. For example, one remains an ex-professor or former sex worker but rarely is someone referred to as an ex-student.

2 Name withheld to protect anonymity.

3 See Chapter 4 for more on this issue.

4 See, for example, the work of Cameron (1997), who discusses the reclamation by feminists of terms generally used to denigrate women, or the work of Mairs (1992) on revaluing language used to describe individuals who are differently-abled.

5 A FingerPrint System Number is a number assigned to each fingerprinted person.

6 See, for example, Giordano, Cernkovich, and Rudolph 2002; Laub and Sampson 2001; LeBel et al. 2008).

Chapter 8: Stigma

1 The type of crime or victim can determine the degree of coverage the crime and trial receives. In his book, *Just Another Indian*, Goulding (2001) made a compelling argument that race is a factor in determining which acts and trials make it into the popular consciousness, thus impacting on the public and personal identity of the convicted person.

2 See, for example, Clear and Dammer 2000; Funk 2004; Harding 2003; Irwin 1970; Petersilia 2001; and Travis and Petersilia 2001.

3 In a morality script, "the self is perceived as criticized and the other as scornful with the individual either experiencing scorn or shaming" (Emde, Johnson, and Easterbrooks 1987, 262).

4 This branding has a historical precedent since, as Shoham and Rohav (1991) note, in many ancient religious stories, a mark was placed on an individual to shame them and warn others. Thus, we see there is an underlying sense that the tattooed person is risky or dangerous. Distinguishing the contemporary use of tattoos from their previous function is the fact that the marks were actively sought by the men.

5 Pseudonym withheld to protect identity.

6 Tertiary deviance is used "to refer to the deviant's confrontation, assessment, and rejection of the negative identity imbedded in secondary deviation, and the transformation of that identity into a positive and viable self-conception ... it is possible for the stigmatized, ridiculed and despised to confront their own complicity in the maintenance of their degraded status, to recover and accept the suppressed anger and rage as their own, to transform shame into guilt, guilt into moral indignation, and victim [we would add 'perpetrator'] into activist" (Kitsuse 1980, 9).

7 See, for example, Day and Schoenrade 1997; Dindia 1998; and Morris, Balsam, and Rothblum 2002.

Chapter 9: Home and Homelessness

1 Names withheld to protect anonymity.

2 Maslow's (1943) hierarchy of needs helps us to understand that the next level towards self-actualization is having a sense of belonging.

Chapter 10: Work and Finance

1 Name withheld to protect anonymity.

2 Name withheld to protect anonymity.

Chapter 11: Interactions

1 See Chapter 4 for more discussion of technologies-of-the-self.

2 See Chapter 6 for more on this topic.

3 It is authentic in that it is characterized by the emotional, spatial, psychological, and social closeness that are the marks of intimacy (Frank 1998).

Final Thoughts

1 For example, Aboriginal prisoners in Canada are more likely to be released on statutory release than on day or full parole (Correctional Investigator Canada 2010; Mann 2009)

Epilogue

1 Her work includes community-based research and conceptualizing (and contributing to) *The Toolkit: Ottawa Area Sex Workers Speak Out* (Purvis, Bruckert, and Chabot 2010), a resource for social service providers inspired by our booklet. This resource was undertaken in collaboration with POWER (Prostitutes of Ottawa-Gatineau Work, Educate and Resist).

Appendix

1 Approval for this research was received from the University of Ottawa Research Ethics Board. As part of the informed consent process, participants were advised aware that this data could be used for publications.
2 *Corrections and Conditional Release Act,* SC 1992, c. 20.

References

Adams, M.L. 2003. "The Trouble with Normal: Postwar Youth and the Making of Heterosexuality." In D. Brock, ed., *Making Normal: Social Regulation in Canada*, 90-103. Toronto: Nelson Thompson Learning.

Agnew, J. 1987. *Place and Politics: The Geographical Mediation of State and Society*. Boston, MA: Allen and Unwin.

Alderman, L. 2008. *In Sickness and in Wealth. Unnatural Causes: Is Inequality Making Us Sick?* San Francisco, CA: California Newsreel.

Andrews, D.A., and J. Bonta. 1995. *A Comprehensive Risk/Needs Assessment of Offender Treatment Planning and Placement*. Scarborough, ON: Pearson.

Baer, L.D. 2005. "Visual Imprints on the Prison Landscape: A Study on the Decorations in Prison Cells." *Tijdschrift voor Economische en Sociale Geografie* 96(2): 209-17.

Baker, M. 1997. *The Restructuring of the Canadian Welfare State: Ideology and Policy*. SPRC Discussion Paper no. 77, Social Policy Research Centre, online: http://nchsr.arts.unsw.edu.au/media/File/dp077.pdf.

Ban Breathnach, S. (n.d.). Thinkexist.com, online: http://thinkexist.com/quotation/.

Baumeister, R., E. Bratslavsky, C. Finkenauer, and K. Vohs. 2001. "Bad Is Stronger Than Good." *Review of General Psychology* 5(4): 323-70.

Beccaria, C. 1764; reprinted 1986. *On Crimes and Punishment*, translated by D. Young. Indianapolis, ID: Hackett Publishing.

Becker, H.S. 1963. *Outsiders: Studies in the Sociology of Deviance*. New York: Free Press.

Black, R. 2002. "Conceptions of 'Home' and the Political Geography of Refugee Repatriation: Between Assumption and Contested Reality in Bosnia-Herzegovina." *Applied Geography* 22(2): 123-38.

Bonilla-Silva, E. 2010. *Racism without Racists: Color-blind Racism and the Persistence of Racial Inequality in the United States*. New York: Rowman and Littlefield.

Bosworth, M. 1999. *Engendering Resistance: Agency and Power in Women's Prisons*. Brookfield, VT: Ashgate Publishing.

Bradley, H. 1996. *Fractured Identities: Changing Patterns of Inequality*. Malden, MA: Polity Press/Blackwell.

Brantingham, P.J., and P.L. Brantingham. 2000. "Police Use of Environmental Criminology in Strategic Crime Prevention." *Police Practice and Research* 1(2): 211-40.

Breese, J.R., K. Ra'el, and G.K. Grant. 2000. "No Place Like Home: A Qualitative Investigation of Social Support and Its Effects on Recidivism." *Sociological Practice* 2(1): 1-21.

Brown, J.D. 1991. "The Professional Ex-: An Alternative for Exiting the Deviant Career." *Sociological Quarterly* 32(2): 219-30.

Brown, M.P. 2000. *Closet Space: Geographies of Metaphor from the Body to the Globe*. New York: Routledge.

Bruckert, C. 2000. *Stigmatized Labour: An Ethnographic Study of Strip Clubs in the 1990s*. PhD diss., Carleton University [unpublished].

–. 2002. *Taking It Off, Putting It On: Women in the Strip Trade*. Toronto: Women's Press.

Butler, J. 1999. *Gender Trouble: Feminism and the Subversion of Identity*. New York: Routledge.

Callard, F.J. 1998. "The Body in Theory." *Environment and Planning D: Society and Space* 16: 387-400.

Cameron, D. 1997. "Performing Gender Identity: Young Men's Talk and the Construction of Heterosexual Masculinity." In S. Johnson and U.H. Meinhof, eds., *Language and Masculinity*, 47-64. New York: Blackwell Publishing.

Canada. 1983. *National Parole Board Report on the Conference on Discretion in the Correctional System*, online: https://www.ncjrs.gov/App/publications/Abstract.aspx?id=96231.

–. 1984. *Report of the Study Group on Murders and Assualts in the Ontario Region*. Ottawa, Canada: Correctional Service of Canada.

–. 1990. *Creating Choices: The Report of the Task Force on Federally Sentenced Women*. Ottawa, ON: Correctional Service of Canada.

–. 2001. *Annual Report of the Correctional Investigator*, 2000-01, 36-38, online: http://www.oci-bec.gc.ca/.

–. 2002a. *Report by the House of Commons Special Committee on the Non-Medical Use of Drugs*. Ottawa, ON: Minister of Supply and Services Canada.

–. 2002b. *Report of the Special Senate Committee on Illegal Drugs*. Ottawa, ON: Minister of Supply and Services Canada.

–. 2007. *From Confinement to Community: The National Parole Board and Aboriginal Offenders*. Parole Board of Canada, online: http://pbc-clcc.gc.ca/infocntr/bklt-eng.pdf.

–. 2010a. *The Changing Offender Profile*, Correctional Service Canada, online: http://www.csc-scc.gc.ca/.

–. 2010b. *Commissioner's Directive: Security Classification and Penitentiary Placement*, Correctional Service Canada, online: http://www.csc-scc.gc.ca/.

Capone, D.L., and W.W.J. Nichols. 1975. "Crime and Distance: An Analysis of Offender Behaviour in Space." *Association of American Geographers* 7: 45-49.

Carr, J. 1975. *Bad: The Autobiography of James Carr*. New York: Dell.

Carroll, L. 1865. *Alice's Adventures in Wonderland*. London: MacMillan.

Casey, E.S. 2001. *J.E. Malpas's Place and Experience: A Philosophical Topography*. Cambridge: Cambridge University Press.

Castel, R. 1995. "Les pièges de l'exclusion." *Lien Social et Politiques* 34: 13-21.

Chase, S.E. 1995. "Taking Narrative Seriously." In R. Josselson and A. Lieblich, eds., *Interpreting Experience: The Narrative Study of Lives, 3*. Thousand Oaks, CA: Sage Publications.

Christie, N. 2004. *Crime Control as Industry* (3rd edition). New York: Routledge.

Clark, W.A.V. 2003. *Immigrants and the American Dream: Remaking the Middle Class*. New York: Guilford Press.

Clear, T.R., and E. Cadora. 2001. "Risk and Correctional Practice." In K. Stenson and R.R. Sullivan, eds., *Crime, Risk and Justice: The Politics of Crime Control in Liberal Democracies*, 51-67. Portland, OR: Willan Publishing.

Clear, T.R., and H.R. Dammer. 2000. *The Offender in the Community*. Scarborough, ON: Thomson Learning.

Cohen, A. 1955. *Delinquent Boys: The Culture of the Gang*. New York: Free Press.

Cohen, S. 1985. *Visions of Social Control*. Malden, MA: Blackwell publishers.

Cohen, S., and L. Taylor. 1972. *Psychological Survival: The Experience of Long-Term Imprisonment* (2nd edition). London: Penguin Books.

Cohen, W.M., and D.A. Levinthal. 1990. "Absorptive Capacity: A New Perspective on Learning and Innovation." *Administrative Science Quarterly* 35(1): 128-52.

Collins, P. 1990. *Black Feminist: Knowledge, Consciousness and the Politics of Empowerment*. Boston: Unwin Hyman.

Comack, E. 2008. *Out There/ In Here: Masculinity, Violence and Prisoning*. Halifax, NS: Fernwood.

Connell, R. 2004. *Masculinities*. Berkeley, CA: University of California Press.

Cooley, C.H. 1902. *Human Nature and the Social Order*. New York: Scribner.

Cope, M. 2003. "Coding Transcripts and Diaries." In N.J. Clifford and G. Valentine, eds., *Key Methods in Geography*, 445-59. Thousand Oaks, CA: Sage Publications.

Cormier, R.B. 1997. "Yes SIR!: A Stable Risk Prediction Tool." *Forum* (Correctional Service of Canada) 9(1): 3-7.

Correctional Investigator Canada. 2010. *Annual Report of the Office of the Correctional Investigator, 2009-10*. Office of the Correctional Investigator, online: http://www.oci-bec.gc.ca/.

Correctional Service of Canada. 1997. *Final Report of the Task Force on Reintegration*. Ottawa, ON: Offender Reintegration Branch, Correctional Service of Canada.

–. 1998. *Implementing the Life Line Concept: Report of the Task Force on Long Term Offenders*. Ottawa, ON: Correctional Service of Canada, online: http://www.csc -scc.gc.ca/.

–. 2003. *Standard Operating Practices*. Ottawa, ON: Correction Service of Canada, online: http://www.csc-scc.gc.ca.proxy.bib.uottawa.ca/.

–. 2007a. *About Parole Officers*. Correctional Service of Canada, online: http://www. csc-scc.gc.ca/.

–. 2007b. *CORCAN Annual Report (2006-2007)*, Correctional Service of Canada, online: http://www.csc-scc.gc.ca/.

–. 2009a. *Long-Term Offenders: Who Are They and Where Are They?* Correctional Service of Canada, http://www.csc-scc.gc.ca/.

–. 2009b. *United Nations Standard Minimum Rules for the Treatment of Prisoners 1975*. Correctional Service of Canada, http://www.csc-scc.gc.ca/.

Correctional Service of Canada Review Panel. 2007. *A Roadmap to Public Safety*. Ottawa, ON: Supply and Services Canada.

Cosgrove, D. 2000. "Sense of Place." In R.J. Johnston, D. Gregory, G. Pratt, and M. Watts, eds., *The Dictionary of Human Geography* (4th edition), 731-34. Malden, MA: Blackwell Publishers.

Cotler, I. (2011). "Feds' Omnibus Bill an Abuse of Democracy." *Hilltimes*, 31 October, online: http://www.hilltimes.com/.

Cresswell, T. 1996. *In Place/out of Place: Geography, Ideology and Transgression*. Minneapolis, MN: University of Minnesota Press.

–. 2004. *Place: A Short Introduction*. Malden, MA: Blackwell Publishing.

Crewe, B. 2007. "Power, Adaptation and Resistance in Late-Modern Men's Prison." *British Journal of Criminology* 47: 256-75.

Cuba, L., and D.M. Hummon. 1993. "Constructing a Sense of Home: Place Affiliation and Migration across the Life Cycle." *Sociological Forum* 8(4): 547-72.

Day, N., and P. Schoenrade. 1997. "Staying in the Closet versus Coming out: Relationships between Communication about Sexual Orientation and Work Attitudes." *Personnel Psychology* 50(1): 147-63.

Dean, M. 1999. *Governmentality: Power and Rule in Modern Society*. London: Sage.

Deane, L., D.C. Bracken, and L. Morrissette. 2007. "Desistance within an Urban Aboriginal Gang." *Probation Journal* 54(2): 125-41.

Delaney, D. 2004. "Tracing Displacements: Or Evictions in the Nomosphere." *Environment and Planning D: Society and Space* 22: 847-60.

Demello, M. 1993. "The Convict Body: Tattooing among Male American Prisoners." *Anthropology Today* 9(6): 10-13.

Devault, M.L. 1990. "Talking and Listening from Women's Standpoint: Feminist Strategies for Interviewing and Analysis." *Social Problems* 37(1): 96-116.

Dindia, K. 1998. "Going into and Coming out of the Closet: The Dialectics of Stigma Disclosure." In B.M. Montgomery and L.A. Baxter, eds., *Dialectical Approaches to Studying Personal Relationships*, 83-108. Mahwah, NJ: Lawrence Erlbam Associates.

Drummond, M. 2007. "Age and Aging." In M. Flood, J.K. Gardiner, B. Pease, and K. Pringle, eds., *International Encyclopaedia of Men and Masculinities*, 10-13. New York: Routledge.

Durlauf, S., and D. Nagin. 2011. "The Deterrent Effect of Imprisonment." In P. Cook, J. Ludwig, and J. McCrary, eds., *Controlling Crime: Strategies and Trade-Offs*, National Bureau of Economic Research, 43-94. Chicago: University of Chicago Press.

Eaton, M. 1993. *Women after Prison*. Buckingham, UK: Open University Press.

Ekland-Olson, S., M. Supanic, J. Campbell, and K.J. Lenihan. 1983. "Post-Release Depression and the Importance of Family Support." *Criminology* 21(2): 253-75.

Emde R.N., W.F. Johnson, and M.A. Easterbrooks. 1987. "The Do's and Don'ts of Early Moral Development: Psychoanalytic Tradition and Current Research." In J. Kagan, S. Lamb, J.D. MacArthur, and C.T. MacArthur, eds., *The Emergence of Morality in Young Children*, 245-76. Chicago: University of Chicago Press.

Entrikin, J.N. 1991. *The Betweenness of Place: Towards a Geography of Modernity*. Baltimore, MD: John Hopkins University Press.

Erickson, R.J., W.J. Crow, L.A. Zurcher, and A.V. Connett. 1973. *Paroled but Not Free*. New York: Behavioural Publications.

Feeley, M.M., and J. Simon. 1992. "The New Penology: Notes on the Emerging Strategy of Corrections and Its Implications." *Criminology* 30(4): 449-74.

Feldman, D.C. 1981. "The Multiple Socialization of Organization Members." *Academy of Management Review* 6(2): 309-19.

Flanagan T.J. 1981. "Dealing with Long-Term Confinement: Adaptive Strategies and Perspectives among Life-Term Prisoners." *Criminal Justice and Behavior* 8(2): 201-22.

Fleming, P., and G. Sewell. 2002. "Looking for the Good Soldier, Svejk: Alternative Modalities of Resistance in the Contemporary Workplace." *Sociology* 36(4): 857-73.

Foucault, M. 1964. *Madness and Civilization*. New York: Pantheon.

–. 1977. *Discipline and Punish: The Birth of the Prison [Surveiller et punir]*, translated by A. Sheridan Trans (2nd edition). New York: Vintage Books.

–. 1978. *The History of Sexuality*, translated by Robert Hurley (volume 1). New York: Random House.

–. 1980a; reprinted 1999. "Governmentality." In G. Burchell, C. Gordon, and P. Miller, eds., *The Foucault Effect: Studies in Governmentality*, 87-104. Chicago: University of Chicago Press.

–. 1980b. "Truth and Power." In C. Gordon, ed., *Power/Knowledge: Selected Interviews and Other Writings 1972-1977*, 107-33. New York: Pantheon Books.

–. 1982. "The Subject and the Power." *Critical Inquiry*, 8, 775-95.

–, 1984/89. "Interview: The Concern for Truth." *Foucault Live*. New York: Semiotext.

–. 1988. "Technologies of the Self." In L.H. Martin, H. Gutman and P.H. Hutton, eds., *Technologies of the self*. Amherst: University of Massachusetts Press.

–. 2004. *Society Must Be Defended: Lectures at the College de France, 1975-76*, translated by D. Macey, 16-42. London: Penguin Books.

Frank. K. 1998. "The Production of Identity and the Negotiation of Intimacy in a 'Gentleman's Club.'" *Sexualities* 1(2): 175-201.

Fried, M. 2000. "Continuities and Discontinuities of Place." *Journal of Environmental Psychology* 20: 193-205.

Funk, P. 2004. "On the Effective Use of Stigma as a Crime-Deterrent." *European Economic Review* 48(4): 715-28.

Gabor, T. 1994. *Everybody Does It!: Crime by the Public*. Toronto: University of Toronto Press.

Galloway, G. 2011. "Crime Falls to 1973 Levels as Tories Push for Sentencing Reform." *Globe and Mail*, 21 July, online: http://www.theglobeandmail.com/.

Garcia, V. 2005. "History of Prisons." In M. Bosworth, ed., *Encyclopaedia of Prisons and Correctional Facilities*. Thousand Oaks, CA: Sage.

Garfinkle, H. 1956. "Conditions of Successful Degradation Ceremonies." *American Journal of Sociology* 61: 420-24.

Ghanem, T. 2003. *When Forced Migrants Return Home: The Psychosocial Difficulties Returnees Encounter in the Reintegration Process*. Refugee Studies Centre Working Paper no. 16. Oxford: Oxford University Press.

Giordano, P.C., S.A. Cernkovich, and J.L. Rudolph. 2002. "Gender, Crime, and Desistance: Toward a Theory of Cognitive Transformation." *American Journal of Sociology* 107(4): 990-1064.

Goff, C. 1999. *Corrections in Canada*. Cincinnati, OH: Anderson.

Goffman, E. 1959. *The Presentation of Self in Everyday Life*. New York: Anchor.

–. 1961a. *Asylums: Essays on the Social Situation of Mental Patients and Other Inmates*. Garden City, NY: Doubleday.

–. 1961b. *Encounters: Two Studies in the Sociology of Interaction*. Indianapolis, IN: Bobbs-Merrill.

–. 1963a. *Behaviour in Public Places: Notes on the Social Organization of Gatherings*. New York: Free Press.

–. 1963b. *Stigma: Notes on the Management of Spoiled Identity*. Englewood Cliffs, NJ: Prentice-Hall.

Gorman-Murray, A. 2006. "Homeboys: Uses of Home by Gay Australian Men." *Social and Cultural Geography* 7(1): 53-69.

Gosselin, L. 1982. *Prisons in Canada*. Montreal: Blackrose Books.

Goulding, W. 2001. *Just Another Indian: A Serial Killer and Canada's Indifference*. Calgary, AB: Fifth House.

Grassin, S. 1983. "Psychopathological Effects of Solitary Confinement." *American Journal of Psychiatry* 140: 1450-54.

Gray, A. 2003. *Strategies and Tactics in Analysis: Research Practice for Cultural Studies.* London: Sage.

Green, J., and N. Thorogood. 2009. *Qualitative Methods for Health Research* (2nd edition). Thousand Oaks, CA: Sage.

Hacking, I. 1990. *The Taming of Chance.* Cambridge: Cambridge University Press.

Hall, S. 1990. "Cultural Identity and Dispora." In J. Rutherford, ed., *Identity: Community, Culture, Difference,* 222-37. London: Lawrence and Wishart.

Hammersley, M., and P. Atkinson. 1983. "Insider Accounts: Listening and Asking Questions." In *Ethnography: Principles in Practice,* 105-26. New York: Tavistock.

Haney, C. 2004. "The Psychological Impact of Incarceration: Implications for Post-Prison Adjustment." In J. Travis and M. Wauls, eds., *Prisoners Once Removed: The Impact of Incarceration and Reentry on Children,* 33-66. Washington, DC: Urban Institute Press.

Hannem, S., and C. Bruckert, eds. 2012. *Stigma Revisited: Negotiations, Resistance and the Implications of the Mark.* Ottawa, ON: University of Ottawa Press.

Harding, D.J. 2003. "Jean Valjeans Dilemma: The Management of Ex-Convict Identity in the Search for Employment." *Deviant Behavior* 24(6): 571-95.

Harding, S. 1987. *Feminism and Methodology.* Bloomington, IN: Open University Press.

Harlow, C. 1999. *Prior Abuse Reported by Inmates and Probationers,* Doc. NCJ 172879, US Department of Justice, Office of Justice Programs, online: http://bjs.ojp.usdoj. gov/content/pub/pdf/parip.pdf.

Harper, S. 2011. *Speech from the Throne.* Here for All Canadians, online: http://www. speech.gc.ca/.

Hebl, M.R., J. Tickle, and T.F. Heatherton. 2000. "Awkward Moments in Interactions between Nonstigmatized and Stigmatized Individuals." In T.F. Heatherton, R.E. Kleck, M.R. Hebl, and J.G. Hull, eds., *The Social Psychology of Stigma,* 275-306. New York: Guilford Press.

Hoggart, M., L. Lees, and A. Davies. 2002. *Researching Human Geography.* New York: Oxford University Press.

hooks, b. 1990. *Yearning: Race, Gender and Cultural Politics.* Boston, MA: South End Press.

Horii, G. 2000. "Processing Humans." In K. Hannah-Moffat and M. Shaw, eds., *The Ideal Prison: Critical Essays on Women's Imprisonment,* 104-16. Halifax, NS: Fernwood.

Howard, J. 1777; reprinted 2000. *The State of the Prisons in England and Wales, with Preliminary Observations, and an Account of Some Foreign Prisons. State of the Prisons in Britain, 1775-1905* (volume 1). London: Routledge/Thoemmes Press.

Hughes, E. 1945. "Dilemmas and Contradictions of Status." *American Journal of Sociology* 50(5): 353-59.

Hunt, S.A., and M.P. Phelan. 1998. "Prison Gang Members' Tattoos as Identity Work: The Visual Communication of Moral Careers." *Symbolic Interaction* 21(3): 277-98.

Institut de recherche et d'informations socio-économiques (IRIS). 2011. *Coûts et efficacité des politiques correctionnelle fédéral.* IRIS, online: http://www.iris-recherche. qc.ca/wp-content/uploads/2011/12/Note-Crime-web2.pdf.

Irwin, J. 1970. *The Felon.* Englewood Cliffs, NJ: Prentice-Hall.

Irwin, J., and B. Owen. 2005. "Harm and the Contemporary Prison." In A. Liebling and S. Maruna, eds., *The Effects of Imprisonment,* 94-117. Portland, OR: Willan.

Ivanova, I., and S. Klein. 2012. *Working for a Living Wage 2012.* Canadian Center for Policy Alternatives, online: http://www.policyalternatives.ca/.

Jackson, M. 2002. *Justice behind the Walls: Human Rights in Canadian Prisons.* Vancouver, BC: Douglas and McIntyre.

Jackson, M., and G. Stewart. 2009. *A Flawed Compass: A Human Rights Analysis of the Roadmap to Strengthening Public Safety.* Online: http://www.justicebehindthe walls.net/resources/news/flawed_Compass.pdf.

Jackson, P. 2001. "Making Sense of Qualitative Data." In M. Limb and C. Dwyer, eds., *Qualitative Methodologies for Geographers: Issues and Debates,* 199-214. New York: Oxford University Press.

Jamal, A. 1998. *Forced Migrants, Forged Histories: Suffering and Idealism in Exile Memory.* MA thesis, University of Oxford [unpublished].

Jamieson, R., and A. Grounds. 2002. *No Sense of an Ending: The Effects of Long-Term Imprisonment amongst Republican Prisoners and Their Families.* Monaghan, Ireland: Seesyu Press.

–. 2005. "Release and Adjustment: Perspectives from Studies of Wrongfully Convicted and Politically Motivated Prisoners." In A. Liebling and S. Maruna, eds., *The Effects of Imprisonment,* 33-65. Portland, OR: Willan.

Jewkes, Y. 2005. "Loss, Liminality and the Life Sentence: Managing Identity through a Disrupted Lifecourse." In A. Liebling and S. Maruna, eds., *The Effects of Imprisonment,* 366-90. Portland, OR: Willan.

Johnson, R., and H. Toch. 1982. *The Pains of Imprisonment.* Beverly Hills, CA: Sage.

Jussim, L., P. Palumbo, A. Smith, and S. Madon, 2000. "Stigma and Self-Fulfilling Prophecies." In T. Heatherton, R. Kleck, M.R. Hebl, and J.G. Hull, eds., *The Social Psychology of Stigma,* 374-418. New York: Guilford Press.

Kateb, G. 2001. "On Being Watched and Known." *Social Research* 68(1): 269-95.

Katz, J. 2006. *The Macho Paradox: Why Some Men Hurt Women and How All Men Can Help.* Naperville, IL: Sourcebooks.

Kimmel, M. 1994. "Masculinity as Homophobia." In E. Ditch, ed., *Reconstructing Gender: A Multicultural Anthology,* 103-9. Boston, MA: McGraw Hill.

Kimmel, M.S., and J. Holler. 2011. *The Gendered Society.* Toronto: Oxford University Press Canada.

Kitsuse, J.I. 1980. "Coming Out All Over: Deviants and the Politics of Social Problems." *Social Problems* 28(1): 1-13.

Kobayashi, A. 2001. "Negotiating the Personal and the Political in Critical Qualitative Research." In M. Limb and C. Dwyer, eds., *Qualitative Methodologies for Geographers: Issues and Debates,* 55-70. New York: Oxford University Press.

Lacy, K. 2007. *Blue-Chip Black: Race, Class, and Status in the New Black Middle Class.* Berkeley, CA: University of California Press.

Larson, C. 1977. *Haven in a Heartless World: The Family Besieged.* New York: Basic Books.

Laub, J.H., and R.J. Sampson. 2001. "Understanding Desistance from Crime." *Crime and Justice,* 28: 1-69.

LeBel, T.P., L. Burnett, S. Maruna, and S. Bushway. 2008. "The 'Chicken and Egg' of Subjective and Social Factors in Desistance from Crime." *European Journal of Criminology* 5(2): 131-59.

LeCompte, M.D., and J.J. Schensul. 1999. *Analyzing and Interpreting Ethnographic Data.* Walnut Creek, CA: AltaMira Press.

Leverentz, A.M. 2006. "The Love of a Good Man? Romantic Relationships as a Source of Support or Hindrance for Female Sex-Offenders. *Journal of Research in Crime and Delinquency* 43(4): 459-88.

Lindstrom, B. 1997. "A Sense of Place: Housing Selection on Chicago's North Shore." *Sociological Quarterly* 38(1): 19-39.

Lofland, J. 1969. *Deviance and Identity.* Englewood Cliffs, NJ: Prentice-Hall.

Luciani, F.L., L.L. Motiuk, and M. Nafekh. 1996. *An Operational Review of the Custody Rating Scale: Reliability, Validity and Practical Utility.* Correctional Service Canada, online: http://www.csc-scc.gc.ca/.

MacDonald, M., and P.M. Connelly. 1989. "Class and Gender in Fishing Communities in Nova Scotia." *Studies in Political Economy* 30: 61-83.

MacGuigan, M. 1977. *Sub-Committee on the Penitentiary System in Canada.* Ottawa, ON: Supply and Services Canada.

Magura, S., A. Rosenblum, C. Lewis, and H. Joseph. 1993. "The Effectiveness of In-Jail Methadone Maintenance." *Journal of Drug Issues* 23(1): 75-99.

Mahalik, J.R., G.E. Good, and M. Carlson. 2003. "Masculinity, Scripts, Presenting Concerns and Help-Seeking: Implications for Practice and Training." *Professional Psychology: Theory, Research and Practice* 34: 123-31.

Mahalingam, R. 2003. "Essentialism, Culture, and Beliefs about Gender among the Arvanis of Tamil Nadu, India." *Sex Roles: A Journal of Research* 49: 489-96.

Mahony, T.H. 2011. *Women in Canada: A Statistical Overview* (6th edition). Statistics Canada, online: http://www.statcan.gc.ca/.

Maidment, M.R. 2006. *Doing Time on the Outside: Deconstructing the Benevolent Community.* Toronto: University of Toronto Press.

Mairs, N. 1992. *On Being a Cripple: Plain Text.* Tucson, AZ: University of Arizona Press.

Mallea P. 2010. "The Fear Factor: Stephen Harper's 'Tough on Crime' Agenda: Canadian Theory of Human Motivation." *Psychological Review* 50: 370-96.

Mann, M. 2009. *Good Intentions, Disappointing Results: A Progress Report on Federal Aboriginal Corrections.* Ottawa, ON: Office of the Correctional Investigator.

Marshall, G., ed. 1994. *Oxford Concise Dictionary of Sociology.* New York: University of Oxford Press.

Martinson, R. 1974. "What Works? Questions and Answers about Prison Reform." *The Public Interest* 35: 22-54.

Maruna, S. 1997. "Going Straight: Desistance from Crime and Life Narratives of Reform." In A. Lieblich and R. Josselson, eds., *The Narrative Study of Lives,* 59-94. Thousand Oaks, CA: Sage Publications.

–. 2001. *Making Good: How Ex-Convicts Reform and Rebuild Their Lives.* Washington, DC: American Psychological Association.

Maruna, S., and R. Immarigeon, eds. 2004. *After Crime and Punishment: Pathways to Offender Reintegration,* 3-26. Portland, OR: Willan Publishing.

Maruna, S., R. Immarigeon, and T. LeBel. 2004. "Ex Offender Reintegration: Theory and Practice." In S. Maruna and R. Immarigeon, eds., *After Crime and Punishment: Pathways to Offender Reintegration,* 3-26. Portland, OR: Willan Publishing.

Maslow, A. 1943. "A Theory of Human Motivation." *Psychological Review* 50: 370-96.

Mason, M. 2010. "Sample Size and Saturation in PhD Studies Using Qualitative Interviews." *Qualitative Social Research,* online: http://www.qualitative-research.net/.

Massey, D.B. 1993. "Power-Geometry and a Progressive Sense of Place." In J. Bird, B. Curtis, T. Putnam, G. Robertson, and L. Tickner, eds., *Mapping the Futures: Local Cultures, Global Change,* 59-69. London: Routledge.

Maur, M., and M. Chesney-Lind. 2002. *Invisible Punishment.* New York: New Press.

May, J. 2000. "Of Nomads and Vagrants: Single Homelessness and Narratives of Home as Place." *Environment and Planning D: Society and Space* 18: 737-59.

McAdams, D.P. 1993. *The Stories We Live by: Personal Myths and the Making of the Self.* New York: William Morrow.

McDonough, J. 2001. *Indelible Impressions: Tattoos and Tattooing in the Context of Incarceration.* MA thesis, University of Ottawa, Ottawa [unpublished].

McDowell, L., and G. Court. 1994. "Performing Work: Bodily Representations in Merchant Banks." *Environment and Planning D: Society and Space* 12(6): 727-50.

McEvoy, K., P. Shirlow, and K. McElrath. 2004. "Resistance, Transition and Exclusion: Politically Motivated Ex-Prisoners and Conflict Transformation in Northern Ireland." *Terrorism and Political Violence* 16(3): 646-70.

McIntosh, P. 1988. *White Privilege and Male Privilege: A Personal Account of Coming to See Correspondences through Work in Women's Studies,* Working Paper no. 189, Wellesley College Center for Research on Women, Wellesley, MA.

Messerchmidt, J.W. 2001. "Masculinities, Crime and Prison." In D. Sabo, T.A. Kupers, and W.J. London, eds., *Prison Masculinities,* 67-72. Philadelphia, PA: Temple University Press.

Milewski, T. 2011. *Texas Conservatives Reject Harper's Crime Plan*. CBC News, online: http://www.cbc.ca/.

Morris, J.F., K. Balsam, and E.D. Rothblum. 2002. "Lesbian and Bisexual Mothers and Non-Mothers: Demographics and the Coming-Out Process." *Journal of Family Psychology* 16(2): 144-56.

Muggeridge, H., and G. Doná. 2006. "Back Home? Refugees' Experiences of Their First Visit back to Their Country of Origin. *Journal of Refugee Studies* 19(4): 415-32.

Mulvey, L. 1975. "Visual Pleasure and Narrative Cinema." *Screen* 16 (3): 6-18.

Munn, M. 2011. "Living in the Aftermath: The Impact of Lengthy Incarceration on Post-Carceral Success." *Howard Journal* 50(1): 233-46.

–. 2012. "Correctional Workers: Managing Rehabilitation, Risk and Responsibility on the Front-Lines." In John Winterdyk and Michael Weinrath, eds., *Adult Corrections in Canada*. Whitby, ON: DeSitter.

–. 2012. *Survey Results: Participant Evaluation of Life Line Services*. Ottawa, ON: St. Leonard's Society of Canada.

Munn, M., and C. Bruckert. 2010. "Beyond Conceptual Ambiguity: Exemplifying the 'Resistance Pyramid' through the Reflections of (Ex)-Prisoners Agency." *Qualitative Sociology Review* 6(2): 137-45.

Murphy, P.J., L. Johnsen, and J. Murphy. 2002. *Paroled for Life: Interviews with Parolees Serving Life Sentences*. Vancouver: New Star Books.

National Clearinghouse on Family Violence. 2008. *When Males Have Been Sexually Abused as Children: A Guide for Men*. Online: http://www.phac-aspc.gc.ca/ncfv -cnivf/pdfs/nfntsx-visac-males_e.pdf.

O'Malley, P. 2001. "Risk, Crime and Prudentialism Revisted." In K. Stenson and R.R. Sullivan, eds., *Crime, Risk and Justice: The Politics of Crime Control in Liberal Democracies*, 89-103. Portland, OR: Willan Publishing.

Ong, A. 1995. "Women out of China: Traveling Tales and Traveling Theories in Postcolonial Feminism." In R. Behar and D. Gordon, eds., *Women Writing Culture*, 350-72. Berkeley, CA: University of California Press.

Oxford English Dictionary. 2008. "Struggle." Oxford: Oxford University Press. Oxford Dictionaries, online: http://www.oxforddictionaries.com/.

–. 2010. "Freedom." Oxford: Oxford University Press. Oxford Dictionaries, online: http://www.oxforddictionaries.com/.

Pager, D. 2007. *Marked: Race, Crime, and Finding Work in an Era of Mass Incarceration*. Chicago, IL: University of Chicago Press..

Parole Board of Canada. 2008. *Policy Manual No. 5(13)*. Ottawa, ON: Government of Canada.

Perron, J. 1991. *Task Force Report on Long-Term Sentences: The Perron Report,* April. Correctional Service of Canada, online: http://www.csc-scc.gc.ca/.

Petersilia J. 2001. "Prisoner Reentry: Public Safety and Reintegration Challenges." *Prison Journal* 81(3): 360-75.

Phillips, P. 1997. "Labour in the New Canadian Political Economy." In W. Clement, ed., *Understanding Canada: Building the New Canadian Political Economy*, 64-84. Montreal and Kingston: McGill-Queen's University Press.

Pinel, E. 2004. "'You're just saying that because I am a woman': Stigma Consciousness and Attributions to Discrimination." *Self and Identity* 3: 39-41.

Pires, A. 1997. "L'échantillonnage." In Groupe de recherché interdisciplinaire sur les méthodes qualitative, ed., *La recherche qualitative: Enjeux épistémologiques et méthodologiques*, 3-54. Montreal: Centre international de criminology comparée, Université de Montréal.

–. 2005. *Non-Directive Interviews for Research.* University of Ottawa, Criminology Department [unpublished manuscript].

Porporino, F. 2004. "Differences in Responses to Long-Term Imprisonment: Implications for the Management of Long-Term Offenders," Government of Canada, online: http://publications.gc.ca/collections/collection_2010/scc-csc/PS83-3-10-eng.pdf.

Pratt, J. 1999. "Governmentality, Neo-Liberalism and Dangerousness." In R. Smandych, ed., *Governable Places*, 133-43. Brookfield, VT: Ashgate Publishing.

Price, K. 2000. "Stripping Women: Worker's Control in Strip Clubs." *Unusual Occupations* 11: 3-33.

Public Safety Canada. 2011. *Corrections and Conditional Release Statistical Overview.* Public Safety Canada, online: http://www.publicsafety.gc.ca/.

Purvis, L., C. Bruckert, and F. Chabot. 2010. *The Toolkit: Ottawa Area Sex Workers Speak Out.* Ottawa, ON: Prostitutues of Ottawa-Gatineau Work, Educate and Resist.

Raju, S. 2002. "We Are Different, but Can We Talk?" *Gender, Place and Culture* 9(2): 173-77.

Ranson, G. 2007. "Fatherhood and Paid Work." In M. Flood, J.K. Gardiner, B. Pease, and K. Pringle, eds., *International Encyclopedia of Men and Masculinities*. New York: Routledge.

Reiman, J., and P. Leighton. 2010. *Rich Get Richer and the Poor Get Prison: Ideology, Class, and Criminal Justice* (9th edition). New York: Pearson.

Reiter, E. 1991. *Making Fast Food.* Montreal and Kingston: McGill-Queen's University Press.

Remy, J. 1990. "Patriarchy and Fratriarchy as Forms of Androcracy." In J. Hearn and D. Morgan, eds., *Men, Masculinities and Social Theory*, 43-54. London: Unwin Hyman.

Rengert, G.F. 1996. *The Geography of Illegal Drugs.* Boulder, CO: Westview Press.

Richards, S.C., and R.S. Jones. 2004. "Beating the Perpetual Incarceration Machine: Overcoming Structural Impediments to Re-Entry." In S. Maruna and R. Immarigeon, eds., *After Crime and Punishment: Pathways to Offender Reintegration*, 221-32. Portland, OR: Willan Publishing.

Richie, B.E. 2001. "Challenges Incarcerated Women Face as They Return to Their Communities: Findings from Life History Interviews." *Crime and Delinquency* 47(3): 368-89.

Rinehart, J. 1996. *The Tyranny of Work: Alienation and the Labour Process* (3rd edition). Toronto: Harcourt Brace.

Ritzer, G. 2004. *The McDonaldization of Society.* Thousand Oaks, CA: Pine Forge Press.

Rives, J. 2008. *The Perfection of Guilt.* Hamilton, ON: MiniMocho Press.

Roberts, J.V., L. Stalans, D. Indermaur, and M. Hough. 2003. *Penal Populism and Public Opinion: Lessons from Five Countries.* New York: Oxford University Press.

Rose, G. 2003. "Family Photographs and Domestic Spacings: A Case Study." *Transactions of the Institute of British Geographers* 28: 5-18.

Rose, N. 1996. "The Death of the Social? Reconfiguring the Territory of Government." *Economy and Society* 25(3): 327-56.

–. 1999. "Powers of Freedom: Reframing Political Thought." Cambridge: Cambridge University Press.

Rose, N., and P. Miller. 1992. "Political Power beyond the State: Problematics of Government." *British Journal of Sociology* 43: 173-205.

Ross, R., and B. McKay. 1980. "Behavioral Approaches to Treatment in Corrections: Requiem for a Panacea." In R.R. Ross and P. Gendreau, eds., *Effective Correctional Treatment,* 37-53. Toronto: Butterworth.

Rossmo, D.K. 1993. "Target Patterns of Serial Murderers: A Methodological Model." *American Journal of Criminal Justice* 17: 1-21.

Sabo, D.F., T.A. Kupers, and W.J. London. 2001. *Prison Masculinities.* Philadelphia, PA: Temple University Press.

Santtila, P., M. Laukkanen, and A. Zappalà. 2007. "Crime Behaviours and Distance Travelled in Homicides and Rapes." *Journal of Investigative Psychology and Offender Profiling* 4(1): 1-15.

Sapers, H. 2010. *A Preventable Death.* Office of the Correctional Investigator, online: http://www.oci-bec.gc.ca/.

Schafer, N.E. 1994. "Exploring the Links between Visits and Parole Success." *International Journal of Offender Therapy and Comparative Criminology* 38(1): 17-32.

Schrock, D., and M. Schwalbe. 2009. "Men, Masculinity and Man Acts." *Annual Review of Sociology* 35: 277-95.

Schwaner, S.L. 1998. "Patterns of Violent Specialization: Predictors of Recidivism for a Cohort of Parolees." *American Journal of Criminal Justice* 23(1): 1-17.

Scraton, P., J. Sim, and P. Skidmore. 1991. *Prisons under Protest.* Milton Keynes, UK: Open University Press.

Scull, A. 1977. *Decarceration.* Englewood Cliffs, NJ: Prentice-Hall.

Sennet, R., and J. Cobb. 1972. *The Hidden Injuries of Class*. New York: Knopf.

Shantz, L., and S. Frigon. 2009. "Aging, Women and Health from the Pains of Imprisonment to the Pains of Reintegration." *International Journal of Prisoner Health* 5(1): 3-15.

–. 2010. "Home Free? The (After)-Effects of Imprisonment on Women's Bodies: The (After)-Effects on Women's Health and Identity." *Aporia* 2(1): 6-17.

Shantz, L., J. Kilty, and S. Frigon. 2009. "Echoes of Imprisonment: Women's Experiences of Successful (Re)integration." *Canadian Journal of Law and Society* 24(1): 85-106.

Shoham, S.G., and G. Rahav. 1991. *La marque de caïn*. Lausanne, Switzerland: L'age d'homme.

Silverstein M. 2001. "The Ties That Bind: Family Surveillance of Canadian Parolees." *Sociological Quarterly* 42(3): 395-420.

Simon, J., and M.M. Feeley (1995) "True Crime: The New Penology and Public Discourse on Crime." In T.G. Blomberg and S. Cohen, eds., *Punishment and Social Control*, 147-80. New York: Aldine de Gruyter.

Smart, L., and D.M. Wegner. 2000. "The Hidden Costs of Hidden Stigma." In T.F. Heatherton, R.E. Kleck, M.R. Hebl, and J.G. Hull, eds., *The Social Psychology of Stigma*, 220-42. New York: Guilford Press.

Snider, L. 2006. "Making Change in Neo-Liberal Times." In G. Bedford and E. Comack, eds., *Criminalizing Women*, 323-43. Winnipeg, MB: Fernwood Publishing.

Snyder, K. 2007. "Bachelors and Bachelorhood." In M. Flood, J.K. Gardiner, B. Pease, and K. Pringle, eds., *International Encyclopedia of Men and Masculinities*, 34-35. New York: Routledge.

Solicitor General of Canada. 1984. *Report of the Advisor Committee to the Solicitor General of Canada on the Management of Correctional Institutions*, Doc. 0-662-13657-8. Ottawa, ON: Canada Ministry of Supply and Services.

–. 1998. *Sentence Calculation: How Does It Work?* Ottawa, ON: Canada Ministry of Supply and Services.

Statistics Canada. 2006a. *A Profile of the Canadian Population: Where We Live*, Census Analysis Series no. 96F0030XIE2001001. Ottawa, ON: Statistics Canada.

–. 2006b. *Women in Canada: A Gender-based Statistical Report*. Ottawa, ON: Statistics Canada.

–. 2008. *Earnings and Incomes of Canadians over the Past Quarter Century, 2006 Census*. Ottawa, ON. Statistics Canada, online: http://www12.statcan.ca/census -recensement/2006/as-sa/97-563/pdf/97-563-XIE2006001.pdf.

–. 2010a. *Adult Correctional Services, Admissions to Provincial, Territorial and Federal Programs*. Statistics Canada, online: http://www.statcan.gc.ca/.

–. 2010b. *Police Reported Crime Statistics in Canada in 2010*. Statistics Canada, online: http://www.statcan.gc.ca/.

–. 2010c. *Women's Participation and Economic Downturn*. Ottawa, ON: Statistics Canada, online: http://www.statcan.gc.ca/.

–. 2011. *Population by Age and Sex*. Ottawa, ON: Statistics Canada, online: http://www.statcan.gc.ca/.

Stiles, B.L., and H.B. Kaplan. 1996. "Stigma, Deviance, and Negative Social Sanctions." *Social Science Quarterly* 77(3): 685-96.

Tewksbury, R., and P. Gagne. 1996. "Assumed and Presumed Identities: Problems of Self-Presentation in Field Research." In J. Miller and R. Tewksbury, eds., *Extreme Methods: Innovative Approaches to Social Science Research*, 72-93. Boston, MA: Allyn and Bacon.

Thomas, E. 2010. *Adult Criminal Court Statistics, 2008/2009*. Ottawa, ON: Statistics Canada, online: http://www.statcan.gc.ca/.

Thompson, E.H., and P.M. Whearty. 2004. "Older Men's Social Participation: The Importance of Masculinity Ideology." *Journal of Men's Studies* 13(1): 5-24.

Thurber, A. 1998. "Understanding Offender Reintegration." *Forum* 10(1): 4-17.

Torres, M. 2007. "Complicit Masculinity." In M. Flood, J. Gardiner, B. Pease, and K. Pringle, eds., *International Encyclopedia of Men and Masculinity*. New York: Routledge.

Travis, J., and J. Petersilia. 2001. "Reentry Reconsidered: A New Look at an Old Question." *Crime and Delinquency* 47(3): 291.

Uggen, C., J. Manza, and A. Behrens. 2004. "Less than the Average Citizen: Stigma, Role Transition and the Civic Reintegration of Convicted Felons." In S. Maruna and R. Immarigeon, eds., *After Crime and Punishment: Pathways to Offender Reintegration*, 261-93. Portland, OR: Willan Publishing.

Viggiani, N. 2007. "Surviving Prison: Exploring Prison Social Life as a Determinant of Health." *International Journal of Prisoner Health* 2(2): 71-89.

Visher, C., N. LaVigne, and J. Travis. 2004. *Returning Home: Understanding the Challenges of Prisoner Reentry*, Maryland Pilot Study: Findings from Baltimore. Washington, DC: Urban Institute.

Weber, M. 1904. *The Protestant Ethic and the Spirit of Capitalism*, translated by Peter Baehr and Gordon C. Wells. Online: http://www.marxists.org/.

West, C., and D. Zimmerman. 1987. "Doing Gender." *Gender and Society* 1(2): 125-51.

White, E. 2002. "Halfway Houses for Federal Offenders: What Do We Know about Them?" *Forum on Corrections Research* 15(1): 22-24, Correctional Service Canada, online: http://www.csc-scc.gc.ca/.

Willis, P. 1981. *Learning to Labor: How Working Class Kids Get Working Class Jobs*. New York: Columbia University Press.

Winterdyk, J. 2006. *Canadian Criminology* (2nd edition). Toronto: Prentice-Hall.

Yalnizyan, A. 2009. *Income Inequity and the Pursuit of Prosperity*. Walter Gordon Massey Symposium, University of Toronto, 10 March, online: http://intraspec.ca/WalterGordonLectureOnIncomeInequality-1.pdf.

Zimbardo, P. 1971. *Testimony to the Committee on the judiciary*. Washington, DC: US Government.

Index

Emmett Macfarlane

Governing from the Bench: The Supreme Court of Canada and the Judicial Role (2013)

Ron Ellis

Unjust by Design: The Administrative Justice System in Canada (2013)

David R. Boyd

The Right to a Healthy Environment: Revitalizing Canada's Constitution (2012)

David Milward

Aboriginal Justice and the Charter: Realizing a Culturally Sensitive Interpretation of Legal Rights (2012)

Shelley A.M. Gavigan

Hunger, Horses, and Government Men: Criminal Law on the Aboriginal Plains, 1870-1905 (2012)

Steven Bittle

Still Dying for a Living: Corporate Criminal Liability after the Westray Mine Disaster (2012)

Jacqueline D. Krikorian

International Trade Law and Domestic Policy: Canada, the United States, and the WTO (2012)

Michael Boudreau

City of Order: Crime and Society in Halifax, 1918-35 (2012)

David R. Boyd

The Environmental Rights Revolution: A Global Study of Constitutions, Human Rights, and the Environment (2012)

Lesley Erickson

Westward Bound: Sex, Violence, the Law, and the Making of a Settler Society (2011)

Elaine Craig

Troubling Sex: Towards a Legal Theory of Sexual Integrity (2011)

Laura DeVries

Conflict in Caledonia: Aboriginal Land Rights and the Rule of Law (2011)

Jocelyn Downie and Jennifer J. Llewellyn (eds.)

Being Relational: Reflections on Relational Theory and Health Law (2011)

Grace Li Xiu Woo

Ghost Dancing with Colonialism: Decolonization and Indigenous Rights at the Supreme Court of Canada (2011)

Fiona Kelly

Transforming Law's Family: The Legal Recognition of Planned Lesbian Motherhood (2011)

Colleen Bell

The Freedom of Security: Governing Canada in the Age of Counter-Terrorism (2011)

Andrew S. Thompson

In Defence of Principles: NGOs and Human Rights in Canada (2010)

Aaron Doyle and Dawn Moore (eds.)

Critical Criminology in Canada: New Voices, New Directions (2010)

Joanna R. Quinn

The Politics of Acknowledgement: Truth Commissions in Uganda and Haiti (2010)

Patrick James
Constitutional Politics in Canada after the Charter: Liberalism, Communitarianism, and Systemism (2010)

Louis A. Knafla and Haijo Westra (eds.)
Aboriginal Title and Indigenous Peoples: Canada, Australia, and New Zealand (2010)

Janet Mosher and Joan Brockman (eds.)
Constructing Crime: Contemporary Processes of Criminalization (2010)

Stephen Clarkson and Stepan Wood
A Perilous Imbalance: The Globalization of Canadian Law and Governance (2009)

Amanda Glasbeek
Feminized Justice: The Toronto Women's Court, 1913-34 (2009)

Kim Brooks (ed.)
Justice Bertha Wilson: One Woman's Difference (2009)

Wayne V. McIntosh and Cynthia L. Cates
Multi-Party Litigation: The Strategic Context (2009)

Renisa Mawani
Colonial Proximities: Crossracial Encounters and Juridical Truths in British Columbia, 1871-1921 (2009)

James B. Kelly and Christopher P. Manfredi (eds.)
Contested Constitutionalism: Reflections on the Canadian Charter of Rights and Freedoms (2009)

Catherine Bell and Robert K. Paterson (eds.)
Protection of First Nations Cultural Heritage: Laws, Policy, and Reform (2008)

Hamar Foster, Benjamin L. Berger, and A.R. Buck (eds.)
The Grand Experiment: Law and Legal Culture in British Settler Societies (2008)

Richard J. Moon (ed.)
Law and Religious Pluralism in Canada (2008)

Catherine Bell and Val Napoleon (eds.)
First Nations Cultural Heritage and Law: Case Studies, Voices, and Perspectives (2008)

Douglas C. Harris
Landing Native Fisheries: Indian Reserves and Fishing Rights in British Columbia, 1849-1925 (2008)

Peggy J. Blair
Lament for a First Nation: The Williams Treaties of Southern Ontario (2008)

Lori G. Beaman
Defining Harm: Religious Freedom and the Limits of the Law (2007)

Stephen Tierney (ed.)
Multiculturalism and the Canadian Constitution (2007)

Julie Macfarlane
The New Lawyer: How Settlement Is Transforming the Practice of Law (2007)

Kimberley White
Negotiating Responsibility: Law, Murder, and States of Mind (2007)

Dawn Moore
Criminal Artefacts: Governing Drugs and Users (2007)

Hamar Foster, Heather Raven, and Jeremy Webber (eds.)
Let Right Be Done: Aboriginal Title, the Calder *Case, and the Future of Indigenous Rights* (2007)

Dorothy E. Chunn, Susan B. Boyd, and Hester Lessard (eds.)
Reaction and Resistance: Feminism, Law, and Social Change (2007)

Margot Young, Susan B. Boyd, Gwen Brodsky, and Shelagh Day (eds.)
Poverty: Rights, Social Citizenship, and Legal Activism (2007)

Rosanna L. Langer
Defining Rights and Wrongs: Bureaucracy, Human Rights, and Public Accountability (2007)

C.L. Ostberg and Matthew E. Wetstein
Attitudinal Decision Making in the Supreme Court of Canada (2007)

Chris Clarkson
Domestic Reforms: Political Visions and Family Regulation in British Columbia, 1862-1940 (2007)

Jean McKenzie Leiper
Bar Codes: Women in the Legal Profession (2006)

Gerald Baier
Courts and Federalism: Judicial Doctrine in the United States, Australia, and Canada (2006)

Avigail Eisenberg (ed.)
Diversity and Equality: The Changing Framework of Freedom in Canada (2006)

Randy K. Lippert
Sanctuary, Sovereignty, Sacrifice: Canadian Sanctuary Incidents, Power, and Law (2005)

James B. Kelly
Governing with the Charter: Legislative and Judicial Activism and Framers' Intent (2005)

Dianne Pothier and Richard Devlin (eds.)
Critical Disability Theory: Essays in Philosophy, Politics, Policy, and Law (2005)

Susan G. Drummond
Mapping Marriage Law in Spanish Gitano Communities (2005)

Louis A. Knafla and Jonathan Swainger (eds.)
Laws and Societies in the Canadian Prairie West, 1670-1940 (2005)

Ikechi Mgbeoji
Global Biopiracy: Patents, Plants, and Indigenous Knowledge (2005)

Florian Sauvageau, David Schneiderman, and David Taras,
with Ruth Klinkhammer and Pierre Trudel
The Last Word: Media Coverage of the Supreme Court of Canada (2005)

Gerald Kernerman
*Multicultural Nationalism: Civilizing Difference, Constituting
Community* (2005)

Pamela A. Jordan
*Defending Rights in Russia: Lawyers, the State, and Legal Reform
in the Post-Soviet Era* (2005)

Anna Pratt
Securing Borders: Detention and Deportation in Canada (2005)

Kirsten Johnson Kramar
Unwilling Mothers, Unwanted Babies: Infanticide in Canada (2005)

W.A. Bogart
*Good Government? Good Citizens? Courts, Politics, and Markets
in a Changing Canada* (2005)

Catherine Dauvergne
*Humanitarianism, Identity, and Nation: Migration Laws in Canada
and Australia* (2005)

Michael Lee Ross
First Nations Sacred Sites in Canada's Courts (2005)

Andrew Woolford
*Between Justice and Certainty: Treaty Making in British
Columbia* (2005)

John McLaren, Andrew Buck, and Nancy Wright (eds.)
Despotic Dominion: Property Rights in British Settler Societies (2004)

Georges Campeau
From UI to EI: Waging War on the Welfare State (2004)

Alvin J. Esau
The Courts and the Colonies: The Litigation of Hutterite Church Disputes (2004)

Christopher N. Kendall
Gay Male Pornography: An Issue of Sex Discrimination (2004)

Roy B. Flemming
Tournament of Appeals: Granting Judicial Review in Canada (2004)

Constance Backhouse and Nancy L. Backhouse
The Heiress vs the Establishment: Mrs. Campbell's Campaign for Legal Justice (2004)

Christopher P. Manfredi
Feminist Activism in the Supreme Court: Legal Mobilization and the Women's Legal Education and Action Fund (2004)

Annalise Acorn
Compulsory Compassion: A Critique of Restorative Justice (2004)

Jonathan Swainger and Constance Backhouse (eds.)
People and Place: Historical Influences on Legal Culture (2003)

Jim Phillips and Rosemary Gartner
Murdering Holiness: The Trials of Franz Creffield and George Mitchell (2003)

David R. Boyd
Unnatural Law: Rethinking Canadian Environmental Law and Policy (2003)

Ikechi Mgbeoji
Collective Insecurity: The Liberian Crisis, Unilateralism, and Global Order (2003)

Rebecca Johnson
Taxing Choices: The Intersection of Class, Gender, Parenthood, and the Law (2002)

John McLaren, Robert Menzies, and Dorothy E. Chunn (eds.)
Regulating Lives: Historical Essays on the State, Society, the Individual, and the Law (2002)

Joan Brockman
Gender in the Legal Profession: Fitting or Breaking the Mould (2001)

Printed and bound in Canada by Friesens

Set in Myriad and Sabon by Artegraphica Design Co. Ltd.

Copy editor: Stacey Belden

Proofreader and indexer: Dianne Tiefensee